AIR
DISASTERS

AIR DISASTERS

Leo Marriott
Stanley Stewart
Michael Sharpe

BARNES
&NOBLE
BOOKS
NEW YORK

This edition published by Barnes and Noble Inc.,
by arrangement with PRC Publishing Ltd

1999 Barnes and Noble Books

ISBN 0-7607-1876-8

M 10 9 8 7 6 5 4 3 2 1

Produced by PRC Publishing Ltd
Kiln House, 210 New Kings Road
London SW6 4NZ

© 1999 PRC Publishing Ltd

Printed in China

The material in chapters 1, 3, 4, 5 and 8
has been reproduced by kind permission
of Ian Allan Publishing Ltd.

Contents

Introduction

Leo Marriott

On May 2, 1952, a de Havilland Comet flown by the British Overseas Airways Corporation (BOAC) ushered in the age of jet-powered air travel when it took off from London's Heathrow airport on the first stage of a flight to Johannesburg. Although the Comet had first flown in 1949, this departure was the first time that fare-paying passengers had been carried by a jet airliner. The graceful silver and white aircraft was the pride of the British aircraft industry and was seen as a world beater, far ahead technically of rival airliners from anywhere else in the world. Even the Comet's own designers must have had little idea of the revolution which jet airliners would bring to the world, shrinking distances, bringing nations closer together, and ultimately bringing the cost of air transport down so that ordinary people could travel cheaply, comfortably, and quickly to anywhere in the world.

Initial response to the introduction of the Comet was overwhelmingly enthusiastic. Passengers were astounded at the levels of comfort and smoothness offered by the new aircraft, and airlines from around the world beat a path to de Havilland's door, placing lucrative and substantial orders. However, within a few months the picture had changed as the Comet was involved in a series of fatal accidents, the causes of which were not immediately apparent.

The dubious distinction of the first fatal accident involving a jet airliner fell to a Comet of Canadian Pacific Airlines which crashed during take off from Karachi on March 3, 1953, although the aircraft was on a positioning flight and there were no passengers on board. A month later, on the first anniversary of the Comet's introduction into service, May 2, Comet 1 G-ALYV broke up in flight en route to Delhi from Calcutta on BOAC's Singapore-London service and 43 passengers and crew were killed. The subsequent inquiry concluded that extreme weather conditions were to blame, in spite of some evidence of metal fatigue.

Serious as this was, worse was to come as two more BOAC Comets disappeared in almost identical accidents. In January 1954, G-ALYP disintegrated in flight above the island of Elba. After a ten-week grounding, the Comets took to the air again until another tragedy took place above the Tyrrhenian Sea. G-ALYY, en route via Rome to Johannesburg, disintegrated killing all on board.

Above: *Following the tragic accidents involving the early Comet 1s, de Havilland and BOAC persevered with the design and the result was the Comet 4C which enabled the airline to start trans-Atlantic jet services in 1958.* Winged Memories/BAe

Below: *The salvaged nose section from the Comet G-ALYZ which crashed on take off at Rome in October 1952. At one time it was planned to use it as the basis for a flight simulator.* Ian James Collection

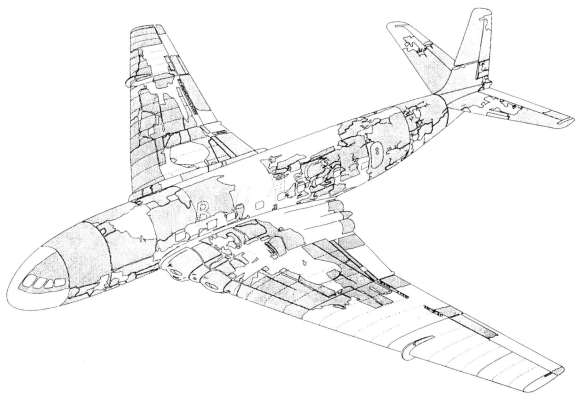

Above: *Diagram showing the amount of wreckage recovered from G-ALYP.*

Below: *Location and direction of main failures on G-ALYP.*

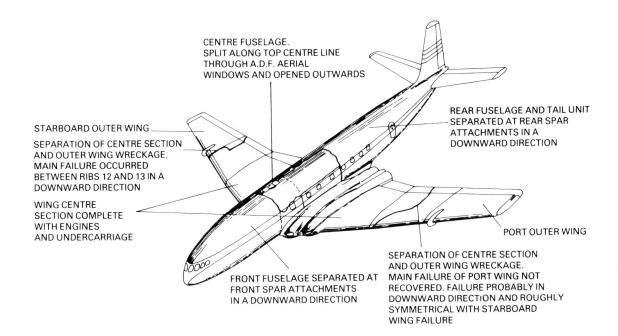

CENTRE FUSELAGE.
SPLIT ALONG TOP CENTRE LINE
THROUGH A.D.F. AERIAL
WINDOWS AND OPENED OUTWARDS

REAR FUSELAGE AND TAIL UNIT
SEPARATED AT REAR SPAR
ATTACHMENTS IN A
DOWNWARD DIRECTION

STARBOARD OUTER WING

SEPARATION OF CENTRE SECTION
AND OUTER WING WRECKAGE.
MAIN FAILURE OCCURRED
BETWEEN RIBS 12 AND 13 IN A
DOWNWARD DIRECTION

WING CENTRE
SECTION COMPLETE
WITH ENGINES
AND UNDERCARRIAGE

PORT OUTER WING

FRONT FUSELAGE SEPARATED AT
FRONT SPAR ATTACHMENTS
IN A DOWNWARD DIRECTION

SEPARATION OF CENTRE SECTION
AND OUTER WING WRECKAGE.
MAIN FAILURE OF PORT WING NOT
RECOVERED. FAILURE PROBABLY IN
DOWNWARD DIRECTION AND ROUGHLY
SYMMETRICAL WITH STARBOARD
WING FAILURE

8

Above: *G-ALYU in the test tank.*

Below: *Detail of ADF aerial windows and the salient features of the disruption to G-ALYP's pressure cabin.*

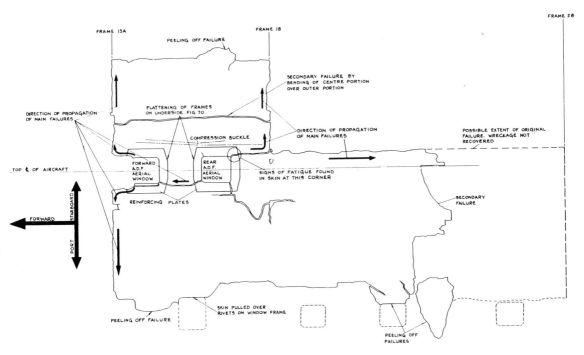

The commercial and political pressure to find the reason for the accidents was intense and one of the biggest investigations in history began with an extensive search of the sea bed off the Italian coast. Eventually, substantial parts of the wreckage were recovered and sent back to the Royal Aircraft Establishment, Farnborough, in the United Kingdom where they were minutely examined while other intact airframes were subjected to a long series of structural tests.

The investigation of aircraft accidents was, by the 1950s, a well established science but the advent of the high flying jets had brought a new dimension to the procedure. The result of the Comet investigation was that—to the amazement of the scientists—after the equivalent of only some 9,000 "flying" hours, there was a catastrophic failure in the pressurized cabin. The culprit? The corner of a cabin window had given way as had the area on the top of the fuselage around the automatic direction finding unit aerials. At a time when accident investigation and fatigue life estimation was just emerging as a precise science, the RAE presented a demonstration of dogged research leading to a solution which was admired throughout the world. The data obtained during the investigation was carefully documented and made available to other manufacturers, including Boeing and Douglas in the United States who were working on the second generation of jet airliners—the Boeing 707 and the Douglas DC-8. The Comet program was saved, de Havilland was able to restart the production lines, but the price of being a pioneer in the field of jet transportation was too high and it never achieved the promise which its early career had shown. Once again, as happens so often in the cause of progress, a great technological leap forward had been accompanied by disaster, the lessons of which had to be learned and digested before progress could be resumed.

In the ensuing decades hundreds of jet airliners have been lost from causes ranging from mechanical or structural failures, as in the Comet accidents, to a variety of human errors and mistakes on the ground or in the air. As each has occurred a lesson has been learned and applied in the endless struggle to make air travel as safe as possible.

The progress of commercial air transport has always been inextricably tied to the issue of safety in the air. In the early pioneering days, flying as a passenger in an aircraft was a risky business and it took a certain amount of courage to embark on a flight. The first fatal airline crash was in December 1920, when a Handley Page O/400 crashed while taking off in fog, killing four people; while in April 1922, the first aerial collision involving civil airliners took place between a DH-18 and a Farman Goliath over France. All seven occupants of the two aircraft were killed.

It was only in the 1930s, when new generations of aircraft with metal airframes, retractable undercarriages, more powerful and reliable engines, and improved methods of control and navigation came into service that safety improved to the extent that commercial airline operations became a viable business proposition. Of course, there were still many accidents but their frequency was low enough not to discourage passengers who flew in ever-increasing numbers.

The Second World War brought a temporary halt to the expansion of civil aviation but the development of new aircraft and equipment during those years meant that airlines in the post-war period were well provided with a range of

Above: *The DC-6 had an alarming propensity to catch fire, but soldiered on to become a successful and reliable airliner. via* Aviation Pictures Library

modern piston-engined aircraft capable of flying a variety of routes, including regular trans-Atlantic and trans-Pacific services. However, these aircraft were still relatively noisy, the piston engines produced a constant and noticeable vibration, and cruising speeds were low, generally around 200mph, although some of the last generation piston-engined airliners such as the DC-7C and the Lockheed Starliner were capable of flying much faster. Nevertheless, a typical trans-Atlantic flight took around 15 to 20 hours and refueling stops at Gander and Shannon were usually necessary. Although some airliners were pressurized, they could still not guarantee to fly above the weather and consequently passengers often experienced discomfort as the aircraft flew through storms and continuous turbulence.

And there were accidents, many caused by the unreliability of the piston engines which became extremely complex and difficult to maintain as efforts were made to squeeze every last horsepower out of the concept. A typical example was the Douglas DC-6, which eventually became one of the most successful and reliable airliners of the period but, initially, had an alarming propensity to catch fire and was grounded on several occasions as attempts were made to rectify the problem. Shortly after one four-month grounding, a DC-6 belonging to United Airlines crashed in flames at Mount Carmel, PA, after a fire broke out in one of the port engines. All 43 people on board perished. British airlines also had their share of disasters, not least being the unexplained disappearance of two Avro Tudors operated by British South American Airways off Bermuda in January 1948 and November 1949.

Against this background, the introduction of the jet airliner was a revolution. It could fly above almost all the weather and its jet engines were potentially more reliable and simpler to maintain. Journey times were cut by half and passengers marveled at the lack of noise or vibration in the pressurized cabin. The Comet disasters were, therefore, doubly newsworthy as not only were they tragedies in themselves, but the whole progress of civil aviation seemed to have been brought to a grinding halt. When the new American aircraft entered service at the end of the 1950s, they were much bigger than the Comet and were technically more advanced. Although their structural integrity was not in question, their greater size and swept wing configuration required complex flying controls and other systems which were initially prone to malfunction or incorrect operation, resulting in a number of accidents. The results of each investigation were immediately passed to the aircraft manufacturer so that modifications could be made and usually an Airworthiness Directive (AD) would be issued by the national regulatory body requiring all operators of that particular aircraft to implement the directive. In the United States, accident investigations were carried out by the Federal Aviation Authority (FAA) and the National Transportation Safety Board (NTSB), while in the United Kingdom the task was delegated by the Civil Aviation Authority to the Air Accident Investigation Board (AAIB). Other developed countries had similar organizations. Protocol demanded that an accident was normally investigated by the country in which it occurred, but in many cases that country would lack the resources or expertise and the task would be assisted by, or delegated to, other agencies such as the FAA or AAIB. Representatives of the aircraft and engine manufacturers would also assist, together with the owners or operators of the aircraft and other experts.

As a result of accident investigations, airworthiness directives would be issued if mechanical or structural failure was responsible, but often the cause would be a human error either by the crew, ground engineers, or air traffic controllers, and in such cases the procedures and equipment used would be reviewed and amended or improved as necessary. In general, throughout civil aviation, a system of reporting and investigation to ascertain cause rather than blame is in force, so that individuals will feel free to contribute freely to any investigation and the investigators will have full access to all information concerning a particular accident. This system of applying the lessons of each accident and incident has led over the years to a substantial and measurable increase in air safety.

When the third generation of jet airliners—such as the Boeing 747 and the DC-10—entered service at the beginning of the 1970s, the structural integrity of the airframes and reliability of the engines had improved to the extent where accidents whose sole cause was a mechanical or structural failure were becoming relatively few. However, this period was also marked by a steep rise in airborne terrorism, which over the next two decades resulted in the loss and destruction of several aircraft as well as causing the loss of many lives. Fortunately, a massive increase in security procedures by airlines and airports has substantially reduced this activity although, unfortunately, it still happens occasionally.

As the reliability of the aircraft improved, there were still numerous accidents caused by crew error either in the actual operation of the aircraft or through navigational errors. In an effort to improve this situation, aircraft manufacturers worked to incorporate the emerging power of digital computers to automate many

Above: *Pan Am ensured that Boeing would go ahead with the 747 by placing an order for 25 aircraft in April 1966. This was a brave decision at the time but these early 747s served the airline well and many were still in service when the airline ceased operations in the 1990s.* ASM Photo

routine tasks and reduce the workload on the flight crew. The pace setter in this field was the European Airbus consortium but Boeing and other American manufacturers were quick to develop their own technology. The use of aviation electronics, commonly known as avionics, has revolutionized the operation and navigation of aircraft and was widely adopted from the early 1980s onward. Traditional flight instrumentation was replaced by computerized graphic displays, while autopilots, autothrottle systems, and inertial navigation systems were all integrated through a digital Flight Management System (FMS). Aircraft such as the Airbus A300/A310 and Boeing 757 and 767 were the pioneers in this field with their so called "glass cockpits" and two-pilot crews that dispensed with the third pilot or flight engineer previously employed. The Airbus A320 and subsequent designs went a stage further, incorporating a computerized "fly by wire" control system with no direct linkage between the pilot and the flying controls. Instead, the pilot signals his intentions by input from his control column while a computer determines what is a safe input to the actual control surfaces and automatically adjusts power settings if necessary.

There is no doubt that today's sophisticated airliners, powered by engines producing up to 100 tons of thrust, could not be safely flown and operated without the use of the complex and integrated computerized systems with which they are equipped. It is also true that flight safety has, on balance, benefited enormously from such advances. Nevertheless, the introduction of this technology has not been without problems, with a number of accidents caused by a crew's unfamiliarity with the new system or else misunderstanding its use and application. Currently, there is a strong movement in the industry to ensure that pilot training programs provide a

13

thorough grounding in the application and operational use of the new and emerging technology.

This recognition of the contribution that properly structured training can make to flight safety has been instrumental in a substantial change in attitudes to the subject. From the earliest days of commercial aviation it has been generally accepted that accidents result mainly from three basic factors: the failure of the aircraft or its equipment, the weather, or pilot error. If an accident cannot be attributed to one of the first two categories, then the pilot must have done something wrong. In recent years few accidents have been attributable to the aircraft itself and in most cases severe weather can be avoided by the use of forecasting facilities, on-board weather radar, and the ability of modern jets to fly well above the worst conditions. This puts the rest down to crew error but, today, there is much greater emphasis on the reasons why pilots make mistakes and every effort is made to reduce these by better design and equipment, and ensuring that operating procedures are made as logical and straightforward as possible. This has resulted in much greater emphasis being placed on the study of so-called "human factors." This looks at the way individuals learn and absorb information, how they react to it, and how they work in conjunction with other crew members and individuals such as engineers, cabin crew, and air traffic controllers. Study of human factors is now a compulsory part of pilot training, teaching them to be aware of pressures and situations which may reduce their ability to make rational decisions.

One vital tool that has evolved from the study of human factors is the concept of cockpit resource management (CRM), which investigates the relationship between the various crew members and the allocation of their tasks and duties, including the vital function of monitoring each other and being able to recognize and prevent errors in a logical manner. This might seem obvious but it has only recently come to the fore with the introduction of automated flight systems which need to be clearly understood and properly monitored. While human factors and CRM have found ready acceptance in many countries, national cultures have made it difficult to implement in some areas where respect for authority and unquestioning obedience is ingrained in young pilots before they start their training. At least one major accident in recent years could have been avoided if the young and relatively junior first officer concerned had more forcefully expressed his concerns about the aircraft's position and these concerns had been properly considered by the senior and autocratic captain. There are many other accidents where this has been a factor, and it is instances such as these that CRM and other methods seeks to prevent.

Human factors also includes the important issue of cockpit ergonomics, a subject that has received much attention in the latest generation of jet airliners such as the Airbus 340 and Boeing 777. Great attention is concentrated on ensuring that controls are logically placed and work in a logical sense, and that instruments and electronic flight information systems (EFIS) can be easily viewed, read and interpreted. A classic example of the importance of ergonomics was the British Midland Boeing 737 which crashed at Kegworth in England in January 1989. In this case the aircraft suffered an engine problem shortly after departure and the crew elected to descend into East Midlands airport—where the airline's technical engineering was based—so that

Above: *The all-digital cockpit of the Airbus A3XX*. Airbus Industrie

the engine could receive attention. In itself this should have been a routine incident, as modern twin-engined airliners such as the Boeing 737 are well able to fly safely on one engine. However, the crew closed down the wrong engine, with the result that there was insufficient power to check descent on final approach. One of the reasons for this fatal error was that the vibration meter for each engine was very small and difficult to read, with little apparent deflection of the pointer between a normal and abnormal reading. Clearer instrumentation might well have prevented this accident. Certainly the pilots made a mistake, but the reasons for the mistake could be identified: this accident is a clear example of one caused by human factors.

One major category of accident which causes considerable concern today is known as Controlled Flight Into Terrain (CFIT). This covers circumstances where an otherwise perfectly serviceable aircraft collides with high ground or rising terrain, or flies into the ground while making an approach to land. This usually occurs as a result of a navigational error by the crew, and consequently human factors and CRM are closely associated with efforts to prevent such accidents. So concerned was the air transport industry about such accidents that a special task force led by the Flight Safety Foundation was set up in 1992 to increase pilot awareness and investigate ways of reducing the number of incidents. Although a significant reduction in overall CFIT incidents has been achieved, there is still a long way to go. In 1997 there were four such incidents involving large jet airliners; there have been 26 in total since 1992, including the Mt. Erebus incident detailed in Chapter 5. Of course, technology can help and in the 1960s a device known as the Ground Proximity Warning System (GPWS) became available and subsequently became mandatory

15

equipment aboard commercial aircraft. GPWS was based on readings from the aircraft's radar altimeter and was designed to alert the pilot if he flew too close to the ground, or if the rate of closure with the ground was excessive. Unfortunately, the early versions of this equipment were prone to false alarms which led many pilots to ignore GPWS warnings and, even when these were eliminated, the device still suffered from a major drawback: basically, it only gave warnings in respect of terrain below the aircraft and not of terrain ahead of the aircraft on its projected flight path. Thus a pilot inadvertently flying toward steeply sloping terrain—such as a cliff or sheer precipice—would not receive any warning until it was too late. This problem has now been addressed with the development of a system known as Enhanced GPWS (EGPWS) and this is now being adopted by the world's major airlines.

Another example of technology coming to the aid of air safety is in the avoidance of aerial collisions. This, of course, is mainly the function and responsibility of the air traffic control system but occasional lapses and errors, either by controllers or pilots, will sometimes put aircraft in a potential collision situation. All commercial aircraft are today fitted with a device known as a transponder which can be interrogated by ground-based ATC radars to provide information on the aircraft's identity and altitude. A Transponder-based Collision Avoidance System (TCAS) has been developed in which each aircraft can send out a low-powered signal to interrogate any transponders in its immediate vicinity and, should the system detect another aircraft in a potentially conflicting situation, it will issue a traffic advisory to the pilot followed, if necessary, by specific instructions to climb or descend to avoid the other aircraft. Like most new systems, the original TCAS was prone to false alarms and air traffic controllers were concerned that this could lead to aircraft making unpredictable maneuvers in busy airspace, making their own task even more difficult. However, a constant refinement of the system and its associated software has eliminated most of the problems and TCAS is becoming increasingly mandatory throughout the world.

Today's accident investigators have some very sophisticated tools available to assist them compared to what was available to the Comet investigators in 1954. In those days almost everything hinged on examination of what wreckage could be discovered and the statements of any survivors or available witnesses. Often the evidence and statements were inconclusive or even conflicting, and the exact cause of a particular accident could often not be determined with any certainty. The introduction of the large jets, with their many and varied complex systems, increased the workload of accident investigators and led to the introduction of Flight Data Recorders (FDR), which greatly assisted them in their work. These devices were fitted in crash-proof containers and usually carried in the tail of the aircraft where they were most likely to survive any impact undamaged. Initially they only recorded basic flight parameters and control surface deflections, but modern FDRs can store a vast amount of data which enable accident investigators to accurately determine and reproduce the chain of events leading up to the accident. When the data is introduced via suitable software to a computer system, a graphic real time representation of the aircraft's maneuvers, together with readouts of any relevant parameters can be constructed, stored, and replayed. Such reconstructions assist not

Above: *An A310 leased to ARIA (Aeroflot Russian International Airlines).* Airbus Industrie

only the accident investigation but are also used as training aids for new pilots and other aviation professionals.

The introduction of the FDR, provided that it can be located following an accident, generally enabled investigators to determine exactly what had happened when an aircraft crashed but did not always make clear why it had occurred. For example, in a CFIT incident, the FDR would show nothing abnormal apart perhaps from a last second attempt by the crew to pull up and avoid hitting the ground, but it would not give any clue as to why the aircraft was flown into that position in the first place. To overcome this problem it eventually became mandatory for transport aircraft to be fitted with Cockpit Voice Recorders (CVR). As can be imagined, this met with considerable resistance from the pilot fraternity, concerned that the recordings would be used for reasons totally unconnected with flight safety and feeling that big brother would always be watching them. Today, however, they are accepted as just another part of the flightdeck equipment and in most cases the recordings are automatically erased at the end of each normal flight.

Use of the CVR recordings enables investigators to determine the crew's reasoning and actions in the period leading up to an accident and have often been quite revealing in cases which would otherwise have remained a mystery. In March 1994 an Airbus A310 operated by the Russian airline Aeroflot suddenly plunged out of control from its normal cruising altitude and crashed into the ground killing all on board. Analysis of the CVR recordings revealed that the captain had allowed his son to sit in his seat and inadvertently operate some of the autopilot controls. The captain was unable to regain control in time to prevent the crash. Without the CVR, the reason for the incorrect operation of the autopilot (as revealed by the FDR) would probably have remained unexplained.

Other recordings available to investigators include those from ground based air traffic control. Recordings of the exchange of radio messages between ATC and the pilot are one of the first things to be checked and in many cases a radar recording will show the track of the aircraft concerned. However, not all parts of the world have good radar coverage and even if recordings are available, the aircraft will often drop below radar coverage before it actually hits the ground. Of course, air traffic control itself may be responsible for an accident. Mistakes by controllers can lead to actual collisions or, as happens, pilots may misinterpret their instructions. Fortunately, such occurrences are rare but the potential for a major disaster remains. Recent examples include a Boeing 747 colliding with an Il-76 transport over India (see Chapter 17), killing all 349 people on board the two aircraft. Perhaps the most serious collision was at Tenerife in 1977 (see Chapter 3) when over 500 people died in a collision on the runway during foggy conditions. In this case, there were errors in the transmission and understanding of radio messages by both ATC and the pilots.

Despite man's ingenuity in building bigger, stronger, more powerful, and better equipped aircraft, the forces of nature are sometimes too strong to resist and weather still plays a significant part in many accidents. In most cases it is a causal factor but not the sole reason. For instance, poor visibility and fog should not cause an accident but will drastically reduce the margin for any errors that the pilot may make. However, there are times when the sheer force of nature is enough to cause a pilot to lose control of an aircraft and, exceptionally, it can literally destroy an aircraft in flight. Perhaps the most dramatic example of this was the BOAC 707 which broke up in severe turbulence near Mount Fuji in Japan. More recently, severe weather is suspected as causing the crash of an Austral airlines DC-9 over Uruguay in October 1997 and it is possible that severe turbulence may have been a factor in the loss of a Silk Air Boeing 737 off Indonesia in December 1997 (although this now seems to have been deliberate suicide by the captain).

When set against the tremendous increase in the amount of civil aviation activity, whether measured in terms of hours flown or passengers carried, air safety has steadily improved to the extent where, statistically, the chances of being killed in an air crash are extremely remote. Nevertheless, the dramatic nature of most disasters coupled with the tendency for the average number of fatalities in a major crash to increase due to the greater size of today's aircraft, can lead to a perception that air travel is still dangerous. In 1997, for example, a total of 1,306 people were killed in air accidents, almost exactly in line with the average for the preceding ten years. Unfortunately, several of the accidents happened over a short period at the end of the year giving rise to speculation, almost totally unfounded, that air safety standards were in decline. The following year saw 21 major accidents (see table opposite). Nevertheless, airlines are beginning to realize that a good safety record is an essential marketing weapon in the cut-throat fight to win passengers and those that fail on this score will eventually fail commercially as well. If nothing else this pressure will ensure that flight safety remains at the very top of their agendas with obvious benefits and reassurance for their passengers and customers.

Major Accidents in 1998

Date	Type	Identity	Operator	Location	Cause
1/11	RJ100	TC-THF	THY, Turkish Airlines	Samsun, Turkey	Not determined
2/2	DC-9-32	RP-C1507	Cebu Pacific Air	Mount Malagana	Not determined/CFIT
2/9	727-223	N845AA	American Airlines	Chicago, IL	Not determined
2/16	A300B4-622R	B-1814	China Airlines	Taipei	Not determined
2/23	727-200Adv	YU-ANU	Chanchangi Airlines	Kaduna, Nigeria	On board fire (ground)
2/26	737-2K3		Chanchangi Airlines	Lagos, Nigeria	Unknown
3/10	707-336C	SU-PBB	Air Memphis	Mombassa, Kenya	Not determined
3/19	727-228	YA-FAZ	Airiana Afghan	Kabul, Afghanistan	Human factors (CFIT)
3/22	A320-214	RP-C3222	Philippine Airlines	Bacolod, Philippines	Mechanical defect
4/16	737-2H4	P4-NEN	Orient Eagle Airlines	Almaty, Kazakhstan	Not recorded
4/20	727-230	HC-BSU	TAME	Bogata	Human factors (CFIT)
5/5	727-282	FAP-351	Peruvian Air Force	Andoas, Peru	Human factors (CFIT)
6/5	727-025F	5Y-BMW	Aero Zambia	Asmana, Ethiopia	Not recorded
7/13	Il-76M	UR-76424	ATI Aircompany	Ras el Khaimah, UAE	Not determined
8/29	Ti154M	CU-T1264	Cubana	Quito, Ecuador	Not recorded
9/02	MD-11	HB-IWF	Swissair	Peggy's Cove, Nova Scotia	On board fire
9/25	BAe146-100	EC-GEO	Paukn Air	Nador, Morocco	Human factors (CFIT)
10/10	727-30	9Q-CSG	Lignes Aeriennes	Kindu, Zaire	Military action
11/14	707	5N-VRG		Ostend, Belgium	Mechanical defect
12/1	747-259B (SCD)	N621FF	Tower Air	Miami, FL	Not recorded
12/11	A310-204	HS-TIA	Thai Airlines	Surat Thani	Human factors

The Ten Worst Aviation Disasters

This list gives brief details of the ten worst disasters involving jet transport aircraft based on the total number of fatalities aboard all the aircraft concerned and including any third party fatalities on the ground. As might be expected, in view of their great capacity, the wide-body jets feature prominently, but this should not be read as an indication of their relative safety or otherwise. Full details of the accidents will be found in the chapters identified.

1. March 23, 1977—Tenerife
Total Fatalities: 583. Aviation's worst accident to date. (See Chapter 3)

2. August 12, 1985—Mount Osutaka, Japan
Total Fatalities: 520. The worst accident involving a single aircraft.
(See Chapter 10)

3. November 12, 1996—Charkhi Dadri, India
Total Fatalities: 349. The worst accident involving an aerial collision.
(See Chapter 17)

4. March 3, 1972—near Paris, France
Total Fatalities: 346. (See Chapter 1)

5. June 23, 1985—near Irish Coast
Total Fatalities: 329. The worst example of terrorism in the air. (See Chapter 9)

6. August 19, 1980—Riyadh, Saudi Arabia
Total Fatalities: 301. The worst case of fire on board an aircraft.
(See Chapter 6)

7. July 3, 1988—Persian Gulf
Total Fatalities: 290. The worst military-related accident. (See Chapter 11)

8. May 25, 1979—Chicago O'Hare, USA
Total Fatalities: 271. (See Chapter 4)

9. December 21, 1988—Lockerbie, Scotland, UK
Total Fatalities: 270. (See Chapter 12)

10. September 1, 1983—Sakhalin Island
Total Fatalities: 269. (See Chapter 8)

1 Near Paris, France, 1972
Turkish Airlines Douglas DC-10-30

Stan Stewart

At 19.19:48hrs local time on a cool summer's evening, American Airlines Flight 96 lifted off from Detroit's Metropolitan Airport. The date was June 11, 1972. Flight 96 was a DC-10-10 scheduled service from Detroit to Buffalo and was lightly loaded with only 56 passengers and 11 crew. It was running about one hour late because of a number of delays, the most notable being the problem in closing the rear cargo door. Difficulties with the door had occurred on a number of occasions and it had taken 18 minutes to close it in Los Angeles. In Detroit it had taken only five minutes to shut the door but the ramp service agent had to use his knee to force down the locking handle. He was sufficiently concerned to mention it to a mechanic who quickly checked the handle and found it safe. On the flightdeck the "door open" light extinguished confirming the door locked.

With the after take-off check complete and the aircraft climbing safely at 250kts, the first officer engaged the autopilot. At 10,000ft the co-pilot set the vertical speed control to 1,000ft/min climb to reduce the climb angle for acceleration from 250kts to the normal cruise speed of 340kts. Passing about 11,500ft, directly over the town of Windsor, with the speed increasing through 260kts, N103AA broke from cloud cover into a clear evening on top.

The flight crew began to relax and to take in the view. Suddenly, without warning, a resounding thud echoed from the rear of the aircraft. The rudder pedals "just exploded" and smacked to the full left rudder position. The captain was resting his feet on the pedals and his right leg was thrown back against the seat with extreme force. First Officer (F/O) Paige-Whitney hit his head on the back of the seat. At the same moment the three thrust levers snapped back to flight idle with the number two (tail) engine throttle hitting the stop with a loud crack. A great rush of air swept past the flight crew throwing dirt and grit into their faces and blinding them with the dust. The stinging effect was like a fire cracker going off below their noses. The captain's headset was knocked from position and as the aircraft jerked, the autopilot automatically disconnected. The captain's first thought was that the windshield had failed, but when his eyes cleared he could see it still in place. Disbelievingly he stretched his hand out to touch the window.

Above: Turkish Airlines took delivery of three DC-10-10s registered TC-JAU (illustrated here), TC-JAV and TC-JAY between December 1972 and February 1973. TC-JAV was the aircraft lost at Paris. A.J. Wright

Below: DC-10 cargo door.

"What the hell was it, I wonder?" called Captain McCormick.

The fire warning bell rang for number two engine and the cabin altitude warning horn sounded indicating the cabin air pressure had reduced to an altitude equivalent to over 10,000ft. The autopilot red "disconnect" light flashed and a red failure flag appeared on the airspeed indicator.

"We've hit something," said the second officer.

The co-pilot had been looking out and had not seen anything of another aircraft so thought it more likely to be disintegration of number two engine. That would explain the fire warning and the rudder problem although the fire indication subsequently proved to be false. Whatever the cause of the trouble, there was no doubting the severity of the problem. In normal circumstances, with the cabin pressurization warning horn sounding, the crew would have been tempted to commence an emergency descent, but the captain was reluctant to force the aircraft into a steep dive until the damage could be assessed. Flying at around 12,000ft few breathing problems would be experienced, although strictly speaking flight crew should wear oxygen masks above 10,000ft.

Captain McCormick retrieved his headset from the back of the seat and quickly radioed Cleveland Center declaring an emergency. There was little information he could give as they didn't know what had happened except that they had a serious problem. The co-pilot still handled the control column, but now relinquished flying to the captain who wanted to "feel out" the controls himself.

"I think it's going to fly," assured the first officer.

The speed fell to 220kts as the DC-10 descended towards the cloud. If they could stay in the clear until the damage was assessed it would make life easier. The captain pulled back on the controls but soon ran out of elevator to arrest the descent. He pushed the thrust levers forward: the wing-mounted engines responded but the tail engine (number two) remained in flight idle. The number two throttle could be moved quite easily and was obviously not attached to anything. However, the power from the wing engines effectively pitched the nose up and the aircraft managed to maintain 12,000ft. By good fortune McCormick had been in the simulator, practicing flying the DC-10 on engine power only, assuming total loss of flying controls with hydraulic failure. The DC-10's engine positions permit relatively effective control when employed in this manner and Captain McCormick became quite adept at the task. He was now able to put his experimental endeavors to good use.

The approach was begun at 20 miles out with 160kts indicated airspeed and a rate of descent of 600–700ft/min. Attempts at reducing speed resulted in unacceptable sink rates. In order to keep the aircraft aligned with the runway the entire approach was conducted with the nose pointing 5–10° to the right. The landing gear was successfully lowered and the remaining flaps extended just before touch-down. The DC-10 landed flat and fast 1,900ft in from the threshold. The landing was smooth, but once on the ground "all hell broke loose." Almost immediately Flight 96 veered off the runway and plowed through the grass. The co-pilot took control of the reverse thrust levers, pulling maximum power on number one engine on the left and cancelling number three. This eased the aircraft left, back on to the hard tarmac of the runway, and the machine stopped about 1,000ft from the end. After the rough landing the captain felt an emergency evacuation might be prudent and activated the alarm. Fortunately, no further danger ensued and all the passengers quickly disembarked down the chutes. In the end only a few minor injuries were sustained. But for good fortune and the skill of the crew, the result could have been much worse.

The next morning National Transportation Safety Board (NTSB) accident investigators arrived on the scene and easily diagnosed the cause of the accident. Scuff marks on the rear cargo door's securing mechanism clearly showed that the door had not been properly locked, in spite of indications to the contrary. As Flight 96 had climbed out of Detroit, the cabin had been pressurized as usual to allow relatively normal breathing for the passengers and crew. The fuselage and doors are designed to prevent the pressurized air from bursting outward into the rarefied atmosphere. Any failure of door, panel or window, however, results in air exhausting rapidly with force. In this case, loads of up to five tons had been placed on the partially locked cargo door. Eventually the latches had sprung under the load and the door had blown open, causing explosive decompression of the aircraft. The door had been torn off by the airflow, damaging the left tailplane in the process. The pressurized cargo hold air had immediately exhausted to the atmosphere via the gaping hole and the cabin air pressure had placed an undue load on the floor. With insufficient venting in the cabin floor area, the floor had simultaneously collapsed, trapping the bar unit in the open cargo door exit. Through the beams of the cabin floor ran control cables, hydraulic pipes and wiring, of which a number had been severed or jammed, resulting in the control difficulties. Fortunately sufficient control systems had remained intact to sustain stable flight. It had been a close-run event and swift and decisive action would be required to prevent a recurrence.

The "Windsor incident," as the near disaster became known, prompted an inquiry by American Airlines, the NTSB, the Federal Aviation Administration (FAA) and McDonnell Douglas into the locking difficulties of the rear cargo door. The manufacturer of the door, Convair, a division of General Dynamics, was also involved. Head of the FAA's Western Regional office was Arvin Basnight, a career public servant whose ability was equal to the task. Shortly after the Windsor incident, on June 13, Dick Sliff, Basnight's head of aircraft engineering, contacted Douglas regarding the cargo door problems. The company's attitude was less than helpful, and it was only after some agitation that information was made available. The documents examined by Sliff revealed that there had been about 100 previous reports of difficulties in closing the door. Some even more damning documents, however, were not revealed. In particular, one written by Dan Applegate, an engineer of Convair, expressed extreme concern with safety aspects of the door. Had Sliff reviewed this information, the story might have been different. In the normal course of events, records received by the manufacturing company from airlines are passed to the FAA for correlation in the form of Maintenance Reliability Reports. In this case, McDonnell Douglas, ever wary of adverse publicity for an aircraft in a highly competitive market, had not honored the arrangement (there was no legal requirement for them to do so) and the FAA was quite unaware of the troubles. Before the Windsor incident, however, the company had already attempted to take matters in hand and had issued Service Bulletins to the airlines operating DC-10s recommending rewiring of the door's electric actuators. It was hoped that, by increasing the power of the actuators with the use of heavier gauge wire, the latches would be driven more fully home. Rewiring of DC-10 cargo doors was still in progress at the time of the incident but Captain McCormick's aircraft had not been modified.

To those involved at the local FAA office the proposed remedy did not seem adequate. If the DC-10 was to continue flying, some interim measure was required until a more effective solution could be devised. The problem was that the actuators were not driving the latch linkage to the over-center position (see diagram on page 29) and it was frequently necessary to shut the doors manually using a hand crank. Before Flight 96 had departed from Detroit, the door had been only partially secured and the locking pin had jammed on the restraining flange. The ramp service agent had then forced the handle home with his knee, distorting the locking pin rods in the process. This had given the false impression that the door had not only closed but had locked, in spite of the fact that the locking pins were not in position. In flight, as the interior pressurized, the enormous force on the latches had been transmitted via the incorrectly positioned latching mechanism to the actuator bolts which had sheared under the strain with the inevitable results.

One simple solution seemed to be provision of a peep-hole of toughened glass through which a locking pin could be checked in position. It was not the complete answer, but something immediate was necessary to help prevent a recurrence of the incident over Windsor. The peep-hole requirement would also be backed by the full force of federal law to ensure the airline's compliance. The document employed to enforce such an order — an Airworthiness Directive (AD) — is issued only in matters concerning safety. The release of the AD, unfortunately for McDonnell Douglas, would make public the circumstances and, being an airworthiness requirement, the costs of the modification would have to be borne by the manufacturer. Early on the morning of June 16, the draft of the AD was telexed to FAA headquarters for approval, but it soon became apparent that consent was not to be forthcoming. Before 09.00hrs, Basnight was telephoned by Jackson McGowan, president of the Douglas Division of McDonnell Douglas. McGowan had talked to Jack Shaffer, the head of the FAA. McGowan told Basnight that he and Shaffer had agreed "the corrective measures could be undertaken as a product of a gentlemen's agreement, thereby not requiring the issuance of an FAA Airworthiness Directive." An AD was not to be issued. A telephone conference was arranged between Douglas, FAA headquarters and the airlines to agree on proposals for modifying the cargo door. Agreement was reached to continue with the wiring program and to placard the doors with a warning for the ground staff not to use a force in excess of 50lb when closing the door handle. How this figure was to be gauged was not explained. It was a totally inadequate response to a very dangerous situation.

On July 6, 1972, the NTSB formally presented its recommendations to the FAA: the door should be rendered "physically impossible" to close incorrectly, modifications should be made to the floor and vents, and the floor strength should be increased. The response at the time from the FAA and McDonnell Douglas was generally to ignore the proposals. Had the recommendations been fully implemented the door-locking problems may have been solved, but the lack of urgency with which they were delivered left a lot to be desired. Without an AD to enforce the issue the airlines flying the 39 DC-10s then in service were slow to apply the modifications. By the end of 1972 18 had still not been altered, and one was still operating without a support plate in 1974.

In the summer of 1972, at the height of the DC-10 cargo door controversy, Turkish Airlines ordered three DC-10-10s, which were delivered in December 1972. In the meantime, Nixon was re-elected. In the course of such events tradition demands that all senior political appointees offer their resignation: the head of the FAA, John Shaffer, acted accordingly. No one was more surprised than Shaffer when his resignation was accepted! Perhaps influenced by Shaffer's imminent departure, the FAA began reviewing its attitude regarding possible floor damage on wide-bodied jets as a result of explosive decompression. The Dutch equivalent of the FAA, the RLD, had been involved since the KLM decision to buy the DC-10, and had been expressing concern for some time. In September 1972, RLD representatives met the FAA and Douglas to discuss the issue. Douglas was quick to point out that the DC-10 floor strength met FAA requirements, but, the Dutch countered, in the light of the Windsor incident the regulations must be considered inadequate. This view was supported by NTSB research. The outcome of the talks was inconclusive with the FAA supporting McDonnell Douglas and agreeing to differ with RLD.

By February 1973 the FAA was beginning to admit the error of its ways and was now urging the big three aircraft manufacturers to consider strengthening floors, increasing venting, and re-routing essential control lines away from the floor. Boeing and Lockheed, perhaps understandably, were indignant at being drawn into the argument surrounding another maker's aircraft. McDonnell Douglas insisted that present regulations were satisfactory. In June 1973, the FAA asked its regional officers to obtain technical details about big jet floors. The reaction of all three manufacturers was predictable as each baulked at the thought of the expense involved in a detailed study. The Dutch had by now reluctantly certificated the DC-10, and the FAA's rather belated attempts at action were not well received. On February 25, 1974, McDonnell Douglas replied stating that if the FAA insisted on a study then the government should bear the cost.

Less than a week later, on March 2, the English and French rugby football teams faced each other in the Parc des Prince in Paris. The estimated 30,000 English fans in attendance swelled the visitors to the city. To make matters worse British European Airways (BEA) ground engineers at Heathrow had called a strike in support of a pay claim and all its European air services were grounded. On the day following the rugby match, Sunday March 3, the chaotic situation at Paris's Orly Airport was compounded by other travelers arriving from elsewhere in Europe. The result was a gigantic headache for BEA staff at Orly as they tried to find seats on other airlines to get their passengers to London.

Turkish Airlines (Turk Hava Yollari — THY) Flight 981 from Turkey to Britain that Sunday was an ideal contender for the beleaguered BEA staff. The aircraft was a DC-10-10 of 345-seat capacity, routing Ankara–Istanbul–Paris–London, and in excess of 200 seats were calculated as being available on the Paris–London sector. The Turkish DC-10, registration TC-JAV, landed on schedule at just after 11.00hrs local time (10.02hrs GMT) with 168 passengers on board. The aircraft parked and 50 passengers disembarked while those in transit remained on board for the stopover. Scheduled departure was local mid-day. Turkish Airlines had a few staff on hand to supervise operations in Paris, but much of the ramp area work was subcontracted to Samor Co. Aircraft loading was one of Samor's responsibilities and its personnel were instructed in DC-10 cargo door closing techniques. After switching on the power, a button was to be pressed to power the actuators. With the door shut the operator was to continue depressing the button for a further 10 seconds to ensure correct positioning of the latches. The external handle was then to be placed flush with the door to engage the locking pins and to close a small vent door (see diagram). This was stated as being the indication that the door was safe. A warning was also issued on the use of any force in closing the door handle. A final check of the locking pin position through the peep-hole was not part of the duties of Samor's staff but was the responsibility of Turkish Airlines. The resident THY ground engineer at Paris, Osman Zeytin, was in Istanbul on a course, and in his absence Flight 981's transit was supervised by another ground engineer, Engin Ucok, who was to continue with the flight to London.

To facilitate procedures at Paris, THY had distributed the baggage and mail throughout the cargo holds. All the load intended for London had been placed in the forward cargo compartment which was not opened. Passengers boarding at Orly had their bags placed in the central compartment while the aft cargo compartment contained only baggage and mail destined for Paris. It was completely emptied. Nothing was loaded in the rear hold and the door was closed at 10.35hrs GMT (all times in GMT) by one of Samor's staff, Mahommed Mahmoudi. He was a 39-year-old Algerian expatriate who could speak two languages fluently, Arabic and French, but who could not read English—so he could not understand the placards by the door indicating the safe and unsafe positions of the locking pins. He had on a number of occasions seen Zeytin, the THY resident ground engineer, place his eye at the peep-hole but he was not aware of its function. Mahmoudi had correctly followed the door closing procedure and nothing had given him cause for concern. THY had experienced numerous difficulties with the opening and closing of TC-JAV's rear cargo door and a number of times it had to be closed using the hand crank, but on this occasion it shut without any undue effort. The final check of the safe condition of the door should have been conducted by one of the THY staff, but neither Zeytin's replacement, the ground engineer Ucok, nor the DC-10's flight engineer, Erhan Ozer, checked the peep-hole. Had they done so they would have seen that the locking pins were not in place. The latches had not been powered home fully and the latch linkage had not been driven to the safe over-center position. As in the Windsor incident all indications were that the door was closed and locked. History was about to repeat itself. But in the Windsor incident the handle had been forced in position with a knee, while Mahmoudi in Paris had placed the handle flush with ease. In fact, it had been almost too easy.

In the Douglas factory at Long Beach, the paper work for TC-JAV clearly stated that the current Service Bulletins had been implemented but, because of an oversight, the requirements of SB 52–37 (extension of the locking pin travel and fitting

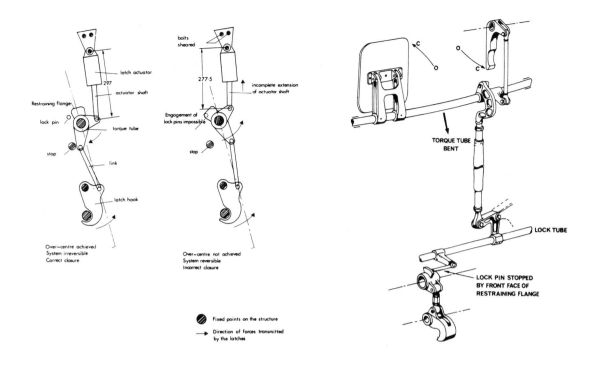

Above: *The problem of forced closure (Left) and DC-10 aft cargo door latch closing system (Right).*

Below: *The faulty adjustments showing how the warning light in the cockpit is actuated (Left); Closing and locking mechanism (Right).*

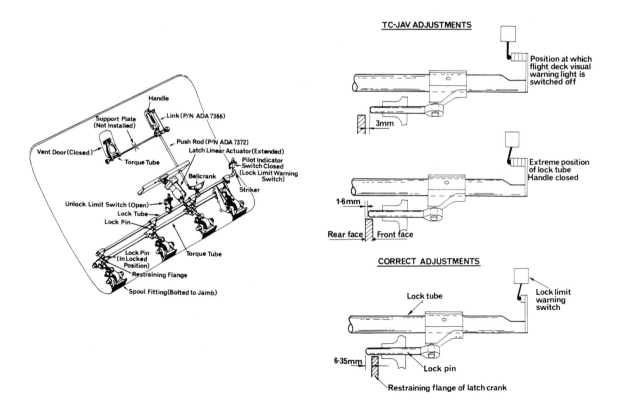

of the locking pin rod support plate) had not been done. After delivery to THY, an adjustment to the locking pin travel was made, but the aircraft was still awaiting fitment of the support plate. By a gross blunder, however, alteration of the locking pin travel was incorrectly applied. Instead of the travel being extended to seat the pin properly when locking the door, or to make obvious the jamming of the door handle with improper setting of the latch linkage, the locking pin travel was actually decreased. Even in the locked position the pins were hardly effective (see diagram).

McDonnell Douglas had calculated that with the locking pin travel extended as required, a force of 215lb was needed to close the handle with the latch linkage incorrectly set, and with the support plate also fitted a force of 430lb (beyond human strength) was necessary. With the locking pin travel decreased as on TC-JAV, a force of only 13lb was required to place the door handle flush with the door still unlocked. The incorrect adjustment also affected the lock limit warning switch which illuminated a "door open" light on the flightdeck to alert crews of incorrect positioning of the lock pins. The mis-rigging resulted in the lock limit microswitch failing to extinguish the flightdeck "door open" warning light, even when the door was locked. At some stage the lock limit switch striker had been extended by the addition of extra shims to permit a more positive contact (see diagram). The result of the tampering was that the flightdeck "door open" light now extinguished even when the door was still unlocked.

To all intents and purposes, therefore, TC-JAV's rear cargo door was closed and locked. Only a visual inspection through the one-inch peep-hole would have indicated the true unsafe condition, and in the absence of the resident ground engineer that was overlooked.

Passengers began to board Flight 981 and take their seats. In all, 216 people were boarded to join those waiting on the aircraft giving a passenger figure of 334. In the confusion 10 or so seats remained unallocated. The crew of 11 (three flight crew and eight cabin staff), plus the ground engineer traveling on board, brought the grand total to 346. The boarding of so many extra passengers in such difficult circumstances resulted in the inevitable delay, and it was not until 11.11hrs that THY first contacted Orly for departure instructions. Flight 981 was assigned departure route 18 from runway 08. Departure route 18 tracked aircraft east and then north to avoid overflying Paris. Boarding was completed by 11.14hrs and engine start was cleared at 11.24hrs to taxi to runway 08. The conditions were fine with a light wind, some patchy cloud, a temperature of 6°C and good visibility. On the flightdeck Captain Nejat Berkoz and his crew of F/O Oral Ulusman and F/E Erhan Ozer completed the before take-off checks and, approaching the runway, changed to "tower" on 118.7MHz. Flight 981 was cleared to line up and take-off, and at 11.30:30hrs the DC-10 weighing 163 tonnes lifted off from the runway. One and a half minutes later "departure" was contacted on 127.75MHz and clearance was received for further climb to flight level 60. The after take-off check was completed and the seat belt sign switched off, but most passengers preferred to remain seated with their lap straps fastened. The autopilot was engaged. TC-JAV reported level at 60 and was instructed to contact Paris (North) on 131.35MHz. On contact with the area controller, Flight 981 was cleared at 11.36hrs for further climb to flight level 230 and instructed to turn left to Montdidier. Five routine communications passed between Flight 981 and Paris (North) in the course of the turn and at 11.38hrs the DC-10 stabilized on a heading of 346°, climbing through flight level 90 at a speed of 300kts. The aircraft interior continued to pressurize as the DC-10 climbed into the rarefied atmosphere, placing a force of almost five tons on the unlocked rear cargo door. At 11.39:56hrs Flight 981 passed 11,500ft climbing over the village of Saint-Pathus at a rate of climb of 2,200ft/min and a speed of 300kts. Suddenly, the door latching mechanism could no longer withstand the strain and the door burst open and tore from the side of the fuselage. The heavily laden rear section of the cabin floor collapsed completely with the force of the explosive decompression and the last two rows of triple seat units above the door, with six passengers and parts of the aircraft, were ejected. The cabin fogged and dust swirled in the rush of air.

On the flightdeck the crew was taken completely by surprise. The throttles snapped closed and the autopilot disconnected. Almost immediately the DC-10 banked to the left and the nose pitched down rapidly.

"Oops. Aw, aw," someone exclaimed. The co-pilot grabbed the controls as Flight 981 dived towards the ground and the cabin pressurization warning horn sounded.

11.40:05hrs, Captain Berkoz: "What happened?"
F/O Ulusman: "The fuselage has burst."
11.40:07hrs, Captain Berkoz: "Are you sure?"

The control cables and hydraulic lines running rearward below the floor were torn from their tracks, or jammed, and elevator and stabilizer controls were lost. The rudder seized at an angle of 10° to the left. There was now no means by which the crew, in spite of their efforts, could regain sufficient control of the aircraft. As the nose dropped the speed began to build up.

11.40:12hrs, Captain Berkoz: "Bring it up, pull her nose up."

At this moment a radio transmission from Flight 981 was received by the radar controller at Paris (North). He could hear a heavy background noise with Turkish being spoken and the noise of the cabin pressurization warning horn sounding. As the crew fought to regain control the transmission continued.

F/O Ulusman: "I can't bring it up—she doesn't respond."

The aircraft continued to accelerate towards the ground. By 11.40:18hrs the nose was pitched down 20° with the speed increasing through 362kts.

11.40:19hrs, F/E Ozer: "Nothing is left."

At 11.40:21hrs, with the DC-10 descending into the more dense atmosphere, the pressurization warning horn ceased. Passing 7,200ft the speed increased to 400kts, and the aircraft continued banking in a left turn as it raced earthwards.

F/O Ulusman: 'Seven thousand feet.'

A second or so later the overspeed warning sounded as the speed edged beyond the "never exceed" speed. At the same moment the Paris (North) controller noticed TC-JAV's flight label disappear from the secondary radar scope. On the primary radar screen a thin sliver of light representing the ejected parts detached itself from the echo and remained stationary while the DC-10's trace curved to the west.

11.40:28hrs, Captain Berkoz: "Hydraulics?"
F/O Ulusman: "We have lost it . . . oops, oops."

At 11.40:31hrs the nose down pitch began progressively to decrease and the speed stabilized at 430kts. The radio transmission being received on the ground abruptly ended at 11.40:41hrs as the controller continued to monitor the DC-10's progress.

11.40:50hrs, Captain Berkoz: "It looks like we are going to hit the ground."
11.40:52hrs, Captain Berkoz: "Speed?"

The overspeed warning continued to sound throughout.

11.40:57hrs, Captain Berkoz: "Oops."

The DC-10's angle of descent stabilized at a shallow angle but the machine continued at great speed towards the ground. TC-JAV was beyond help. At 11.41:04hrs and 11.41:06hrs further short radio transmissions were received by the ground controller from the DC-10. These were the last to be heard. Flight 981 struck the trees of the Ermenonville forest at 11.41:08hrs at a speed of 430kts in almost level flight, but with the wings banked 17° to the left. At 11.41:31hrs the DC-10 impacted in a rugged valley at a place known as Bosquet De Dammartin, 20 miles northeast of Paris, only 77 seconds after the door burst open. The aircraft "cut a swath through the forest some 700m long by 100m wide," and literally disintegrated as it struck. All 346 on board perished. With the force of the impact TC-JAV exploded into a million tiny pieces and scattered over a wide area. There was virtually no fire. Nothing had a chance to burn.

In the control center the radar controller watched helplessly as the echo disappeared from his screen. Many times he tried in vain to contact Flight 981 and with no reply he raised the alarm. Soon a large-scale rescue operation was put into action and the first rescuers arrived on the scene at 12.15hrs. There was little they could do except start to clean up the mess. Experts who witnessed the devastation stated that they had never seen an aircraft disintegrate so completely over such a wide area.

Within 22 minutes of the disaster, even before the first rescuers arrived at the site, the BBC broadcast news of the crash. It was the accident the world had feared: the first involving a fully laden wide-body jet since their introduction into service only four years earlier. The worst previous had killed 176 when a Boeing 707 crashed on landing at Kano, Nigeria, returning with Muslims from a pilgrimage to Mecca in

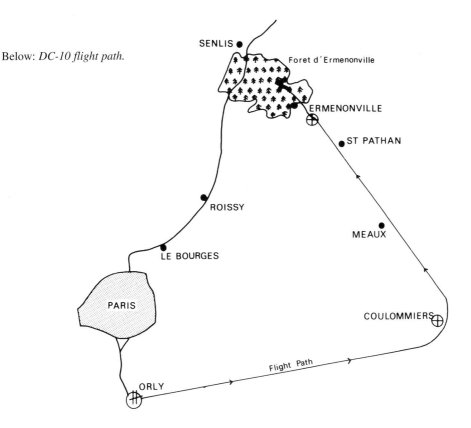

Below: *DC-10 flight path.*

SENLIS ●

Foret d´Ermenonville

ERMENONVILLE

● ST PATHAN

● ROISSY

MEAUX ●

LE BOURGES ●

PARIS

COULOMMIERS

Flight Path

ORLY

January 1973. The THY DC-10 catastrophe, with all 346 on board killed, was at the time the worst disaster in civil aviation history. Only hours after the accident, journalists were on the scene to report the details to the world—and the spreading of the news attracted thousands of the morbidly curious in search of a glimpse of the carnage. Police were required to keep the sightseers at bay.

Immediately FAA and NTSB investigators arrived in France from the U.S. to examine the wreckage. Inspection of the door soon revealed the cause of the tragedy. The next day, March 7, the FAA at last issued an Airworthiness Directive requiring application of the modifications outlined in the previous Service Bulletins. Butterfield, the new head of the FAA, ordered an investigation into his own organization's handling of the DC-10 cargo door affair. During this inquiry, a survey of the records of problems experienced with the cargo door between October 1973 and March 1974 revealed 1,000 separate incidents. The report was submitted on 19 April 1974 and was highly critical of the cargo door design and the system which permitted its certification. A special sub-committee of the House of Representatives also reviewed the affair and determined that between the Windsor incident of June 1972 and the Paris crash of 1974, "through regulator nonfeasances, thousands of lives were unjustifiably put at risk." Demands by the FAA for wide-body floor strengthening were followed in July 1975 with the introduction of legislation requiring all wide-body floors to withstand the decompressive effect of a 20sq ft (the area of the DC-10 rear cargo door is a little over 14.5sq ft) hole appearing in the fuselage.

The report of the official inquiry clearly outlined the imperfections of the cargo door latching mechanism and the risks entailed in its faulty operation. "All these risks," the report concluded, "had already become evident 19 months earlier, at the time of the Windsor incident, but no efficacious corrective action had followed."

2 San Fernando, Chile 1972 TAMU Fairchild-Hiller FH-227D-LCD

Michael Sharpe

At 08.05hrs on the morning of October 12, 1972, a Fairchild-Hiller FH227D-LCD, chartered by members of a Uruguayan amateur rugby team took off from Carrasco airport, Uruguay, bound for Santiago in Chile. The team, known as the "Old Christians," were greatly looking forward to a repeat of the previous year's fixture, and, to help meet the cost of chartering the aircraft from the Uruguayan Air Force, some members of the player's families came along to fill empty seats. Prominent members of the team, who were mainly in their late teens or early 20s, included Marcelo Pérez the first team captain, Roberto Canessa, one of three medical students in the party, and Nando Parrado who worked at his father's firm manufacturing nuts and bolts. The aircraft was capable of carrying 52 passengers, but for this trip it was carrying 40 plus the five crew members. As the Fairchild moved out over Montevideo, then across Buenos Aires, the high-spirited team settled down to what they hoped would be a pleasant 3½-hour journey across Argentina, followed by a quick 30 minute hop across the Andes and into Chile.

The twin turboprop Fairchild FH-227 is a license-built version of the Fokker F-27 Friendship. Fairchild's stretched (6ft 6in) FH-227 version, which first flew in January 1966, was adopted by many South American operators as a replacement for the venerable Douglas DC-3. This particular aircraft was a FH-227D aircraft powered by Rolls-Royce Dart RDa.7 Mk 532-7L engines and registered to the Uruguayan Air Force (Fuerza Area Uruguay) as T-571. The aircraft commander was Colonel Ferradas. However, flying this morning was his co-pilot Lieutenant Lagurara who, although older than Ferradas, had bailed out of a Lockheed T-33 jet trainer earlier in his career and was now flying under Ferradas' watchful eye. Ferradas himself had over 20 years of experience and had flown this aircraft on numerous occasions.

By aeronautical standards the Fairchild was in top condition, having only logged 792 hours of flight time. By choosing to leave at 08.00hrs, Ferradas planned to cross the Andes before noon thus avoiding treacherous postmeridianal turbulence and, if weather conditions were clear, there would be four routes available to him after Mendoza: the Juncal, Nieves, Alvarado, or Planchon Pass. The route via

Above: *Survivors stand beside the FH-227.* CORBIS/Bettmann

Juncal Pass was the most direct, but if visibility became poor then this passage became impossible. In these conditions the Fairchild had a maximum ceiling of 22,500ft, yet some of the peaks awaiting them on the Juncal route forced a ceiling of 26,000ft. The routes via Alvarado and Nieves were also useless in poor weather as there were no radio beacons en route.

As the hours rolled past Nando Parrado, sitting with his best friend Panchito Abal, talked of cars, girls, and rugby. The other passengers were also engrossed in conversations, played cards, or read books and comics, while the land below them changed from luscious, rectangular fields of crops and plantations dotted amongst the endless pampas, to the more harsh, arid land at the foothills of the cordillera. Suddenly, steward Ramirez, came from the cockpit and announced that due to weather conditions they would be making an unscheduled landing at Mendoza. After an overnight stop, in the late morning of Friday, October 13, the members of the team and their families began filtering in little groups back to Mendoza Airport from their various hotels—some of the players accompanied by Argentine girls whom they had met dancing the night before! However, Col Ferradas and Lt Lagurara were still wrestling with the big dilemma that had yet to be resolved: was it now safe to cross the mountains?

Meteorological reports indicated that weather conditions along their flight path were improving. Even though a flight across the pass at Juncal was impossible in the Fairchild, there was a strong chance that by early afternoon the pass at Planchon would be clear. It would mean flying at a time of day that was normally considered risky, but they felt sure they could fly above the turbulence. They were undoubtedly influenced by the fact that they left with only one other alternative—to fly back to Montevideo—as it was against regulations for a military aircraft to stay on Argentine soil for more than 24 hours. Ferradas consulted the pilot of a cargo plane recently arrived from Chile and was told that although turbulence was very strong, an aircraft such as the Fairchild, equipped with the latest navigational equipment, should have no difficulties; it was even suggested they fly through the Juncal Pass. This information seems to have persuaded Ferradas, who decided they would fly not via Juncal, but across the safer pass of Planchon. After announcing these plans to his impatient passengers, the colonel was greeted with a roar of approval.

At 14.18hrs local time Lagurara lifted the Fairchild off Mendoza's main runway. For many of the jubilant souls on board 571, it was to be their last good look at civilization. Earlier, one of the players had joked about the condition of the Argentine cargo plane as it taxied toward them at Mendoza airport. One of the Argentine girls had retorted with prophetic vision, "At least it got over the Andes, which is more than yours will."

The treachery presented by the cordillera is not simply the great height of some of its peaks (although the highest, Aconcagua, which rises to nearly 23,000ft is higher than the Fairchild's maximum operating ceiling). Unpredictable weather conditions present as great a hazard. As the Fairchild continued its ascent into the icy atmosphere above the snow line, currents of air from the east rising up to meet the mountains were running straight into cyclonic winds roaring up the valleys from the Pacific coast. This head-on collision of conflicting weather systems was creating

36

violent high altitude turbulence. It is one of the peculiarities of the prevailing weather conditions in the region and can leave aircraft completely at its mercy.

The cargo plane pilot had good reason to be confident in the Fairchild. As well as being equipped with a standard Automatic Direction Finder radio compass, it was also fitted with the more up to date VHF Omnidirectional range, known as VOR, navigational aid. At 15.08hrs, as was normal, the crew tried to tune to the radio beacon at Malargüe, but found that it was blocked. Lagurara then turned the Fairchild into air lane G17 while maintaining an altitude of 18,000ft. He estimated that they would pass over Planchon, the central point of this mountain route and the point where air traffic control in Santiago would take over from Mendoza, at 15.21hrs.

As they flew toward the boundaries of Argentine dominion in the Andes, a blanket of cloud began to cloak the ridges and snow filled valleys beneath them. This wasn't a major issue as visibility above cloud was still good and, in any case, visually identifying Planchon under a blanket of snow would have been tricky to say the least. With total faith in his calculations Lagurara radioed Santiago ATC at 15.21hrs and told them that he was over the Pass of Planchon. He then informed them that he would be passing over Curic, a small town in Chile, at 15.32hrs.

What Lt Lagurara and Col Ferradas had failed to notice was that, earlier, as they had banked the aircraft into air lane G17, the moderate tail wind had changed to a strong head wind—and their ground speed had decreased from 210 to 180 knots. At 15.24hrs the crew again radioed Santiago and announced "Checking Curicáo and heading toward Maipu," then turned the aircraft 90° and headed north from their previous course. Santiago accepted the crew's account of their position, although now they were flying almost blind, guided only by a faulty calculation. The ATC then authorized Lagurara down to 10,000ft for his approach to Pudahuel Airport.

At 15.30hrs, moments after Lagurara had reported his height as 3,000ft, the aircraft flew into more cloud and began to shake with air turbulence. The "No Smoking" and "Fasten Safety Belt" signs were switched on and, as steward Ramirez delivered Ferradas' bitter tea, Lagurara asked him to control the high-spirited passengers in the cabin, some of who were tossing a rugby ball back and forth. Ramirez told them to put it away; the plane was going to "dance a little bit" as they ran into some heavier weather. Then Ramirez took up his hand at the game of Truco with the other steward and the navigator.

Again they became engulfed by another cloud, but this time the plane shook and was tossed about inside the weather system. As the bravest passengers in the cabin tried to mask their fear by behaving normally, in the cockpit, the pilots assessed their instruments searching for any signs of trouble. At that moment, the Fairchild hit another air pocket and sank a few hundred feet while still engulfed entirely by cloud.

In the cabin, Roberto Canessa instinctively asked the lady next to him on the other aisle if she was scared. "Yes," she replied, "Yes I am." As the boys chanted, "Conga," Canessa again passed the ball down to one of the other passengers, he in turn passed it on and, as the cry of "Olé, Olé, Olé" went up, they were suddenly swallowed inside another vacuum and dropped about another 300ft.

As they emerged through the cloud base Lt Lagurara and Col Ferradas must have gasped at what they saw—not the green plains of Chile thousands of feet below, but the jagged peaks and ridges of the Argentine Andes all around them. Instantly Lagurara tried to climb. Further back, Nando Parrado looked out of his passenger window and his view was just as terrifying—rocky ridges a mere ten feet away from the tip of the wing. Someone asked "Are we supposed to fly this close?" The reply was a muted "I don't think so."

Lagurara hauled the stick back to the stop and threw the throttles forward, urging the aircraft upward. Gradually the nose lifted as the aircraft clawed through the thin air searching for lift. In the passenger cabin people began to pray and braced themselves for the impact as the scream of engines at full throttle echoed though the mountains. Then there was a splintering crash as the starboard wing was torn away by a ridge and flicked back across the fuselage cutting the tail clean off. Instantly, the steward, the navigator, and three of the players were sucked out into the icy air still strapped into their seats. The aircraft bounced crazily across the rocky ridge then smashed into another ridge that snapped the port wing back, causing the port propeller to slash into the outer skin of the fuselage.

Like a bullet, the wingless aircraft shot over the ridge and hurtled toward a mountain peak beneath. Somehow it cleared the peak, landing smoothly on its belly on the steep, snow-covered face of the other side. Inside, amid the screaming, a brave few opened their eyes and were horrified to find themselves skimming over the snow at 200 knots! Two more unfortunates were sucked from the gaping hole at the rear. Those that remained inside the fuselage and strapped into their seats suddenly felt themselves catapulted forward as the seat mountings failed with the enormous stress of deceleration. The passengers furthest forward were flung into the wall of the forward baggage compartment with terrible force.

The aircraft twisted crazily as it careened down the mountain. With the freezing mountain air gushing inside, those who were still conscious, or not engrossed in prayer, steeled themselves for the oncoming impact. As the aircraft hurtled towards what must have felt like certain doom, a terrified voice shouted "Jesus, Jesus, little Jesus, Help us!" and with the words still hanging in the air the mangled aircraft thudded to a halt. In an instant silence returned to the bleak mountain peak.

They had come to a stop against a deep bank of snow. After a silent moment of reorientation, groans of agony and then muffled shrieks began to sound out from the twisted chaos of metal, plastic, and flesh.

In the aftermath heroes were to emerge who worked tirelessly to help free their friends and families from the buckled seats. Roberto Canessa, the medical student, worked calmly with his medic friend Zerbino assessing and assisting the many casualties and, without any basic First Aid equipment they were forced to improvise. Captain Pérez took it upon himself to oversee and organize people as effectively as possible, helping to move wreckage and hunting for anything that could be of any use to them. Whilst he was dealing with the many injuries a player named Platero approached Canessa and asked if he was okay. Canessa blinked then looked again. Platero had what looked like a three-foot steel rod sticking out of his stomach. He told him he was fine, and to go and help others. As he turned, Canessa wrenched the bar from his gut as well as what looked like six inches of his intestine with it.

Above:The Fairchild-Hiller FH-227 was a stretched Fokker F.27. Austin T. Brown/Aviation Picture Library

While some of the younger players were seated on the snow taking in the utter desolation they noticed a figure running down the hill toward them. It was their friend Carlos Valeta who had been sucked from the fuselage. They shouted and beckoned him, he seemed to hear them and come across their way a little. Suddenly, Valeta altered direction again and began tumbling down the mountainside, never to be seen again. Nando Parrado was still in a state of unconsciousness. If he had come round it would be to find that his mother had been killed instantly and his sister was hanging on to life by the thinnest thread.

One of the players hit upon the idea of laying cushions out in front of him and using them to cross the deep snow. When he finally made it to the cockpit, he found Ferradas was dead, but Lagurara was still breathing, just. He looked closer, the instrument panel was buried deep into their chests. When he returned with help they fed the dying man snow as he begged for water and his pistol. They replied that they couldn't give him his gun, as the Roman Catholic church did not endorse suicide. After a failed attempt to contact Santiago by radio, they discovered that the radio's batteries were in the tail.

At around 16.00hrs it started to snow, and it was then that Canessa hit upon the idea that probably kept them alive throughout that first miserable night—they would take the seat covers off and use them as blankets. Out of 45 passengers and crew, 13 had died instantly, the question that remained now was who would survive the night at this mind numbing altitude—already at just 18.00hrs it was dark and the temperature had plunged below freezing.

After the Fairchild had disappeared off radar in Santiago, the task of finding them fell to the Chilean Search and Rescue squad. Ten days continuous searching was the agreed international convention, but once again bad weather was to play its part in the story. After eight days, two of which had to be abandoned because of the inclement weather, the search was called off. At various times over the next two and a half months, searches were resumed and then abandoned. To compound an almost impossible rescue operation, the roof of the Fairchild was painted white and was invisible from the air. Furious with the bureaucracy that hampered the rescue of their relatives, the families mounted their own rescue operation orchestrated by ham radio from Uruguay. One father, Carlos Páez Vilaró, maintained an incredible one man pan-Andes search right until the very end.

The resilience and weakness of the human spirit is never more utterly exposed as in a crisis and with every passing day the survivors' food supply diminished and their crisis deepened; eight bars of chocolate, five bars of nougat, some caramels, dates and dried plums, a packet of salted biscuits, two tins of mussels, one tin of salted almonds, and some small jars of jam is not a substantial amount of food for 28 people. Marcelo Pérez had the boys organized into different teams. Canessa was head of the medical team, although he refused to allow his talents to be so narrowly utilized. Others with more serious injuries were in charge of making water out of snow from the device invented by one of the players out of aluminum sheets that harnessed solar power. As the days went past, many different aircraft flew over and the spirits of the men dwindled as no help appeared.

The sleeping arrangements were murderous. Packed like sardines, head to tail, the survivors huddled together under Canessa's "blankets." In the howling dead of night, unfortunate souls who needed to urinate stepped on their friend's broken bones and every time someone moved in their sleep, everyone was forced to move.

Eventually, Nando Parrado came out of his coma. On waking he was told by Canessa, "Your mother died at once in the crash. Her body is out in the snow. But don't think of that. You must help Susana." Parrado heroically nursed and warmed his sister day and night until, eventually and inevitably, she passed away like her mother had done before her. With his mother and sister dead, Parrado resolved to make good on remarks he had made to Carlitos Paez about walking out of the mountains. Paez had already deemed this feat to be impossible, telling Parrado that he would freeze to death in the snow.

"Not if I wore enough clothes," Parrado replied.

"Then you'd starve to death. You can't climb mountains on a little piece of chocolate and a sip of wine."

"Then I'll cut the meat from one of the pilots," said Parrado. "After all, they got us into this mess."

The meager provisions soon petered out and as the weeks slowly slipped past, every man and woman who wished to stay alive was forced to accept the fact that cannibalism was their only chance of survival. It was a heart-rending decision for the survivors, all of them schooled in devout Catholicism. Eating human flesh became akin to the act of holy communion central to Catholic belief and every gruesome meal was undertaken with heavy quasi-religious overtones. Although the Roman Catholic church later accepted the practice *in extremis* they decided not to endorse the way that the survivors had chosen to think of it.

Although exploratory groups went out into the mountains, on one momentous trip finding the tail of the wrecked fuselage, few believed they would ever be found. Six weeks into their ordeal, after watching badly injured friends slip away, eating human meat to remain alive and after surviving an avalanche that cruelly smashed into their shelter killing many friends including Captain Pérez, and after bad weather had kept them trapped inside for days, Parrado and Canessa set off to find help, spurred on by the knowledge that if they couldn't find it all of them would die, lonely and starving, on the freezing mountainside. Seventy days after the Fairchild had first crashed, Nando Parrado and Roberto Canessa finally made contact with a Chilean peasant whom they spotted on the opposite bank of a river in a remote Chilean valley, but their unkempt appearance frightened him away. Returning the next day with a group of villagers, the peasant threw Parrado and Canessa a pen and paper wrapped inside a handkerchief. When he received the paper back it read, "I come from a plane that fell in the mountains. I am Uruguayan. We have been walking for ten days."

The next day, December 22, 1972, Parrado returned to the scene of the crash in a helicopter and the first six survivors were airlifted off the mountain. The rescue was extremely hazardous due to the air currents, so medical and food supplies and three rescue workers were dropped to assist the last eight. Finally, 72 days after crashing, the last eight brave men were lifted from the mountains to join their friends and families once again in civilization. Out of 45 souls on board the Fairchild only 16 were to survive the ordeal. An inquiry board later attributed the crash to pilot error.

3 Tenerife, Canary Islands, 1977 Pan American Boeing 747-121 and KLM Boeing 747-206B

Stan Stewart

On Sunday, March 27, 1977, a bomb exploded in the passenger terminal at Las Palmas Airport, damaging the check-in area and injuring a number of people. A separatist organization, the Movement for the Independence and Autonomy of the Canaries Archipelago, was believed responsible. The Canary Island group is a Spanish possession lying just off the west coast of North Africa, and is rich in tourism. The capital, Las Palmas, is situated on the east coast of Grand Canary Island, and a short distance to the west lies another island of the group, Tenerife, with the main town of Santa Cruz and its airport, Los Rodeos.

The explosion at Las Palmas was followed by a warning of the possibility of a second bomb, and as a precaution the authorities closed the airport. As a result all flights were diverted to Los Rodeos Airport on Tenerife. The organization demanding independence from Spain, making its presence felt at the beginning of the tourist season, had achieved the desired result of gaining publicity for its cause. Unknown to the perpetrators, however, their efforts that day were to be completely overshadowed by future events. The Las Palmas blast killed no one but, unintended by the bombers, triggered a sequence of occurrences which, in the end, led to a catastrophe of horrific proportions.

Pan American Flight PA1736, a Boeing 747 registration N736PA on charter to Royal Cruise Lines, departed Los Angeles on the evening of March 26 local date (01.29hrs GMT, March 27) with 275 passengers for New York and Las Palmas. On the stop-over at JFK a further 103 passengers boarded, bringing the total to 378. The crew of 16 was changed. At 07.42hrs (all times GMT) Flight PA1736, call sign Clipper 1736, departed Kennedy for Las Palmas under the command of Captain Victor Grubbs, with First Officer (F/O) Robert Bragg and Flight Engineer (F/E) George Warns. Tending the passengers' needs were 13 flight attendants. About 1½ hours after the Clipper's take-off from New York, KLM Flight KL4805 departed from Amsterdam at 09.00hrs also en route to Las Palmas. The KLM Boeing 747, registration PH-BUF, was operated by the Dutch airline on behalf of Holland International travel group, and on board were 234 tourists bound for a vacation in the Canary Islands, plus one travel guide. After disembarking the passengers,

Above: *The burnt out debris of what remains to this day the worst disaster in aviation history.*
CORBIS/Hulton-Deutsch Collection

PH-BUF was scheduled as Flight KL4806 to fly back to Amsterdam with an equal-ly large group of returning holidaymakers. The Dutch crew rostered for the round trip was commanded by Captain Jacob van Zanten, a senior KLM training captain, and with him on the flightdeck were F/O Klass Meurs and F/E William Schreuder. There were 11 cabin staff to look after the charter passengers.

As both Boeing 747s converged on Las Palmas, the bomb was detonated in the terminal building about one hour before KLM's arrival. With closure of the airport Flight KL4805 simply diverted to Los Rodeos on Tenerife pending the reopening of the airport, and landed at 13.38hrs GMT, the same time as local. Pan Am's arrival from New York was also affected, but Flight PA1736 landed at Los Rodeos at 14.15hrs, about 30 minutes behind KLM. The weather was clear and sunny. Many aircraft were diverted from Las Palmas that day and, with Tenerife's own week-end traffic, Los Rodeos was becoming overcrowded.

The Dutch crew, concerned that there might be insufficient time for them to com-plete the round trip back to Holland, contacted Amsterdam on high frequency long range radio. Crews were advised to liaise with Amsterdam in order to establish a limit to their duty day. Captains were bound by this limit and could be prosecuted under the law for exceeding their duty time. Amsterdam replied that if the KLM flight could depart Las Palmas by 19.00hrs at the latest, they would not exceed their flight time limitation.

Shortly after Pan Am's arrival, at about 14.30hrs, Las Palmas was declared open and aircraft began to depart for Grand Canary Island. Since the Clipper charter flight's passengers were still on board, they were prepared for a quick departure. Two company employees joined the flight in Tenerife for the short hop to Las Palmas and were placed in the jump seats on the flightdeck, bringing the total on board to 396; 380 passengers and 16 crew. As the aircraft on the holding area positioned between the two 747s were permitted to depart, Pan Am called for clearance in turn. When start-up was requested, the controller explained that although there was no air traffic delay they might have to wait. Taxiing via the parallel taxi route past the main apron was not possible because of overcrowding, and the holding area exit on to the runway was probably blocked by KLM. The other aircraft parked on the holding area, being smaller in size, had managed to pass behind the KLM 747 on their departure for Las Palmas. Unable to follow suit, N736PA was trapped until the Dutch aircraft moved.

The KLM passengers were summoned from the terminal building, but it took time to bus them back to the aircraft and reboard the flight. Of those who landed in Tenerife only the Dutch company travel guide remained behind, giving a total on board of 248; 234 passengers and 14 crew. In the meantime, many aircraft were arriving at the reopened Las Palmas Airport and it, too, was becoming congested. Los Rodeos was co-ordinating the situation with Las Palmas personnel and soon news came through of a further delay for the Dutch flight. As yet no gate was available for KLM and Captain van Zanten had no choice but to wait. The Dutch crew maintained close contact with Tenerife tower over their departure time and expressed concern over the delay. They had now been on the ground for over two hours. It was unlikely a speedy turn-round could be expected in Las Palmas owing to the congestion, so to ease the situation the Dutch captain made the somewhat late decision to refuel at Tenerife. Since they were still awaiting departure clearance owing to the unavailability of the gate at Las Palmas, it would save time on the transit to refuel there for the return Tenerife–Las Palmas–Amsterdam journey. The fueling process, however, would take about 30 minutes.

The Pan Am crew, still hemmed in on both sides, was far from happy with this decision. N736PA was free to leave at any time but could not do so until KLM moved. The American first officer and flight engineer walked out on to the tarmac to measure the distance behind KLM but confirmed that there was insufficient space. Captain Grubbs had been listening in on KLM's radio conversation with the tower and knew of the Dutch captain's desire to leave as early as possible but, unaware of KLM's tight schedule, he felt the Dutch were further delaying both their departures unnecessarily. Clearance for Captain van Zanten to start could come through at any moment but would now have to wait completion of KLM's refueling. To complicate matters, the weather was beginning to deteriorate. Los Rodeos Airport is at an elevation of 2,000ft in a hollow between mountains and is often subject to the presence of low-lying cloud, reducing visibility. In fog, the moisture content and, therefore, visibility remains relatively constant, but with low cloud drifting across an airport the visibility can change rapidly from several miles to zero in a matter of minutes. Clouds of varying density from light to dark were blowing down the departure runway 30 with the northwesterly 12–15kts wind. At times the runway visibility increased to about two miles and at other times dropped to half a mile. The runway centerline lights were inoperative, making judgement on take-off more difficult. There was also heavy moisture in the air with the passage of the clouds, and aircraft were frequently required to use windscreen wipers to clear the view when taxiing.

The time was now about 16.30hrs and the Pan Am crew had been on duty for 10 hours. They were beginning to feel the strain and were looking forward to their rest after the short 25-minute hop to Las Palmas. The KLM crew had been on duty for eight hours, but they still had to complete the round trip back to Amsterdam. Three hours remained to the deadline for departure out of Las Palmas, but with the weather worsening, this time limit could easily be compromised if they had to wait for the clouds to clear. As it was, the duty limit had not yet been confirmed, and even with fuel on board the transit through Las Palmas could be slow. If the crew ran out of hours and PH-BUF got stuck in Las Palmas, there would be more than a few problems for the ground staff, such as finding 250 beds at short notice. The crew would also be late back to Amsterdam and the aircraft would miss the next day's schedules. It was hardly surprising that the Dutch crew were keen to get away. The Americans, too, irritated at being held back by KLM, would also be happy to leave.

Permission for KLM to depart did not come through until refueling was almost finished and vindicated van Zanten's decision to complete the process in Tenerife. As the Clipper crew waited, the American passengers were invited to view the flight-deck, and questions about the flight were answered. At 16.45hrs van Zanten signed the fuel log and at 16.51hrs, with pre-start checks completed, KLM requested start-up. Alert to the situation, Pan Am heard KLM's radio call.

"Aha," said Captain Grubbs, "he's ready!"

The Clipper also received start clearance as KLM was starting engines and the two crews prepared to taxi. Owing to the prevailing northwesterly wind, both aircraft had to enter the runway from the holding area for runway 12 and taxi right to the far end of the 11,150ft (3,400m) runway, a distance of over two miles, for take-off in the opposite direction on runway 30.

At that time the control tower had three radio frequencies available—121.7MHz, 118.7MHz, and 119.7MHz. Only two controllers were on duty, so 118.7MHz was used for ground taxi instruction and 119.7MHz, the approach frequency, for both take-off and approach communication. KLM was cleared to taxi at 16.56hrs but was instructed to hold short of the runway 12 threshold and to contact approach on 119.7MHz. On establishing contact, Flight KL4805 requested permission to enter and back-track on runway 12. Clearance was received to taxi back down the runway and to exit at the third turn-off, but almost immediately the controller amended the taxi instruction. KLM was directed to back-track the runway all the way, then to complete a 180° turn at the end and face into the take-off direction. The first officer acknowledged the instruction but the captain, now concentrating on more pressing matters, was beginning to overlook radio calls.

The visibility was changing rapidly from good to very poor as they taxied along the runway and it was proving difficult to ascertain position. The approach controller issuing taxi instructions could see nothing from the tower so was unable to help. One minute later the KLM captain radioed the approach controller asking if they were to leave the runway at taxiway Charlie 1. Once more KLM was instructed to continue straight down the runway.

Pan Am received taxi instructions on the ground frequency of 118.7MHz and was also directed to hold at the 12 threshold. Captain Grubbs was happy to wait until after KLM's departure but almost immediately was cleared to follow the Dutch flight. The instruction was given to back-track on the runway and leave by the third exit, but because of the ground controller's heavy Spanish accent the crew had a great deal of trouble understanding the clearance. With better communications the captain might well have established his preference to hold position, but since several attempts were required to comprehend a simple direction it was obviously going to be easier to comply with the controller's wishes. Pan Am was given instructions to back-track on the ground frequency so the Dutch crew, already changed to approach, were at first unaware that the Americans were following behind. As Flight PA1736 began its journey down the runway, ground cleared Captain Grubbs to contact approach. At 17.02hrs KLM now heard the Pan Am crew call approach control and request confirmation of the back-track instruction.

"Affirmative," replied approach, "taxi into the runway and leave the runway third, third to your left, third."

By now the Americans had been on duty for over 11½ hours and were feeling tired. The Dutch crew had been on duty for over 9½ hours, of which about 3½ hours had been spent waiting on the ground at Tenerife. The visibility began to drop markedly and fell to as low as 300ft in the path of the two Boeing 747s taxiing down the runway. It was difficult to spot the exits. Thick cloud patches at other parts on the airport reduced visibility right down to zero. All guidance was given via the radio as no one could see anyone else and Los Rodeos was not equipped with expensive ground radar. Captain van Zanten, when approaching taxiway Charlie 4, again asked his co-pilot if this was their turn off, but the first officer repeated that the instruction had been given to back-track all the way to the end. The KLM crew had switched on the wipers to clear the moisture and suddenly, through the mist, could see some lights. The first officer confirmed the sighting.

"Here comes the end of the runway."

"A couple of lights to go," replied the captain. Approach then called asking Flight 4805 to state its position.

17.02:50hrs, Approach R/T: "KLM 4805, how many taxiway did you pass?"
17.02:56hrs, KLM 4805 R/T: "I think we just passed Charlie 4 now."
17.03:01hrs, Approach R/T: "OK. At the end of the runway make a 180 and report ready for ATC [Air Traffic Control] clearance."

The KLM crew now asked if the centerline lights were operating and the controller replied he would check. The Americans were still not sure of the correct turn-off because of the language difficulties and once again asked for confirmation that they were to exit the runway at the third exit.

Above: *The KLM 747 would have been in this attitude and, as here, just off the ground when it hit Pan Am's flight 1736.* via John Stroud

Below: *A Pan Am 747.* John Stroud

17.03:36hrs, Approach R/T: "Third one sir, one, two, three, third, third one."
17.03:39hrs, PA1736 R/T: "Very good, thank you."
Approach R/T: "Clipper 1736, report leaving the runway."

The Clipper replied with his call sign. As the Americans continued down the runway the taxi check was commenced. Instruments and flying controls were checked, the stabilizer was set and the flaps were positioned for take-off, etc. Meanwhile, the Pan Am crew was also trying to spot the turn-offs from the runway in order to count along to the third one, but were having a great deal of trouble in seeing properly. They passed and recognized the 90° taxi exit but were unable to see the taxiway markers so were unsure how many turn-offs they had passed. The allocated exit involved following a "Z"-shaped pattern to maneuver on to the parallel taxiway and was going to be difficult for the large Boeing 747 to negotiate. Finding Charlie 3 was also proving to be difficult since its shape was similar to Charlie 2.

As KLM approached the end of the runway the controller called both aircraft regarding the centerline lights.

Approach R/T: "For your information, the centerline lighting is out of service."

Each flight acknowledged in turn and checked the minimum visibility required for take-off in such circumstances. By now KLM was commencing the turn at the end of the runway and much was on the captain's mind. Turning a large aircraft through 180° on a narrow runway requires a degree of concentration and temporarily distracted the captain from other duties. The time was now almost 17.05hrs and the restriction for departure out of Las Palmas was rapidly approaching. If they didn't depart soon they could easily miss it. By seeming good fortune the visibility had improved sufficiently for take-off and with a reduction in moisture the wipers were switched off. If they could get away quickly in the gap in the weather everything should be fine. As the take-off approached, the captain, having to concentrate on so many items, "seemed a little absent from all that was heard on the flightdeck." He called for the check list.

KLM F/O: "Cabin warned. Flaps set ten, ten."
KLM F/E: "Eight greens."
KLM F/O: "Ignition."
KLM F/E: "Is coming—all on flight start."
KLM F/O: "Body gear."
KLM F/E: "Body gear OK?"

The turn was now almost complete with the aircraft lining up on runway 30.

KLM Capt: "Yes, go ahead."

The visibility now improved to over half a mile, but a cloud could be seen ahead moving down the runway. There was just enough time to get away. The Pan Am aircraft was approaching exit Charlie 3 at this stage, half way along the two-mile-long runway, but in the bad conditions was unobserved by KLM. Nothing could be seen of the locations of the 747s from the tower. The two aircraft faced each other unseen in the mist.

KLM F/O: "Wipers on?"
KLM Capt: "Lights are on."
KLM F/O: "No . . . the wipers?'
KLM Capt: "No I'll wait a bit . . . if I need them I'll ask."
KLM F/O: "Body gear disarmed, landing lights on, check list completed."

At 17.05:28hrs the captain stopped the aircraft at the end of the runway and immediately opened up the throttles.

KLM F/O: "Wait a minute, we don't have an ATC clearance."

The KLM captain, being a senior training pilot, had a lack of recent route practice and was more used to operations in the simulator. In the simulator radio work is kept to a minimum on the grounds of expediency in order to concentrate on drills and procedures, and take-offs are often conducted without any formalities. Such an oversight, although alarming, can perhaps be explained by the circumstances. On closing the throttles the captain replied, "No, I know that, go ahead, ask." The first officer pressed the button and asked for both take-off air traffic clearances.

KLM F/O R/T: "KLM4805 is now ready for take-off and we are waiting for our ATC clearance."

Pan Am arrived at exit Charlie 3 just as approach began to read back KLM's ATC clearance. Having miscounted the turn-offs, they missed their designated taxi route and continued on down the runway unaware of their mistake. They were still about a mile from the threshold and out of sight of KLM. It was now over two minutes since the approach controller's last call to Pan Am requesting him to report leaving the runway, and in the KLM crew's desire to depart, the fact that Pan Am was still in front of them, not having cleared the runway, was being overlooked.

17.05:53hrs Approach R/T: "KLM4805, you are cleared to the papa beacon, climb to and maintain flight level nine zero. Right turn after take-off, proceed with heading zero four zero until intercepting the three three five radial from Las Palmas VOR [VHF omnidirectional range radio beacon]."

Towards the end of this transmission, and before the controller had finished speaking, the KLM captain accepted this as an unequivocal clearance to take-off and said, "Yes." He opened up the thrust levers slightly with the aircraft held on the brakes and paused till the engines stabilized.

17.06:09hrs KLM F/O R/T: "Ah, roger sir, we're cleared to the papa beacon, flight level nine zero . . ."

As the first officer spoke the captain released the brakes at 17.06:11hrs and, one second later, said, "Let's go, check thrust." The throttles were opened to take-off power and the engines were heard to spin up. The commencement of the take-off in the middle of reading back the clearance caught the first officer off balance and during the moments which followed this, he "became noticeably hurried and less clear."

KLM F/O R/T: ". . . right turn out, zero four zero, until intercepting the three two five. We are now at take-off.'

The last sentence was far from distinct. Whatever was said the rapid statement was sufficiently ambiguous to cause concern and both the approach controller and the Pan Am first officer replied simultaneously.

17.06:18hrs Approach R/T: "OK . . ."

In the one-second gap in the controllers' transmission, Pan Am called to make their position clear. The two spoke over the top of each other.

17.06:19hrs Approach R/T: ". . . stand-by for take-off, I will call you."

Pan Am F/O R/T: "No, uh . . . and we are still taxying down the runway, the Clipper 1736."

The combined transmissions were heard as a loud three-second squeal on the KLM flightdeck causing distortion to the messages. Had the words been clearer the KLM crew might have realized their predicament but, only moments later, a second chance came for them to assess the danger. The controller had received only the Clipper call sign with any clarity but immediately called back in acknowledgement.

17.06:20hrs Approach R/T: "Roger, papa alpha 1736, report the runway clear."

On this one and only radio call the controller, for no apparent reason, used the call sign papa alpha instead of Clipper.

17.06:30hrs Clipper R/T: "OK we'll report when we're clear."
Approach R/T: "Thank you."

In spite of these transmissions, the KLM Boeing 747 continued to accelerate down the runway. The words were lost to the pilots concentrating on the take-off but they caught the flight engineer's attention. He tentatively inquired of the situation.

KLM F/E: "Is he not clear, then?"
KLM Capt: "What did you say?"

KLM F/E: "Is he not clear, that Pan American?'
KLM Capt: "Oh, yes."

The co-pilot also answered simultaneously in the affirmative and the flight engineer did not press the matter. The KLM aircraft continued on its take-off run into the path of Pan Am. It is difficult for most people to understand how anyone as experienced as the Dutch captain could have made an error of such magnitude. For those used to regular hours and familiar surroundings, with nights asleep in their own time zone and frequent rest periods, it may be impossible to comprehend. But the flying environment can place great strain on an individual. Constant traveling in alien environments, long duty days, flights through the night and irregular rest patterns can all take their toll. The Dutch crew had been on duty for almost 9½ hours and still had to face the problems of the transit in Las Palmas and the return to Amsterdam. Lack of recent route experience for the captain, especially in these trying conditions, did not help. The pressure was on to leave Los Rodeos as early as possible and the weather was not making it any easier. A gap in the drifting cloud had presented itself and the captain had taken the opportunity to depart.

Close concentration was required on the take-off as clouds were once again reducing visibility. At such moments the thought process of the brain can reach saturation point and can become overloaded. The "filtering effect" takes over and all but urgent messages, or only important details of the task in hand, are screened from the mind. Radio communications, which were being conducted by the first officer, were obviously placed in a low priority in the minds of both the pilots once the take-off had been commenced. The controller's use of papa alpha instead of Clipper—the only occasion that day on which this identification was used—reduced the chances of registering the transmission. On the Clipper flightdeck the crew was sufficiently alarmed by the ambiguity of the situation to comment although they were not as yet aware that the KLM had started his take-off run.

Pan Am Capt: "Let's get the hell out of here."
Pan Am F/O: "Yeh, he's anxious, isn't he."
Pan Am F/E: "Yeh, after he held us up for an hour and a half . . . now he's in a rush."

The flight engineer had no sooner finished speaking when the American captain saw KLM's landing lights appear, coming straight at them through the cloud bank.

Pan Am Capt: "There he is . . . look at him . . . that . . . that son-of-a-bitch is coming."
Pan Am F/O: "Get off ! Get off ! Get off!"

Captain Grubbs threw the aircraft to the left and opened up the throttles in an attempt to run clear. At about the same time the Dutch first officer, still unaware of Pan Am's presence, called "Vee one," the go or no-go decision speed. Four seconds later the Dutch crew spotted the Pan Am 747 trying to scramble clear.

KLM Capt: "Oh!!"

The Dutch captain pulled back hard on the control column in an early attempt to get airborne. The tail struck the ground in the high nose up angle leaving a 20m long streak of metal on the runway surface. In spite of the endeavors of both crews to take avoiding action, however, the collision was inevitable. The KLM 747 managed to become completely airborne about 5,000ft down the runway, near the Charlie 4 turn-off, but almost immediately slammed into the side of Pan Am. The nosewheel of the Dutch aircraft lifted over the top of Pan Am and the KLM number one engine, on the extreme left, just grazed the side of the American aircraft. The fuselage of the KLM flight skidded over the top of the other but its main landing gear smashed into Pan Am about the position of Clipper's number three engine. The collision was not excessively violent and many passengers thought a small bomb had exploded. Pan Am's first class upstairs lounge disappeared on impact, as did most of the top of the fuselage, and the tail section broke off. Openings appeared on the left side of the fuselage and some passengers were able to escape by these routes. The Pan Am air-craft had its nose sticking off the edge of the runway and survivors simply jumped down on to the grass. The first class lounge floor had collapsed, but the flight crew, plus the two employees in the jump seats, managed to leap below into what was left of the first class section and make their escape. On the left side the engines were still turning and there was a fire under the wing with explosions taking place. The main landing gear of the KLM flight sheared off on impact and the aircraft sank back on to the runway about 500ft further on. It skidded for another 1,000ft and as it did so the aircraft slid to the right, rotating clockwise through a 90° turn before coming to a halt. Immediately an extensive and violent fire erupted engulfing the wreckage.

The controllers in the tower heard the explosions and at first thought a fuel tank had been blown up by the terrorists, but soon reports of a fire on the airport began to be received. The fire services were alerted and news of the emergency was trans-mitted to all aircraft. The fire trucks had difficulty making their way to the scene of the fire in the misty and congested airport, but eventually the firemen saw the flames through the fog. On closer inspection the KLM aircraft was found completely ablaze. As they tackled the conflagration another fire was seen further down the run-way, assumed to be a part of the same aircraft, and the fire trucks were divided. It was then discovered that a second aircraft was involved and, since the KLM flight was already totally irrecoverable, all efforts, for the moment, were concentrated on the Pan Am machine.

Of the 396 passengers and crew aboard the Pan Am flight only 70 escaped from the wreckage and nine died later in hospital. 335 were killed. All 248 aboard the KLM aircraft perished. On that Sunday evening of March 27, 1977, 583 people lost their lives, and as if to mock those in fear of flying, the accident happened on the ground. It stands on record as the world's worst disaster in aviation history.

As the survivors were being tended in Santa Cruz, firemen at the airport contin-ued to fight the infernos on the runway. In the end, in spite of the intense blaze, the firefighters managed to save the left side of the Pan Am aircraft and the wing, from which 30,000–40,000lb of fuel were later recovered. It was not until the afternoon of the following day that both fires were completely extinguished.

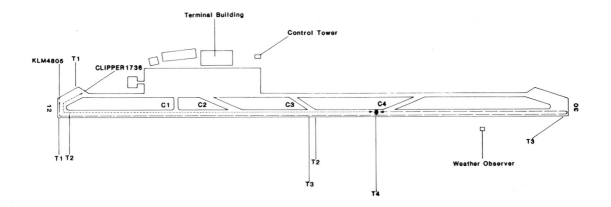

Above: *Tenerife runway details showing relative positions of the aircraft at different times (T1, T2, T3) and point of impact (T4).*

Below: *The position of the aircraft at the point of impact.*

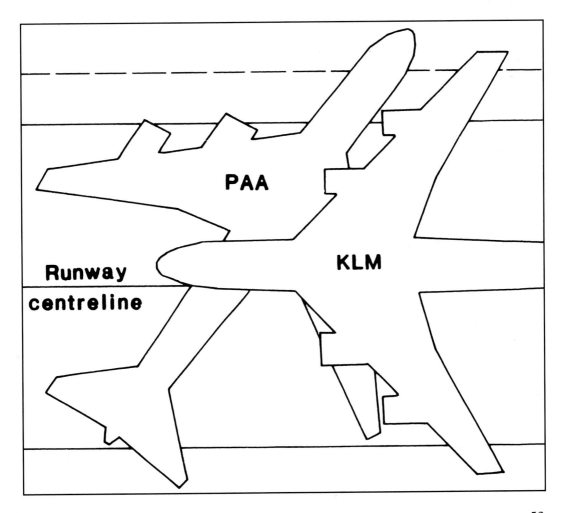

4 Chicago O'Hare, USA, 1979
American Airlines Douglas DC-10-10

Stan Stewart

merican Airlines DC-10-10, registration N110AA, began taxying at 14.59hrs central daylight time (19.59hrs GMT) to the 10,000ft 32 Right runway at Chicago's O'Hare International Airport. The date was May 25, 1979. The weather was clear with 15 miles' visibility and the temperature was 63°F. A fresh wind blew from 020° at 22kts. The DC-10 was operating Flight 191, a scheduled service from Chicago to Los Angeles, and on board were 258 passengers and 13 crew. On the taxi to the runway the before take-off checks were commenced and the trailing-edge flaps were set to 10°. The leading edge flaps, known as slats, set automatically in sequence. The take-off data card showed V1, the go or no-go decision speed as 139kts, the rotation, or lift-off, speed as 145kts and V2, the safe take-off speed required in the air in the event of an engine failure at V1, as 153kts. All speeds were checked and confirmed correctly set on the airspeed indicator using small bugs to mark the speeds. Approaching the threshold of 32 Right, Flight 191 was cleared into position and instructed to hold. Captain Walter Lux operated the radio while F/O James Dillard prepared to fly the sector. The F/E was Alfred Udovich. As the DC-10 moved into position on the runway, take-off clearance was received.

15.02:38hrs, Chicago Tower R/T: "American 191, cleared for take-off."
15.02:46hrs, Capt Lux R/T: "American 191 under way."

Two seconds later F/O Dillard opened the thrust levers and N110AA, at a gross weight of 379,000lb, began a rolling take-off. F/E Udovich accurately set the power and established take-off thrust by 80kts. During the take-off run left rudder was used to compensate for the strong cross-wind. The machine accelerated rapidly along the runway and at 139kts Captain Lux called "Vee one." The DC-10 was now committed to take-off. As the speed continued to increase all systems operated normally. The DC-10 accelerated satisfactorily along the runway until, just two seconds before lift-off, a major emergency occurred. Number one engine seemed suddenly to lose power. At that moment observers on the ground saw smoke and vapor emanating from the vicinity of the engine.

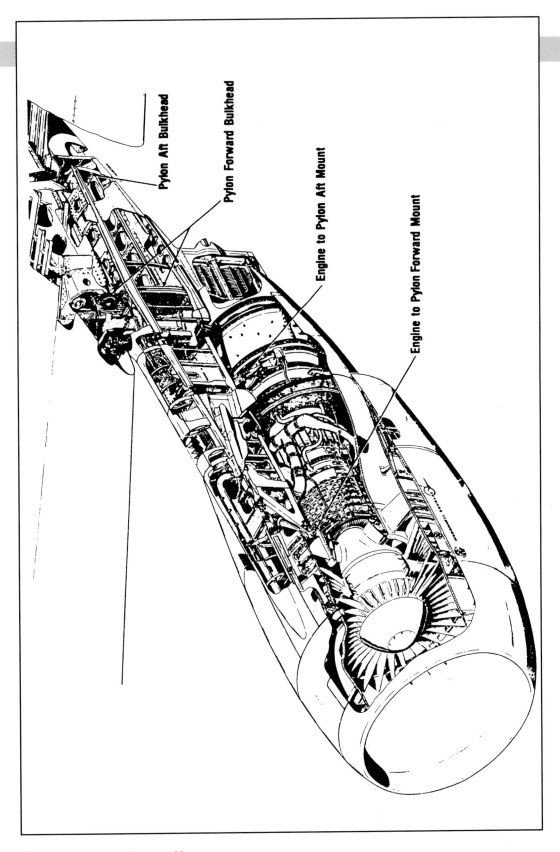

Pylon Aft Bulkhead

Pylon Forward Bulkhead

Engine to Pylon Aft Mount

Engine to Pylon Forward Mount

Above: *Engine and pylon assembly.*

Above: *American Airlines DC-10.* Via John Stroud

Below: *Firemen battle the flames.* Associated Press Photograph

"Damn," someone shouted in the cockpit.

The pilots were unable to see either the wings or the engines from the flightdeck so were unaware of the full extent of the unfolding drama. The left wing-mounted engine and its connecting pylon detached completely from the wing and the whole assembly shot upwards and tumbled backwards over the wing, smashing onto the asphalt. As the engine/pylon unit separated, a three-foot section of the wing leading edge was ripped out and vital hydraulic and electrical lines were severed. As a result important systems were lost, but, owing to a sequence of unfortunate failures, warning devices were inhibited and there was no indication on the flightdeck of the additional problems. Unaware of the extent of the damage, the crew simply followed standard procedures for engine failure on take-off, which is a well-practiced maneuver in the simulator.

As the engine separated, the lift-off speed of 145kts was reached and the captain called "rotate." F/O Dillard pulled back on the control column and at 20.03:38hrs, with 10° nose-up attitude, the DC-10 became airborne. The take-off run had lasted 50 seconds and used 6,000ft of runway. During rotation the speed had increased through the V2 speed of 153kts and had reached V2+6, 159kts, by lift-off. The DC-10 became airborne with the left wing slightly down and aileron was applied to bring the wings level. The aircraft continued to accelerate and the significance of the left wing dropping, specifically at 159kts, was lost to the crew. Unknown to the pilot, the left outboard leading edge slats had retracted inadvertently, but on the flightdeck there was no indication of the event. With such a configuration the left wing tip would stall if the speed were to drop to 159kts and positive control would be required to prevent the aircraft from rolling to the left.

F/O Dillard applied right rudder to compensate for loss of power on the left side and managed to hold the aircraft straight with the heading stabilizing at 326°. A number of important flight instruments which would have indicated the situation were supplied by the number one generator electrical busbar and had failed with the loss of number one engine. Power from the other generators should have been relayed to the number one busbar, but a protection system had operated indicating the occurrence of a major electrical fault on the component. In the few seconds after take-off, however, there was little time for trouble-shooting. To reach the electrical and generator reset panel the flight engineer had to reposition his seat, release the safety belt, and get out of the seat.

The first officer's instruments operated normally and he continued to fly the aircraft. American Airlines engine failure procedures called for a V2 climb-out speed of 153kts—6kts below the left wing tip stall speed—and Dillard pitched the nose-up to the 14° angle displayed on the flight director for a two-engined climb. The vertical speed indicator displayed an initial climb of 1,150ft/min and at 20.03:47hrs, nine seconds after lift-off, the aircraft had accelerated to 172kts at about 140ft above the ground. Aileron and rudder controls maintained the wings level and the heading relatively stable, and the nose-up angle and rate of climb remained constant. With the nose held up at 14° the speed began to decelerate from 172kts to the recommended two-engine V2 climb speed of 153kts. With positive rate of climb established the gear should have been selected up but there was hardly time to take action before the flight began to go seriously wrong. On decelerating towards 153kts, the speed fell steadily until at 159kts the left wing tip stalled. There was little or no indication of buffeting, which would have been masked by the light turbulence anyway, and the stick shake system, which would normally alert the crew to a stall situation, had been rendered inoperative. As far as the crew was concerned, all the flaps and slats were positioned correctly and the desired V2 climb speed of 153kts was satisfactory. Had they been aware of the impending stall the nose would have been lowered immediately to increase speed and a safe climb-out would have been possible. Instead, the left wing tip began to drop abruptly and the aircraft nose to yaw to the left as the stall developed. With a clearer understanding of the condition it would still have been possible to achieve a safe climb-out, even with an engine failure and the asymmetric slat condition, as long as positive action was taken to maintain the wings precisely level. The minimum speed for controlling the damaged aircraft in the air, with wings level, was as low as 128kts. As soon as the left wing banked 4°, however, the wingtip stall speed of 159kts was the minimum speed at which directional control could be maintained, even with the two operating engines at take-off power.

At 20.03:58hrs, 20 seconds after take-off and with the aircraft only 325ft above the ground, the aircraft began rolling to the left and the left wing banked over 5°. With the speed edging below 159kts, directional control was lost, although the situation was not readily apparent to the pilot. Without an increase in speed for which the crew, up to this point, could see no need, the aircraft was beyond recovery. The effect was sudden and catastrophic. The DC-10 continued a rapid roll to the left in spite of large inputs of aileron and rudder in an attempt to maintain directional control. Only 20-odd seconds had passed since lift-off and there was no time to think. The F/O continued to follow the flight director but the nose began to drop, even with full up elevator. At 20.04:06hrs, 28sec after take-off, the DC-10 banked 90° to the left and the nose dropped below the horizon. The wings continued to roll through the vertical and the nose pitched down rapidly to 21°, in spite of full opposite aileron and rudder controls and almost full up elevator being applied. At 20.04:09hrs, after only 31sec of flight and less than one mile from the end of the runway, the left wing tip struck the ground. The aircraft exploded and broke apart, and was completely demolished on impact. Debris scattered over an open field and mobile home park and a fierce fire erupted. Within a short time little remained of Flight 191. All 271 passengers and crew aboard the DC-10 perished and two people on the ground were killed. It was, and still is, the worst accident in American aviation history.

Examination of N110AA's engine pylon recovered from the wreckage on the runway disclosed a 10in fracture on one flange which had originally been caused by over-stressing. Fatigue cracking was also evident at both ends of the fracture indicating the damage had been present for a period of time. During take-off the weakened section had been overloaded and separation of the pylon from the wing had occurred. As a result of these findings the FAA ordered a fleet-wide inspection of the DC-10. The checks revealed that a further nine Series 10 aircraft had suffered damage—four American Airlines, four Continental Airlines and one United Airlines— including two Continental Airlines aircraft which had been repaired. Discrepancies in certain clearances as well as a number of loose, failed, and missing fasteners were also

TAKE-OFF ENGINE FAILURE
FLAPS 15° OR LESS OR 22°

This procedure assumes indication of engine failure where the take-off is continued. Each take-off should be planned for the possibility of an engine failure. Normal take-off procedures ensure the ability to handle an engine failure successfully at any point.

If an engine failure occurs when making a Standard Thrust take-off, Standard Thrust on the remaining engines will produce the required take-off performance. If deemed necessary, the remaining engines may be advance to Maximum Take-Off Thrust.

Speed . . . . CLIMB OUT AT V_2 UNTIL REACHING 800 FEET AFL
OR OBSTACLE CLEARANCE ALTITUDE, WHICHEVER IS HIGHER,
THEN LOWER NOSE AND ACCELERATE.

At 0°/EXT Min Maneuver Speed,
Flaps . . . . UP

At V_2 + 50 60 ,
Slats . . . . .RETRACT
    If returning to land, slats may be left extended.

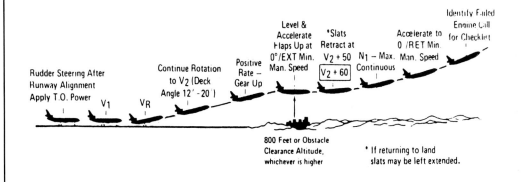

Above: *The American Air Lines' engine failure procedure.*

found. Examination of the flange fractures established a similarity of the failure modes and prompted an extensive analysis and testing program of the DC-10 engine/pylon assemblies. The FAA, ever wary of the adverse publicity received following the Paris DC-10 crash, launched a most thorough investigation. The facts which were eventually revealed made disturbing reading.

Evidence of broken fasteners, which did not account for the accident, was found on 31 aircraft. The deficiencies in quality control which had produced these results were traced in part to the disruption caused in 1974 when moving the pylon assembly line from Douglas's factory in Santa Monica to Huntington Beach. Many skilled workers were upset by the change and refused to move. Finding replacements was not easy. In addition to the broken fasteners, the minimal manufacturing clearances at the pylon-to-wing attachment point resulted in maintenance difficulties which made the occurrence of pylon flange damage more likely. This chance of damage was increased by maintenance methods adopted by some airlines.

As early as May 1975, and again in February 1978, McDonnell Douglas issued DC-10 service bulletins requiring maintenance of parts of the engine pylon at the convenience of the operators. The procedure called for dismantling of the complete engine and pylon assembly which was normally accomplished by first removing the engine then detaching the pylon from the wing. American Airlines engineers, while working on four DC-10-30 aircraft in 1977, evaluated the possibility of removing the engine and pylon as a single unit using a modified forklift-type truck. United Airlines was already performing these tasks using an overhead hoist. The technique was calculated to save 200 man hours per aircraft and, from a safety point of view, would reduce the number of fuel, hydraulic, and electrical disconnects from 79 to 27. The airline contacted McDonnell Douglas with its proposal, and the manufacturer, with neither the authority to approve nor disapprove their customers' maintenance actions, simply stated that they would not encourage the procedure. At that time, FAA approval of an airline's maintenance methods was not required either, and they were not consulted on the proposed changes. American Airlines, with other DC-10 operators, including Continental Airlines, decided to adopt the process and a considerable number of single-unit engine/pylon assemblies were removed in this manner. The use of a forklift truck to lower and raise the assembly required a great degree of precision on the part of the controller. Post-accident investigations revealed that of the 175 occasions of U.S. airlines removing engines and pylons for maintenance procedures, 88 had been conducted with the engine and pylon as a single unit, 12 of these had been lowered and raised using an overhead hoist and 76 using a forklift truck. All incidents of pylon flange fractures involved use of the forklift vehicle.

In December 1978, Continental Airlines engineers were removing an engine/pylon unit using the forklift truck method when a noise "like a pistol shot" was heard. An inspection revealed fracture of a pylon flange. The flange was repaired and the aircraft was returned to service. Again, in February 1979, a similar "pistol shot" was heard when a misunderstanding arose between the forklift operator and the lead mechanic. The nose of the engine was lowered instead of raised, resulting in fracture of the flange. Once more the damage was simply repaired.

Above: *American Airlines lost a second DC-10 following an aborted take off at Dallas Fort Worth in 1988 but in this case nobody was killed.* ASM Photo

Continental Airlines examined the incidents and concluded that they were both caused by maintenance errors. The FAA rules governing the reporting of incidents occurring both during maintenance and in service are extensively defined, but in this case the regulations did not seem adequately to outline what constituted a major repair. Also, Continental's mishaps, considered by the airline as maintenance errors, seemed to fall between two categories. As a result there did not seem a requirement to inform the FAA of the incidents and, as in the case of the DC-10 rear cargo door problems, the FAA was totally unaware of the events.

At the occurrence of the Continental Airlines flange fracture in 1978, McDonnell Douglas had sent an engineering specialist to assist in the repair. He was simply informed that the crack had happened when lowering the pylon. The engineer wrote a report on the fracture explaining that it had apparently occurred when the pylon shifted during lowering. An account of this damage was circulated to airlines with a list of other events in a document known as an Operational Occurrence Report, but it was camouflaged by the trivia of other incidents: an air conditioning unit malfunction, a lightning strike, and an injury to a flight attendant. American Airlines did not even recall receiving the Operational Occurrence Report. Once again a major fault had been discovered by one airline but a breakdown in communications had resulted in improper dissemination of the information. American Airlines continued to remove engine/pylon assemblies as a single unit without any knowledge of the inherent dangers.

At the end of March 1979, the accident aircraft underwent modifications. On removal of the left engine/pylon unit it is possible that inadvertent creep down of the lifting truck forks, and/or misalignment of the engine stand on the fork lift, over-stressed the pylon flanges. Unknown to the engineers, a 10-inch fracture had occurred on one of the flanges. The aircraft had been returned to service in this condition after maintenance and the crack had continued to weaken during the eight weeks of operation before the accident. Finally, the structure had been sufficiently weakened to fail under normal load and the complete engine and pylon had separated from the wing on the take-off out of Chicago.

But why had the aircraft crashed? Engines had failed before, and had even fallen off, as had other aircraft parts, and the crew had been able to recover successfully. What circumstances had caused such tragic results on May 25, 1979? The answer lay in the complications of the DC-10 design philosophy and on the approved engine failure procedures. On separation of the engine and pylon from the wing, three feet of the wing leading edge had been torn off and hydraulic and electrical cables had been severed. The damage had resulted in fracture of the numbers one and three hydraulic lines for the extension and retraction of the left wing outboard leading edge slats. Other aircraft designs included mechanical devices which positively locked out the slats when extended, but the DC-10 did not incorporate such a mechanism. Instead, the DC-10's slats were simply held extended against the air loads by trapped hydraulic fluid in the operating lines. One FAA regulation required symmetric operation of the slats, even with hydraulic problems, and on the DC-10 this was satisfied by a single valve controlling the inboard slats, left and right, and by mechanically linked valves controlling the outboard slats, left and right, which were attached to the inboard slats. The arrangement ensured uniform operation of the flaps, including taking into account hydraulic failures. In the event, however, it was still considered that asymmetric failure of the outboard slats was a possibility and that a chance remained of the DC-10 being exposed in flight to one set of outboard slats extended and the other retracted. To satisfy the regulations in this respect it was ably demonstrated in flight that with an outboard asymmetric slat condition the DC-10 could be flown safely within the normal range of departure and approach speeds. As an added precaution a slat warning light was introduced which was designed to illuminate when the positions of any slat disagreed with the flap/slat lever position. In addition, a stick shaker was available to operate if early onset of a stall condition, including that induced by asymmetric slat, was detected by the system. If a pilot experienced such an event with the accompanying warning signals, he would simply lower the nose to increase speed and fly out of danger. It seemed an adequate and reasonable design.

According to FAA regulations, any newly designed aircraft was required to be capable of continued flight and landing after "any combination of failures not shown to be extremely improbable"; the definition of "extremely improbable" being one chance in a billion. Studies showed that the probability of an uncommanded slat retraction, specifically during the take-off phase, ranged from one chance in a hundred million to two chances in a billion per flight. The consequences, therefore, had to be considered and Douglas complied. An examination of the asymmetric situation at the lower take-off speeds was not conducted in flight although an analysis showed that with all engines operating safe speeds could be achieved. The analysis also

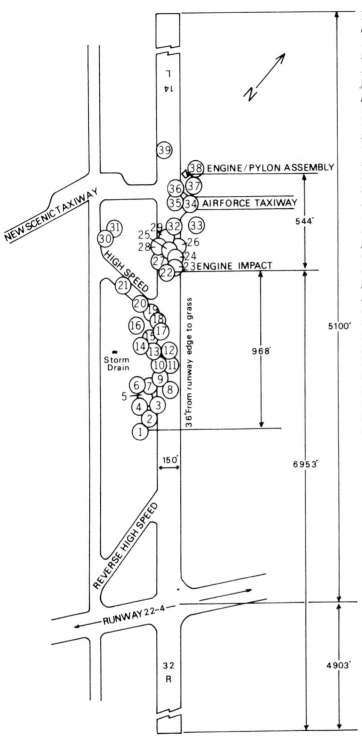

Left: *Distribution of engine/pylon and associated wreckage.*

1 Pylon fairing (fiberglass); 2 Seal and torn metal; 3 Pylon fairing (fiberglass); Pylon thrust line shim washer; 5 Flange from pylon thrust link bushing; 6 Pylon pneumatic fitting; 7 Sheet metal AUB 7108-413; 11 Control bracket AUN-7020-1. NUN 6001-401; 12 Piece of mono ball (thrust line); 13 Thrust link washer; 14 Wing leading ARB 1065-1GS # Mac 22 (wing leading edge to pylon interface edge with Jay Box); 15 Control bracket AUN 7009-1 (four pulleys); Bolt match to No 21; 17 Sheet metal ARB 1680 (bulkhead type); 18 Fuel line with DBL wall coupling with fuel drain T coupling; Fan cowl ASL 0209-2 (275 707-04); 20 Acoustic material; 21 Sheared bolt and nut 0.5in diameter; 22 Engine pylon impact; 23 Inlet acoustic face sheet piece; 24 Right side cowling pieces, CSD Sv door; 25 Cowling piece; 26 Cowling inlet; 27 Right side fan cowl (piece) 28 Fan blades; 29 Engine drain; 30 Right hand fan cowl; 31 Front spar attach bulkhead piece; 32 Pylon thrust line bushing; 33 CSD generator gearbox; 34 Section of front spar attach bulkhead; 35 Ignition unit; 36 Reverser actuator; 37 Hinged cowling; 38 Control bracket; Fuel line (pylon).

showed, however, that with a simultaneous engine failure and asymmetric flap retraction the safety margin might be compromised. A mathematical probability study concluded that the combination was "extremely improbable" and the design was accepted as complying with the requirements. FAA regulations "did not require the manufacturer to account for multiple malfunctions resulting from a single

63

failure," and the likelihood of an engine/pylon assembly detaching from a wing, which might have triggered such a sequence, was not considered. McDonnell Douglas deemed "the structural failure of the pylon and engine to be of the same magnitude as the structural failure of a wing." Since the loss of a wing, and in Douglas's opinion a pylon assembly, was an unacceptable occurrence, these structures were "designed to meet and exceed all the foreseeable loads of the life of the aircraft." The consequences arriving from such failures were not considered. It was logical not to analyse the loss of a wing since continued flight was impossible, but pylon structures had failed in the past and flight had been sustained. An analysis based on the loss of an engine/pylon assembly might have "indicated additional steps or methods which could have been taken to provide these systems essential to continued flight." To be fair to the designers, it seems an almost impossible task to predict accurately every likely sequence of events as the result of a failure. In aviation, however, the most unlikely events can and do happen. On May 25, 1979, the seemingly impossible occurred and an engine/pylon assembly detached from N110AA's wing. "The design and interrelationship of essential systems as they were affected by the structural loss of the pylon" led to catastrophic results.

As the pylon detached hydraulic and electrical lines were ripped out. Normally, when an engine fails, systems continue to function as their power source is automatically switched to the pumps and generators driven by the operating engines. On the DC-10, for example, although the hydraulic systems are independent of each other, the number one hydraulic system, in the event of a number one engine failure, is sustained by its pumps being driven by hydraulic fluid from number two system. Likewise, number one electrical system, in the event of number one engine failure, is sustained by the number one generator busbar being supplied with electrical power from the other engines' generators. The vulnerability of supply lines to a pylon detachment resulted in the tearing out of numbers one and three hydraulic lines. Number one system was lost completely and number three system began discharging fluid, although it continued to operate normally in spite of the leak owing to the short duration of the flight. Had the aircraft continued to fly, only number two hydraulic system would have remained, but aircraft in the past had been landed safely in such a condition. The left outboard leading edge slats were operated by hydraulic lines supplied by numbers one and three systems. Fracture of the slat operating lines had resulted in discharge of the trapped hydraulic pressure locking out the slats, and uncommanded slat retraction had ensued under aerodynamic loads.

The severing of electrical wire bundles within the failed pylon resulted in a short circuit of the number one electrical system. A protective circuitry detected the fault related to the number one generator busbar and automatically isolated the component from other parts of the electrical system. A relay device, designed to supply electrical power from the other generators, tripped and left the number one busbar dead. The flight engineer might have been able to restore power, if the fault had cleared, by operating switches on the electrical and generator reset panel, or by restoring some power by closing the emergency power switch, but the lack of time precluded any such action. With the number one generator busbar isolated, electrical power supply from that source was cut off and a number of items, including some flight and engine instruments, were lost. More importantly, the slat disagree warning light system and the stall warning system were rendered inoperative. The slat disagree warning light remained extinguished in spite of the asymmetric slat condition and resulted in the crew being unaware of the situation. Only one stick shaker system was installed, on the captain's side and, with lack of electrical power to the stick shaker motor, it also failed to function. Even had power been available to the motor, the warning would not have activated at the stall speed related to the asymmetric slat condition, as the computer sensing the position of the left outboard slat was inoperative as well. As a result no prior warning of the stall condition was received and the only indication the pilot had of the onset of the stall was when the aircraft began an abrupt roll and yaw to the left. The DC-10's two-engine climb-out procedure as practiced by a number of airlines and approved by the FAA was intolerant of such an unlikely situation. Crew were trained to fly in such circumstances at a speed equivalent to V2, and the aircraft's flight director was programed to indicate a nose-up angle at which this speed could be achieved. When DC-10 control was first evaluated, based on the asymmetric leading edge slat situation, it was assumed the appropriate warning devices would be functioning. The separation of the number one engine/pylon assembly, followed simultaneously by uncommanded retraction of the left outboard leading-edge slats and loss of the slat disagreement and stall warning systems, plus an array of failure flags on the flightdeck, did not give the crew a chance. As a result of the disaster which befell N110AA, operators were recommended to accept engine-out climb speeds in excess of V2, up to V2+10, so long as obstacle clearance was not compromised.

Three days after the crash the FAA ordered an inspection of engine pylons, and, on June 4, backed these demands by requiring further inspection of engine and pylon assemblies which had been removed and replaced during maintenance. Results of these inspections revealed damage to engine pylons which greatly alarmed the FAA. On June 6, 1979, the authority's chief administrator, Langhorne Bond, took the unprecedented action of issuing an emergency order of suspension and grounded all DC-10s worldwide. It was feared that the DC-10 design did not meet FAA requirements and the aircraft type certificate was suspended "until such time as it can be ascertained that the DC-10 aircraft meets the certification criteria." A total of 270 DC-10s, operated throughout the world by 41 airlines, was affected by the order. The longer range DC-10-30 aircraft, in which no faults had been found, was also included in the grounding, and McDonnell Douglas and a number of airlines operating the type protested at the FAA actions. A month after the Chicago crash, and more than two weeks of grounding, authorities outside the US began to lift the suspension, subject to stringent inspection and maintenance procedures, without American approval. The FAA refused to rescind the order until their own investigation was complete, and countered by issuing an instruction on 26 June prohibiting the "operation of any Model DC-10 aircraft within the airspace of the United States." It was not until after five weeks of enforced grounding of American registered DC-10s, on July 13, 1979, that the FAA, satisfied that the DC-10 did meet its requirements and that stricter inspection and maintenance procedures were being implemented, terminated the emergency suspension order and permitted the DC-10s to fly again.

5 Mt. Erebus, Antarctica, 1979
Air New Zealand Douglas DC-10-10

Stan Stewart

In the years 1839 to 1843 a British expedition led by Captain James Clark Ross sailed around Antarctica. In an area which now bears his name, Ross penetrated to the southern limits of the Pacific Ocean. There he discovered two towering volcanoes which he named Terror and Erebus in honor of his gallant ships. Erebus, from the Greek for darkness, signified the gloomy region between Earth and Hades.

With the advent of cheap and fast jet travel, remote and far off places like Antarctica became a focus of public interest. Air New Zealand put forward plans to operate two chartered DC-10 services in February 1977 and the air service license was duly obtained. The proposal for summer flights over the south magnetic pole was soon changed to overflying the more interesting McMurdo Sound area, with the impressive sights of active Mt. Erebus (at 12,450ft) and the Victoria Land glaciers.

Fraught with all the dangers that overflying this inhospitable land far from New Zealand entailed, Antarctica's unpredictable weather is made more worrying by the problems of navigation. The magnetic compass is unusable close to the magnetic pole and reference to the true pole is difficult owing to the rapidly converging meridians. Instead, grid navigation is employed, whereby a grid aligned with the Greenwich Meridian is superimposed on charts and all navigational directions are expressed with reference to the grid. The practice can be confusing with true south becoming grid north, thus applying only one north direction over the whole polar area. Without such a plan, an aircraft proceeding over the Pole would suddenly switch from heading south to heading north (or vice versa) while continuing in the same direction.

The first Air New Zealand overflight of Antarctica was on February 15, 1977: from the beginning the trips proved to be popular and at the start of the next summer additional flights were undertaken. To improve sightseeing a minimum safe altitude of 6,000ft was established within McMurdo Sound. If cloud conditions existed, aircraft were only permitted to descend to this altitude in a specifically defined area. These instructions remained in force until October 1979 when the beacon was withdrawn. The minimum acceptable cloud base height was 7,000ft for such a procedure, and descent from 16,000ft to 6,000ft was to be monitored by radar. In the sector designated by the airline, radar coverage above 6,000ft could only be achieved with

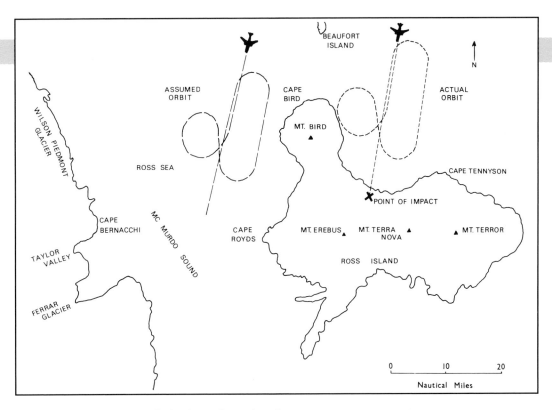

Above: *Antarctica, intended flight plan and actual track.*

the greatest of difficulty because of the outmoded equipment ANZ used and which was unacceptable to the controllers at McMurdo. In practice, however, weather conditions proved good and the visibility excellent in the unpolluted atmosphere. On these and subsequent flights, permission was requested and granted from McMurdo ATC for aircraft to depart from the planned track and fly freely in the area.

In August 1978 the airline's newly acquired ground computer was being programed with the company's routes. During this process the destination of the Antarctic flight track was changed from the beacon at Williams Field to overhead the Dailey Islands. This avoided overflying the active volcano—but the change of track was unintentional. A small but significant error had been made when one digit of the flight path was entered incorrectly into the computer. The co-ordinates of the beacon (or to be exact, Williams Field) 77° 53.0´S; 166° 48.0´E were inserted as 77° 53.0´S; 164° 48.0´E. This had the effect of moving the track about 27 miles west, a fact which went undetected. From then on the computer printed the more logical but incorrect route. This new direct routing from Cape Hallett to the position over the Dailey Islands (marked as McMurdo), now took Air New Zealand down the center of the 40-mile wide McMurdo Sound.

On November 9, 1979, a briefing took place for two remaining flights scheduled for November. Of the five present, Captain Collins and F/O Cassin would be on the flight on November 28. Topographical maps were shown but without the intended route marked; on routine flights, crews normally carry charts overlayed with route tracks, but none were available. Copies of other maps were at hand for home study, each clearly showing the military route passing down the middle of McMurdo Sound. Also available was an actual flight plan from a trip made only two days earlier. On it were typed the latitude and longitude of positions along the route (waypoints) which would be inserted into the on-board navigation computer on the day of the flight. Due to the lack of charts, the exact track and position of the end waypoint at McMurdo were not obvious. All this was examined, and notes taken for further home study.

Captain Collins had a small notebook, which he used for such information. Sightseeing procedures, including suitable viewing altitudes, were discussed and authorization was given for flights to depart from track and to descend to any altitude approved by the controllers at McMurdo. The briefing was conducted as on previous occasions, except for noting that the beacon at Williams Field had been withdrawn. Cloud break procedures using the beacon let-down pattern would not be possible, and all descents to lower altitudes would have to be in sufficiently clear skies. As an added precaution, Air New Zealand raised the minimum visibility requirements to 12 miles for Antarctic operations and also stipulated that for descent by VMC (visual meteorological conditions) there were to be no snow showers in the area.

Past experience of Antarctic flights had shown that VMC normally prevailed and that aircraft, while still in contact with controllers, could sightsee at will, flying freely under VFR in the McMurdo area. Now with the radio beacon inoperative descent would also have to be negotiated in VMC. Without VMC, flights would have to divert to the secondary viewing area to the south magnetic pole. Later, on the simulator, grid navigation techniques were outlined and the VMC descent procedure practiced.

On November 14, 1979, Captain Leslie Simpson left for Antarctica. The weather was fine and good for sightseeing. The aircraft departed early from track and flew past the glaciers of the Victoria Land coast before turning to fly visually across the sound toward McMurdo Station while descending to 2,000ft. Although the beacon at Williams Field was unserviceable, another radio aid used by the military, the tactical air navigation aid (TACAN), was operating. This transmits both bearing and range data, but only range from the transmitter is available to civil aircraft. On crossing the programed track down McMurdo Sound, Captain Simpson noted from his distance measuring equipment (DME) that the distance to the TACAN was greater than he expected. Suspecting a computer navigation error he overflew the TACAN, but all proved satisfactory. The distance from the TACAN to the McMurdo end of track waypoint was shown to be 27 miles, when Captain Simpson assumed it to be nearer 10 miles. On his return he informed Captain Johnson, mentioning that crews should be apprised of this knowledge. Captain Johnson misunderstood him and assumed that he was referring to changing the end of track waypoint from the withdrawn NDB to the operating TACAN, a distance of only 2.1 miles. This misleading information was duly passed by Captain Johnson to the navigation section for analysis. The machinery of the airline was slow to respond and it was not until the following week that the end of track waypoint change was implemented.

At home on the evening of November 27, Captain Jim Collins sat down to review the material and notes collected at the Antarctic briefing held 19 days earlier. He also plotted the co-ordinates of the track waypoints from the flight plan details on his own large Antarctic topographical chart. Although this was quite outside normal requirements the conscientious Captain Collins wanted to have no doubt of the route in his own mind. After studying the details for about two hours he retired early to bed.

Tuesday night was the time of the week for updating the stored computer information and Mr. L. Lawton, the navigation section superintendent, and Mr. B. Hewitt, his chief navigator, were receiving navigational data. By an unfortunate circumstance the flight plan retrieved for checking was one of the original copies which displayed the direct route from Cape Hallett to the Williams Field NDB. It was, therefore, a simple task to change the co-ordinates stored in the computer to those pertaining to the TACAN (77° 52.7′S; 166° 58.0′E) and nothing more was thought of it. The effect, however, was to move the end waypoint of McMurdo 27 miles back east to the TACAN near Williams Field, moving the track again over the top of Mt. Erebus.

Next morning the flight crew assembled in the dispatch office. The normal complement of captain, co-pilot and flight engineer was increased to five, with an extra first officer and flight engineer being required by law for the extra long duty day. With Captain Collins were F/O Greg Cassin and F/O Graham "Brick" Lucas, and F/E Gordon Brooks and F/E Nick Maloney. A very experienced and competent crew, although none of the pilots had been to Antarctica before and only F/E Brooks had operated on one of the earlier trips. With the briefing complete, the paperwork was collected and the crew made their way to the DC-10, ZK-NZP. No one at any time mentioned the vital change of the end waypoint co-ordinates or of the significance of the track change. The "flash ops" message which should have alerted the crew to the change was missing from the flight plan. Somewhere along the line the system had broken down.

On board Air New Zealand's Antarctic Flight 901 that day were a total of 237 passengers. Pre-departure checks included inserting the route co-ordinates via a push-button keyboard into the three on-board area inertial navigation systems (AINS), totally self-contained computer navigation units. The AINS can be coupled to the autopilot to navigate with extreme accuracy over thousands of miles without the aid of ground stations. The waypoint data keyed into the AINS was carefully cross-checked for accuracy against the flight plan co-ordinates, but checking the digits of the computer-generated flight plan was not part of crew procedures. The alteration of only four digits would not be noticed among the mass of other figures. But the AINS, by an insidious series of errors, was now programed to fly towards Erebus.

Before departure the flight plan details were transmitted to the military personnel at McMurdo Station. By a further mistake, however, the transmitted flight plan had the TACAN co-ordinates omitted and simply displayed the word McMurdo in their place. The controllers at McMurdo Station, assuming the track remained unchanged, were also still programed to accept Flight 901 down the center of the Sound.

At 08.17hrs local New Zealand time (19.17hrs GMT Tuesday—local New Zealand time GMT+13 hours, including one hour summer daylight saving) DC-10 Zulu Papa pushed back from the gate and took-off for the five-hour flight south to McMurdo. The aircraft departed close to its maximum weight of 250 tonnes, with 109 tonnes of fuel for the journey. On the journey, the latest McMurdo weather reports were relayed from Oceanic Control at Auckland forecasting better weather. Crossing 60°S the flight crew prepared for grid navigation techniques, aligning the gyro compasses with grid. Tracking almost due true south they would now be heading grid north. By now Flight 901 was in contact with the US Navy controllers at McMurdo air traffic control center (ATCC), known as Mac Center, and received reports that weather in the area was not as good as expected. The cloud was down to 3,000ft over Ross Island and the McMurdo area, but with the visibility below cloud an excellent 40 miles. Captain Collins's decision to continue or divert to the south magnetic pole had to be made by the Balleny Islands and a conference would have ensued with the captain feeling pressure to fulfil his obligation to the passengers. After assessing the situation the decision was made to continue.

The DC-10 continued towards the Cape, then rounded the point for the 390-mile leg down to McMurdo. Approaching 200 miles north of the Sound, the passengers were informed that they would descend through the cloud and would shortly enter McMurdo underneath the layer. Before descent, Collins conducted a thorough crew briefing, outlining his intention of following the computer track into the McMurdo area below cloud before starting sightseeing. If weather conditions were poor they would climb out of the region at about Bird reporting point, 23 miles to the end waypoint. The aircraft was flying in clear air with the Victoria Land glaciers on the right. Ahead Erebus, and the other Ross Island peaks, were obscured by cloud at 15,000ft.

At 12.17hrs Ross Dependency Antarctic time (for convenience Antarctic local mean time [LMT] is used throughout) the "before descent" check was completed. Only the altimeters needed to be reset on descent to local area pressure setting. Approaching 150 miles north of McMurdo the decision was made to commence descent.

12.17:13hrs, Capt Collins: "I think we'll start down early here."
F/O Cassin: "OK, I'll see if I can get hold of them on VHF."

So far communications had been on high frequency (HF) long-range radio, but Flight 901 was now within the 200-mile range of very high frequency (VHF) transmissions. Attempts at VHF contact failed but did not give undue cause for alarm.

12.18:05hrs, Mac Center HF R/T: "We have a low overcast in the area at about 2,000ft and right now we're having some snow, but visibility is still about 40 miles . . . I can give you an update on where the cloud areas are around the local area."
12.18:29hrs, F/O Cassin R/T: "Yes, 901, that would be handy. We'd like to descend to flight level one six zero."
12.18:41hrs, Mac Center HF R/T: "Kiwi 901, Mac Center, descend and maintain flight level one eight zero."
12.18:52hrs, Mac Center HF R/T: " . . . It looks like the clear areas around McMurdo area are at approximately between 75 and 100 miles to the northwest of us, but right now over McMurdo we have a pretty extensive low overcast. Over."
12.19:14hrs, F/O Cassin R/T: "Roger, New Zealand 901, thanks."

Ahead they could see the clouds marking the shores of McMurdo Sound.

12.19:22hrs, F/E Maloney: "That'll be round about Cape Bird, wouldn't it?"

F/O Cassin: "Right, right."

12.19:39hrs, F/E Maloney: "Got a low overcast over McMurdo."

Captain Collins: "Doesn't sound very promising, does it?"

12.19:56hrs, Mac Center HF R/T: "Within a range of 40 miles of McMurdo we have radar that will, if you desire, let you down to 1,500ft on radar vectors. Over."

12.20:07hrs, F/O Cassin R/T: "Roger, New Zealand 901, that's acceptable."

Captain Collins: "That's what we want to hear."

As the nose pitched down for descent to flight level 180, Captain Collins lifted the PA handset and spoke to the passengers, "We're hopeful we'll be able to give you a look at McMurdo today." The distance on the AINS indicated 114 miles but there was still no range information from the TACAN displayed on the distance measuring equipment (DME) to confirm accuracy. While the aircraft descended, the autopilot was still locked into the AINS which earlier land sightings had shown to be navigating satisfactorily. The pack ice could be seen below scattered cloud, while ahead, areas completely free of cloud could be seen. At this point F/E Maloney relinquished the engineer's position to F/E Brooks, but remained on the flightdeck observing. F/O Lucas stayed off the flightdeck throughout, viewing the scene from another window. Further futile attempts at VHF contact with Ice Tower at Williams Field were made.

The estimated aircraft weight of 119.5 tonnes at 1,500ft was checked and the minimum speed required of 252kts confirmed—suitable for flight within the McMurdo area. At 12.24:51hrs the aircraft leveled off at flight level 180. The crew confirmed AINS navigation track selection and height automatically captured by the autopilot. On HF, Mac Center called again to suggest re-attempting VHF contact at 80 miles. Several times Cassin and Collins tried the two VHF frequencies of 134.1MHz and 126.2MHz on both sets, but to no avail. The problem, however, was not equipment, but terrain. VHF transmissions, TACAN signals, and radar pulses are all "line of sight"; the radio emissions can pass through most buildings or structures but not through mountains or over the horizon. The AINS-programed track inexorably led Flight 901 towards Erebus, placing the mountain between the transmitters and the aircraft—blocking all signals. HF signals, on the other hand, reflect from ionized layers in the sky and bounce back to earth, so are not affected by terrain.

At this stage it seemed pointless to continue at flight level 180 towards McMurdo Sound as cloud layers covered Erebus and Ross Island right down to a base of 2,000ft over Williams Field. Visual descent for Flight 901 required only co-ordination with radar control, but even that was proving difficult. The only contact with McMurdo was via HF with Mac Center at McMurdo Station. The radar controllers were situated in Ice Tower at Williams Field, about two miles south of McMurdo Station, with only VHF available. Contact with the radar controllers had to be via the HF link with Mac Center personnel, who then had to pass messages to Ice Tower by way of their own link. There was also no source of bearing signal as an accurate check of the AINS. Equipment to receive TACAN bearings was not available to civil aircraft and the NDB had been notified as having been withdrawn. However the radio beacon was operating, the Americans had rescinded their original decision. But the crew were not told, so were unlikely to try a radio beacon which they believed unavailable.

At about 60 miles north of McMurdo (as indicated by the AINS,) the thin 10,000ft layer below dispersed and large clear areas appeared. By descending into these open spaces well away from the cloud at Ross Island the aircraft could enter the Sound below the cloud layer to be picked up by radar at 40 miles. Had the DC-10 been in the process of landing the same procedure would have been followed.

12.31:01hrs, Capt Collins: "I'll have to do an orbit here, I think."
12.31:08hrs, Capt Collins: "It's clear out here if we get down."
F/E Brooks: "It's not clear on the right-hand side here."
F/O Cassin: "No."
12.31:20hrs, Capt Collins: "If you can get HF contact tell him that we'd like further descent. We have contact with the ground and we could . . . descend doing an orbit."
12.32:07hrs, F/O Cassin HF R/T: "We'd like further descent and we could orbit in our present position which is approximately 43 miles north, descending VMC."
12.32:08hrs, Mac Center HF R/T: "Roger, Kiwi New Zealand 901, VMC descent is approved and keep Mac Center advised of your altitude."
12.32:10hrs, F/O Cassin HF R/T: "Roger, New Zealand 901, we're vacating one eight zero. We'll advise level."

As the aircraft started descent, the captain disconnected the autopilot from the AINS track and turned the heading control knob to initiate a right-hand orbit. Flight 901 was now operating under VFR, although still co-ordinating with Mac Center.

12.34:21hrs, Capt Collins PA: "Captain again, ladies and gentlemen. We're carrying out an orbit and circling our present position and we'll be descending to an altitude below cloud so that we can proceed to McMurdo Sound."

At the same time Brooks, spotted the Wilson Piedmont Glacier on the right.

12.34:21hrs, F/E Brooks: "There's Wilson."
12.35:15hrs, F/O Cassin: "Transponder is now responding."

Halfway round the turn Flight 901 ventured just sufficiently west of Erebus to permit reception of "line of sight" signals and passed within radar range. A light on the radar transponder indicated that radar had picked them up at about 40 miles distance, and clearly indicated the accuracy of the AINS.

12.35:20hrs, F/E Maloney: "Still no good on that frequency, though?"
F/O Cassin: "No."

Another attempt was made at VHF contact which this time proved successful.

12.35:36hrs, F/O Cassin VHF R/T: "Roger, 901, you are now loud and clear also. We are presently descending through flight level one three zero, VMC, and the intention at the moment is to descend to one zero thousand."

To the south they could see a broken layer of cloud lying across their track, but most of the cloud appeared to be over Ross Island. Flying above the frozen sea the air was mainly clear. As the aircraft completed the right-hand orbit VHF transmissions were once again blocked by Erebus. Six times Ice Tower attempted to re-establish contact.

12.36:32hrs, F/O Cassin: "We've lost him again."

The DC-10 leveled off as the autopilot captured 10,000ft. Radar contact was short lived but sufficient to reassure the crew of their position. No indication was given by Ice Tower of their imminent danger; perhaps contact had been too fleeting to catch the controllers' attention, or they assumed the DC-10 had started sightseeing. Flight 901 was now operating under VFR, with the crew responsible for their own progress.

F/O Cassin: "I'll go back to HF, Jim."
Capt Collins: "I've got to stay VMC here, so I'll be doing another orbit."
12.38:38hrs, F/O Cassin HF R/T: "901, we briefly had contact on one three four one. We've now lost contact. We're maintaining 10,000ft, presently 34 miles to the north of McMurdo."

Several unsuccessful attempts were made on VHF, including a call on the guard frequency of 121.5MHZ. Both sets were checked and the squelch confirmed off.

Capt Collins: "Tell him we can make a visual descent on a grid of one eight zero and make a visual approach to McMurdo."

The idea was to descend in VMC in a race track pattern by turning left on to true north for a few miles before turning left again back on track towards the Sound.

12.42:01hrs, F/O Cassin HF R/T: "901, still negative contact on VHF. We are VMC and we'd like to let down on a grid of one eight zero and proceed visually to McMurdo."
12.42:05hrs, Mac Center HF R/T: "New Zealand 901, maintain VMC. Keep us advised of your altitude as you approach McMurdo."

Mac Center also requested Flight 901 to report ten miles from McMurdo. The big jet banked left in a descending turn and headed due north, continuing down to 2,000ft. The crew confirmed the autopilot set to capture 2,000ft altitude and the speed hold engaged. On the right could be seen what appeared to be the western escarpment of Mount Bird. As the DC-10 dropped lower they could see below the edges of the distant cloud layers and visibility was at least 40 miles.

12.42:49hrs, Capt Collins: "We're VMC around this way so I'm going to do another turn in."

Collins banked the aircraft in a descending left turn to head south and pick up the track towards McMurdo. Peter Mulgrew now took his seat on the flightdeck.

12.42:59hrs, Capt Collins: "Sorry, haven't got time to talk, but . . . "
Mulgrew: "Ah well, you can't talk if you can't see anything."

Captain Collins commented that at 50 miles they were still not picking up VHF. With no line-of-sight signal reception on VHF, TACAN or radar, perhaps alarm bells should have been ringing. The earlier transponder light illumination, however, may have given the impression that radar contact was established and they may also have assumed that at low altitudes they were still out of VHF range. They also felt that the TACAN channel frequency was incorrect and re-checked it several times. While the aircraft banked to the left large black patches marking breaks in the ice could be seen all around — an island, or was it just a black patch? It was difficult to tell. If land it had to be Dunlop Island by Victoria Land coast. Looking to their left in the direction of turn and not viewing straight ahead, they would have only caught a glimpse. Had Peter Mulgrew taken his seat earlier he may have recognized something, but the area now lay to their right, out of view from the flightdeck.

12.43:27hrs, Mulgrew: "There you go. There's some land ahead."
Capt Collins: "I'll arm the nav again."

The AINS was now re-engaged to navigate the aircraft via the autopilot. All round visibility was 40 miles and ahead they could see the ice-covered sea stretching to the horizon. Mac Center came up again on HF and requested reports on the cloud layers.

12.44:47hrs, F/O Cassin HF R/T: "Roger, New Zealand 901, 50 miles north the base was one zero thousand. We are now at 6,000 descending to 2,000 and we're VMC."

Jim Collins turned to speak to Peter Mulgrew.

12.45:26hrs, Capt Collins: "We had a message from the Wright Valley and they are clear over there."
Mulgrew: "Oh good."
12.45:31hrs, Capt Collins: "So if you can get us out over that way …?"
Mulgrew: "No trouble."
12.45:36hrs, Mulgrew: "Taylor on the right now."

In the distance he could see what appeared to be the edge of Taylor Valley lying just to the south of Cape Bernacchi. It would not yet be in view for the passengers.

Mulgrew PA: "This is Peter Mulgrew speaking again folks. I still can't see very much at the moment. Keep you informed soon as I see something that gives me a clue as to where we are. We're going down in altitude now and it won't be long before we get quite a good view."

Passing through 3,000ft the crew checked from charts the edges of land they could see on either side. These confirmed their approach down the middle of McMurdo

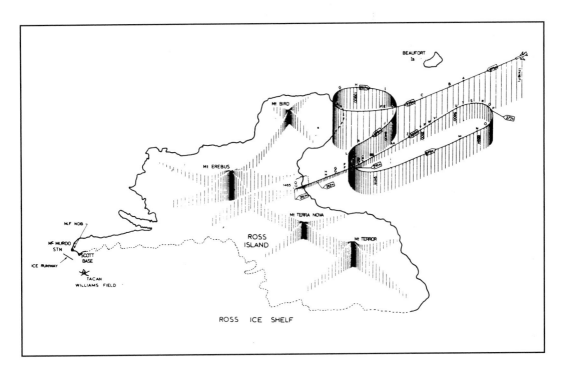

Above: *The last minutes of TE901.*

Sound. Had a check been made of the latitude and longitude readout displayed continuously above the pilots' heads their true position would have been indicated, but at that time ANZ procedures only required use of the overhead co-ordinates at pre and post flight, or if one system was in disagreement.

12.46:39hrs, F/E Brooks: "Where's Erebus in relation to us at the moment?"
Mulgrew: "Left, about 20 or 25 miles."
F/O Cassin: "Yep, yep."
12.46:48hrs, F/E Brooks: "I'm just thinking of any high ground in the area, that's all."

Mulgrew checked the position from a map.

Mulgrew: "I think it'll be left."
F/E Maloney: "Yes, I reckon about here."
Mulgrew: "Yes . . . no, no, I don't really know."
12.47:02hrs, Mulgrew: "That's the edge."

The DC-10 now levelled at 2,000ft with the speed hold engaged and the AINS still navigating on track. The cloud ahead continued to lower to its 2,000ft base.

12.47:43hrs, Capt Collins: "We might have to pop down to 1,500ft."
F/O Cassin: "Yes, OK. Probably see further anyway."

The aircraft dipped its nose in gentle descent.

12.47:49hrs, F/O Cassin: "It's not too bad."

Mulgrew looked about and checked the chart details against the coast lines on both sides.

Mulgrew: "I reckon Bird's through here and Ross Island there. Erebus should be here."

At 1,500ft the autopilot captured the height and the DC-10 sped on at 260kts over the sea ice. Further discussion ensued on the problem with the TACAN. All looked ahead for a glimpse of the buildings at McMurdo Station. The sea ice of what appeared to be McMurdo Sound stretched over what could only be the Ross Ice shelf to a distant horizon. However, the horizon ahead began to melt from view.

12.48:46hrs, Capt Collins: "Actually, these conditions don't look very good at all, do they?"
Mulgrew: "No they don't."

Concerned at the lack of VHF contact, Collins requested Cassin to try again.

12.49:08hrs, Mulgrew: "That looks like the edge of Ross Island there."

But it wasn't Ross Island. They were, in fact, flying south into Lewis Bay, the shores of which bore a remarkable resemblance to those at the head of McMurdo Sound. Lying in the DC-10's path, obscured from sight by a freak of nature, was the giant Mount Erebus. In spite of the endeavors of the crew to navigate with safety and accuracy, the aircraft was most certainly not where the crew, or the controllers, expected it to be. F/E Brooks, positioned further back than the two pilots, was not happy.

12.49:24hrs, F/E Brooks: "I don't like this."

Visibility, however, was still 40 miles and the passengers were happily snapping shots with their cameras. Sunlight streamed into the cabin.

12.49:25hrs, Capt Collins: "Have you got anything from him?"
F/O Cassin: "No."

Still no VHF reception. It was now several minutes since the last radio contact.

12.49:30hrs, Capt Collins: "We're 26 miles north. We'll have to climb out of this."

Their intention was to turn and back-track. Cassin insisted it was clear on the right. Collins, with Mulgrew, was looking to the left and preferred to turn in that direction.

12.49:35hrs, Mulgrew: "You can see Ross Island? Fine."
12.49:38hrs, F/O Cassin: "You're clear to turn right. There's no high ground if you do a one eighty."

Above: *A DC-10 crew carries out its pre-departure checks. Incorrect procedures were a contributory factor in the loss of the Air New Zealand DC-10 over Mt. Erebus.* ASM Photo

Capt Collins: "No . . . negative."

The captain pulled the heading select knob to disengage the AINS tracking. The DC-10 adjusted slightly as it settled on the heading already selected on the heading cursor. Collins prepared to turn left. Suddenly the ground proximity warning system (GPWS) sounded a monotone warning. "Whoop, whoop. Pull up. Whoop, whoop" the electronic voice intoned. The warning must surely be false. They were in the middle of McMurdo Sound with nothing visible ahead. Regulations, dictated obedience, so the crew immediately commenced the drill calmly and efficiently. Captain Collins disconnected the autopilot and pulled back on the control column with his left hand, lifting the nose about 15°. Simultaneously he pushed forward the throttles with his right hand. The flight engineer called out the heights on the radio altimeter.

12.49:48hrs, F/E Brooks: "Five hundred feet."
GPWS: "Pull up."
F/E Brooks: "Four hundred feet."
GPWS: "Whoop, whoop. Pull up. Whoop, whoop. Pull up."

Collins, in a firm, calm voice, asked the flight engineer to set the engine power.

Capt Collins: "Go-around power, please."
GPWS: "Whoop, whoop. Pull— . . . "

The DC-10 struck the lower slopes of Mount Erebus and shattered into a million pieces. The underbelly smashed 13 feet deep into the ice and snow as the two wing engines chewed into the mountainside. Instantly a great fire ball erupted and in a fraction of a second all 257 people on board perished. The tail engine ran on a few seconds longer, catapulting the tail fin and sections of the cabin up the slope. The inferno raged for some time, melting the ice beneath and blackening the wreckage. As the last of the flames subsided a dark scar 1,968ft long slashed the snowy whiteness.

Flight 901 had been unseen since it departed from Auckland and by late afternoon concern was growing. At 20.00hrs New Zealand local time it was announced on the news that the aircraft's fuel would by now have run out — the DC-10 was presumed lost. At 01.00hrs, local time, a US Navy Hercules spotted the dark line of wreckage.

On the evening of 29 November a Hercules aircraft departed from Christchurch for Antarctica with personnel from the police, Air New Zealand, the press, and the accident investigation branch. Within a few days recovery work was underway and the flight data recorder and the cockpit voice recorder tapes were found. By mid-December the results had been analysed and aircraft malfunction ruled out.

Rumors spread—talk of low flying in cloud and pilot error surfaced, also of a flight plan computer error. A directive from the CEO, Morrie Davis, forbade employees to talk to the press and a file was opened by the company for all relevant documents. All surplus material and flight papers not relating to the accident were to be destroyed, but too often the decision to discard or file data was in the hands of the very airline employees who might be implicated in the disaster. Many papers simply disappeared.

By the beginning of March, Chief Inspector Ron Chippendale's interim accident reported was delivered to the Minister of Civil Aviation. Shortly afterwards it was announced that a Commission of Inquiry would be established to investigate the cause of the accident, but would not be convened until after Chippendale's final report. Since the interim report clearly implicated the crew, there seemed little doubt that the pilots would be found at fault. One pilot above others, Captain Gordon Vette, placed his career at stake to fight for his colleagues. Much of Vette's evidence on visual perception and associated problems was subsequently presented at the Commission of Inquiry and helped lead to a full explanation of the disaster.

In Auckland, meanwhile, battle lines were being drawn between two distinct groups of antagonists: on the one side senior Air New Zealand management and executive pilots, prepared to sacrifice a crew to the accusation of pilot error to save the name of the airline, and on the other side colleagues of the deceased flight crew and the New Zealand Airline Pilots' Association (NZALPA). It was to be a bitter confrontation which was to lead all the way to the Privy Council in Great Britain.

By June 20, the Chief Inspector's final report was ready for the July Inquiry. The government, with a vested interest in Air New Zealand, gave top priority to the printing of the report. The result was a foregone conclusion. "The probable cause of the accident was the decision of the captain to continue flight at low level towards an area of poor surface horizon definition when the crew was not certain of their position, and the subsequent inability to detect the rising terrain which intercepted the aircraft's flight path."

The conclusion was based on five main points:
1. The change in the computer flight path from McMurdo Sound to Lewis Bay did not mislead the crew. 2. The crash was caused by the pilots descending beneath 16,000ft contrary to the airline's instructions. 3. The crew was not certain as to their position. 4. The aircraft's radar would have depicted the mountain terrain ahead. 5. The captain headed the aircraft toward cloud-covered high ground appearing to the pilot as an area of limited visibility or whiteout.

The Royal Commission of Inquiry conducted by Judge Peter Mahon opened on July 7, 1980, and sat for many months. The evidence presented by the airline was in keeping with Chippendale's report. The crew, somehow, should have detected the change in the co-ordinates leading to the alteration of track. No permission had been given for descent below 16,000ft on the approach to Mount Erebus, that the captain had elected to do so was the primary cause of the accident. Air New Zealand was adamant; none of the airline's management or executive pilots could be swayed.

Much material relating to the accident simply disappeared. In the course of the Inquiry the Chippendale report and Air New Zealand's stance came in for much criticism. The airline's briefing material was considered inadequate and ill-informed and contained a number of mistakes. Only whiteout in snow shower conditions was considered. The fact that sector whiteout could occur in clear conditions and was not an unusual phenomenon in Antarctica but an everyday event was never conveyed to the crews. As Flight 901 flew south towards Erebus they faced a lowering cloud base meeting rising snow-covered ground, with the sun in the north shining from behind. By misfortune, the lower cliff face which might have given a visual reference was obscured by a fog bank which completed the ramp effect.

A film of the accident site taken the day after the crash actually recorded the formation of this same fog bank. Light striking the snow-covered slope deflected upwards from the ice crystals and reflected back from the lower surface of the cloud. Such diffusion of light deceives the eye into seeing ahead a limitless vista and distant horizon. Crews were never warned of these dangerous effects. The visual deception was completed by the amazing similarity between the entrance to Lewis Bay and the head of McMurdo Sound. Captain Vette, demonstrated quite clearly how the crew had been tricked. The cliffs of Cape Bird to the right of Lewis Bay, for example, lay on a bearing similar to what would be expected of the cliffs at Cape Bernacchi to the right of McMurdo Sound. Although the Cape Bird cliffs were only one-third of the size they stood at almost exactly one-third of the distance from the DC-10's flightpath, and gave a similar impression of size.

The airline was also criticised for not supplying charts with the actual route marked thereon. Without adequate charts Captain Collins had plotted his own route with subsequent results. The sequence of blunders by the navigation section, amounting to over 50 in all, was found to be the primary cause of the accident.

The report by the Royal Commission was submitted in April 1981, and completely exonerated the crew of any blame. "In my opinion," wrote Judge Mahon, "neither Captain Collins nor F/O Cassin nor the flight engineers made any error which contributed to the disaster, and were not responsible for its occurrence."

6 Riyadh, Saudi Arabia, 1980
Saudi Arabian Airlines Lockheed
Tristar 200

Leo Marriott

The Lockheed Tristar was similar in size and capacity to the McDonnell Douglas DC-10 and although popular with passengers it failed to make a really significant market penetration and production ceased after a total of 250 aircraft had been delivered. Despite having now been in service for almost 30 years it has maintained a good safety record and has been involved in relatively few serious accidents. In fact there have been only four fatal accidents involving the Tristar although two aircraft were destroyed in ground incidents, one as the result of terrorist action. However, one of the accidents was almost unique in the history of flight safety with all 301 occupants being killed by the effects of a fire aboard an aircraft which had completed a safe landing and came to rest structurally intact.

This bizarre incident began at 18.08hrs GMT on August 19, 1980, when a Saudi Arabian Airlines Lockheed Tristar 200, registration HZ-AHK, took-off from Riyadh Airport for a flight to Jeddah on the Red Sea coast. The flight number was SV163, SV being the designator for Saudi, and it was actually the second leg of a flight from Karachi from where it had departed at 13.32hrs. Taking two hours 34 minutes en route to Riyadh, all passengers were offloaded on arrival for customs clearance while the aircraft was refueled and prepared for the next sector. Subsequently the passengers were re-embarked together with others who were joining the flight at that point, so that by the time it taxied away from the gate at 17.50hrs there were a total of 301 persons on board. This figure included 14 crew in addition to the 287 passengers among whom were 15 infants. After the usual delays associated with taxiing and waiting for ATC clearances the Tristar got airborne and turned on course for Jeddah via Airway Green Five Three, climbing steadily through the evening sky to its cleared cruising level, 35,000ft. With after take-off checks completed, the crew were beginning to settle into the normal routine when the calm of the flightdeck was disturbed by visual and aural warnings of a fire in the after cargo compartment, designated C-3. This occurred as the aircraft was climbing through 14,500ft but it then took over four minutes before the captain recognized the seriousness of the situation and decided to return to Riyadh. Part of the delay was caused by difficulties which the crew, and particularly the flight engineer, experienced in trying to

Above: *A Saudi Airlines Lockheed Tristar 200 taking off from Geneva. This is an identical aircraft to the one lost at Riyadh.* Robbie Shaw

Below: *SV163 flight profile.*

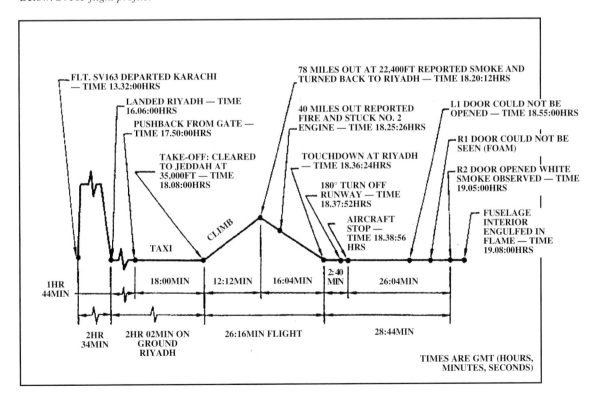

FLT. SV163 DEPARTED KARACHI — TIME 13.32:00HRS

LANDED RIYADH — TIME 16.06:00HRS

PUSHBACK FROM GATE — TIME 17.50:00HRS

TAKE-OFF: CLEARED TO JEDDAH AT 35,000FT — TIME 18.08:00HRS

78 MILES OUT AT 22,400FT REPORTED SMOKE AND TURNED BACK TO RIYADH — TIME 18.20:12HRS

40 MILES OUT REPORTED FIRE AND STUCK NO. 2 ENGINE — TIME 18.25:26HRS

TOUCHDOWN AT RIYADH — TIME 18.36:24HRS

180° TURN OFF RUNWAY — TIME 18.37:52HRS

AIRCRAFT STOP — TIME 18.38:56 HRS

L1 DOOR COULD NOT BE OPENED — TIME 18.55:00HRS

R1 DOOR COULD NOT BE SEEN (FOAM)

R2 DOOR OPENED WHITE SMOKE OBSERVED — TIME 19.05:00HRS

FUSELAGE INTERIOR ENGULFED IN FLAME — TIME 19.08:00HRS

CLIMB

TAXI

1HR 44MIN

18:00MIN

12:12MIN

16:04MIN

2:40 MIN

26:04MIN

2HR 34MIN

2HR 02MIN ON GROUND RIYADH

26:16MIN FLIGHT

28:44MIN

TIMES ARE GMT (HOURS, MINUTES, SECONDS)

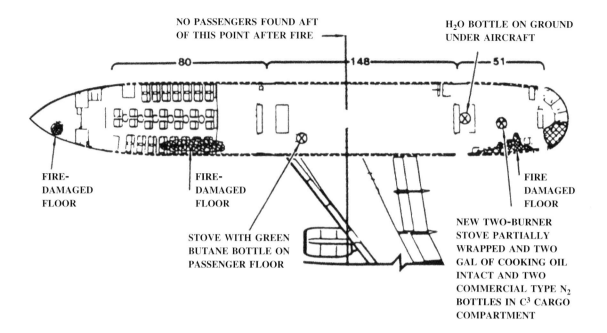

NO PASSENGERS FOUND AFT
OF THIS POINT AFTER FIRE

H₂O BOTTLE ON GROUND
UNDER AIRCRAFT

FIRE-
DAMAGED
FLOOR

FIRE-
DAMAGED
FLOOR

FIRE
DAMAGED
FLOOR

STOVE WITH GREEN
BUTANE BOTTLE ON
PASSENGER FLOOR

NEW TWO-BURNER
STOVE PARTIALLY
WRAPPED AND TWO
GAL OF COOKING OIL
INTACT AND TWO
COMMERCIAL TYPE N₂
BOTTLES IN C³ CARGO
COMPARTMENT

Above: *Drawing showing what the investigators found inside the Tristar.*

locate the correct procedures for dealing with such a situation. The airline had split its emergency procedures into three sections listed under Emergency, Abnormal, and Additional. Consequently some time was wasted looking through the Abnormal procedures before the correct information was found in the Emergency section. By the time that this had been located and a decision to return had been made, the flight engineer had gone back to the passenger cabin and quickly returned with confirmation that there were signs of an actual fire.

By now it was 18.20hrs local time and the still climbing aircraft had reached an altitude of 22,000ft when the First Officer contacted Riyadh ATC with the message "One Six Three, we are coming back to Riyadh." In answer to the obvious query from the ground, he provided the amplifying message, "We got fire in the cabin, please alert the fire trucks." Riyadh then advised the pilot that the aircraft was 78 miles out and cleared it to begin a descent and return for a landing on runway zero one. Obviously ATC had not quite understood the nature of the problem as they queried if there was an engine on fire but were told again that the fire was in the cabin. This initial exchange was rounded off with a request for the number of persons on board which was met with the answer, "Don't know exactly, think we have a full load."

The flight engineer again went back to the cabin and returned to report that there was just some smoke in the rear of the cabin area. In fact, right up to the last moment the engineer appeared to play down the seriousness of the situation and, although this is a common reaction in such circumstances, his attitude may have caused the captain to underestimate the seriousness of the problem. Nevertheless, the flight engineer did also report that the passengers in the rear of the aircraft were panicking and asked if the fire trucks were standing by on the ground. The captain answered to the affirmative but then asked the first officer to confirm this again with ATC.

By this time the aircraft was descending steadily back towards Riyadh and was passing through 12,000ft when a further aural fire smoke alarm sounded. This was cancelled by the flight engineer who said, "I think its alright now." Despite this, a further alarm sounded 30 seconds later and shortly after that the captain discovered that the throttle for number two engine was stuck. This was the tail mounted engine and he announced his intention to shut it down, although in fact did not do so until the aircraft was about to land. The time was now 18.25:26hrs, just over 10 minutes after the first fire alarm had sounded, and some 10 minutes before the Tristar finally landed. By now, reports from the cabin crew had positively confirmed that there was an actual fire in the cabin and also that there was difficulty in keeping the passengers under control. The cabin crew were subsequently commended for their actions in attempting to calm and re-assure the passengers, and they made repeated requests to the captain for a decision on whether to evacuate the aircraft after landing. Engrossed in flying the aircraft, he appeared to ignore these requests for some time.

As the approach continued, the first officer asked Riyadh ATC to tell the fire trucks to go to the rear of the aircraft when it landed. This information was relayed, although it is evident from the recordings of prolonged conversations between the tower and the rescue services that there was still some confusion as to the exact site of the fire. At 18.29hrs another report from the cabin staff about thick smoke in the cabin caused the flight engineer to check the smoke detectors again and, amazingly, he pronounced that there was no indication of smoke! At 18.30hrs the captain began the final approach check list and two minutes later reported the runway in sight and was cleared to land. Shortly afterward he shut down the number two engine and reported that he was on engines numbers one and three when the tower cleared him to land. In response to further requests from the cabin crew directed via the flight engineer he positively refused permission to evacuate the aircraft saying, "Tell them, tell them not to evacuate!"

As the stricken airliner swept over the runway threshold, the Cockpit Voice Recorder (CVR) picked up the flight engineer making the routine height callouts, "fifty. . . forty. . . thirty. . ." However at this point it ceased to function and vital evidence of the last minutes of this drama was lost. Nevertheless, the aircraft touched down safely on runway zero one at 18.36:24hrs, some 21.5 minutes after the first fire alert. As the Tristar approached and landed, several witnesses saw smoke coming from the rear of the aircraft although the fire crews on the ground could see no actual fire and this information was relayed, via ATC, to the captain. After touchdown the aircraft continued down the runway and turned off onto a taxiway before finally coming to rest two minutes and 40 seconds later—an inordinately long time in the circumstances. The controller in the tower asked the aircraft if they wanted to taxi to the ramp or shut down in their present position and one of the crew answered, "Standby. . . okay, we are shutting down the engines now and evacuating." Despite this, nothing appeared to happen and there were frantic exchanges between the fire crews and the tower concerning the appearance and rapid spread of flames from the rear of the aircraft, coupled with requests for the flight crew to shut down the engines so that the aircraft could be approached. When this was relayed to the aircraft, the reply received was, "Affirmative, we are trying to evacuate now." This was the last transmission received from the aircraft. The time was 18.40:33hrs, now four minutes after touchdown.

The fire trucks had followed the Tristar after it had landed and were now ranged around the aircraft but the crews did not attempt to move in and open the doors while the engines were still running. Eventually, after a few minutes, they were shut down at 18.42:18hrs, over three minutes after the aircraft had come to a stop and, presumably, somebody on the flightdeck was still alive at that time. The crash crews now tried to open up the doors but due to poor training and a lack of suitable equipment it took them almost 20 minutes before the number two door on the starboard side was opened at 19.05hrs. By this time it was far too late and all 301 occupants were dead; killed either by the inhalation of smoke and toxic fumes, or burnt to death by the fire which had gutted the whole interior.

Once the fire had eventually been extinguished and the gruesome task of removing the bodies, many burnt or charred beyond recognition, had been completed, the investigation of the accident began. There were two questions to be addressed. The first was concerned with establishing the cause and origin of the fire which had precipitated the return to Riyadh, and the second was to look at the actions of the crew to determine the exact sequence of events which had prevented a successful evacuation of the aircraft after it had landed safely. As far as the cause of the fire was concerned there were a number of possibilities to be considered, but many of these were quickly eliminated by detailed forensic tests of various components and the results of pathological examination of the victims. Some of these tests were carried out by the Metropolitan Police Forensic Science Laboratory in London, or at the Royal Aircraft Establishment, Farnborough. Others were carried out by Lockheed themselves and at the US Federal Aviation Authority Technical Center. The deliberate placing of an incendiary device was ruled out by these means as was any possibility that the fire had started in the passenger cabin, although the latter had to be considered. It was not unknown on this type of flight for passengers, not familiar with the normal constraints of air travel, to carry cooking stoves and even attempt to light them while in flight. Indeed at least one such appliance was found in the Tristar's passenger cabin and another in the rear cargo hold. However the facts known about the spread of the fire did not accord with its origin in the cabin.

A number of areas in the after lower deck of the aircraft were also investigated. These included the "cheek" area in the aerodynamic fairing aft of the wing root and adjacent to the rear cargo hold, and another area aft of the rearmost cargo hold, but both were eventually eliminated. Having examined all of these possibilities, the balance of probability was that the fire had started in the rear of the three underfloor cargo holds, designated C-3, and indeed this hypothesis accorded with all the known facts. The actual sequence of events probably began with an item of cargo igniting and eventually generating enough smoke to trigger the "B" smoke detector system which was the first indication on the flightdeck that anything was amiss.

Above: *The wreckage of HZ-AHK, showing the damage to the passenger compartment and cockpit.*
Associated Press Photograph

Subsequently the "A" system detector was also triggered and this would have confirmed the location of the fire to the crew. When the flight engineer went aft a few minutes later and reported "just smoke in the aft," this would indicate that already the ceiling of C-3 was burning through and smoke was penetrating into the eight inch void between the top of the cargo hold and the cabin floor. From here it was free to spread transversely across the aircraft and into the cabin through the side-wall exhaust grills. At the same time the heat and flames could have melted the nylon fairlead rollers supporting the throttle cable to No.2 engine which passed through this void and caused them to stick to the cable, restricting its movement. This would have explained why the captain reported the throttle to number two engine as being stuck at about 18.25hrs.

By 18.26hrs one of the cabin staff had actually observed flames in the left rear cabin, indicating that it was spreading through the void below the cabin floor and up the sidewalls. An overheat signal from a sensor alongside the C-3 compartment, which triggered at 18.32hrs, and a false alarm that the rear cargo door was open caused by damage to the electrical harness at that point also supported the theory of the fire originating in C-3 and spreading from that point. Although the actual cause of the initial combustion was never traced, the investigators reached a positive conclusion that the basic sequence of events was as described.

They then turned to the conduct of the crew and while many incorrect and illogical actions were identified and pinpointed, it proved impossible to state with any certainty the motives behind these. Initially, despite some delay in accepting that there actually was a fire on board and determining the correct course of action to follow in that event, they made the correct decision to return to Riyadh to make a priority landing. The major failing appears to have been that the captain failed to instruct the cabin crew to evacuate the aircraft as soon as possible after landing. Indeed, as has been seen, he positively instructed them to the contrary. Inexplicably he failed to order the use of oxygen masks on the flightdeck or to remind the cabin crew to do so. Initially, this omission was of little consequence, at least on the flightdeck as all the evidence indicated that the cockpit crew were not affected by smoke or toxic fumes, at least until after the aircraft had landed safely. The first officer, despite his limited experience on the aircraft, came in for criticism in the accident report on the grounds that he was not assertive enough. Presumably the thought was that if he did realize the seriousness of the situation he failed to convey this to the captain who, for some reason, failed to react appropriately to the growing indications that there was very serious fire on board and that a rapid evacuation after landing was essential.

In the circumstances the obvious course of action after landing would have been to have stopped as quickly as possible on the runway, open the doors, deploy the escape chutes and evacuate the aircraft as quickly as possible. To have done this efficiently would have required positive instructions and briefing to the cabin crew before landing. Instead the aircraft made a normal landing without excessive braking and then taxied slowly clear of the runway before coming to rest. It was calculated that this added a critical two minutes to the period in which the aircraft was in motion on the ground and it was just after this time that a flash fire was thought to have swept through the cabin and flightdeck, incapacitating all aboard to the extent that they were unable to attempt any form of evacuation. This probably happened as the engines were being shut down and is believed to have occurred as a result of the air condition packs being turned off after landing—a normal procedure which had the unintended effect of shutting off the supply of fresh air to the cabin. In turn this depleted the amount of oxygen and allowed a build up of other combustible and toxic gases which eventually built up to a critical proportion and were ignited spontaneously by flames from the rear of the cabin. Up to that point, the investigators considered that most of the occupants would have survived if an evacuation had been begun but thereafter there was little hope and the failure of the rescue services to enter the aircraft was the final tragic link in the chain. While admitting that, individually, the firemen had done their best in the circumstances, the final report was scathing in its criticism of their organization and training, and noted that they lacked suitable protective clothing and were not equipped with suitable tools to force an entry into the aircraft. Nor had they been trained in such procedures with the Tristar aircraft despite the fact that several were in the Saudi Airlines fleet based at Riyadh.

Apart from their comments on the actions of the flightcrew and ground personnel, the investigators also looked at the FAA regulations concerning firefighting arrangements in various compartments as they affected the Lockheed Tristar. For this purpose the C-3 cargo hold was designated as a Class D compartment and the main provision required that any fire therein could be completely confined without

Above: *Tristar 200 taxying. The baggage compartment in which the Riyadh fire started was on the lower deck, immediately aft of the wing.* Robbie Shaw

endangering the aircraft or its occupants. Additional requirements covered the need to exclude any hazardous smoke, flames, or gases from the crew and passenger compartments, as well as adequate ventilation to ensure that any fire did not progress beyond safe limits. The US National Transportation Safety Board (NTSB) carried out extensive tests and determined that, although the design of the Tristar's cargo compartment complied with the regulations, these themselves were actually inadequate and inappropriate for the large volume holds of wide-bodied aircraft. However the FAA did not agree with the NTSB findings and made no specific recommendations to improve matters although the manufacturers, Lockheed, did implement their own modification scheme which reduced the possibility of any fire burning through the roof of the compartment.

Despite the technical arguments, at the end of the day some 301 lives were lost mainly because of human errors. The reasons why the captain or other members of the flightdeck crew failed to respond effectively to the situation will never be known. However, in the past decade the importance of human factors and the proper management and integration of the skills of all members of the flight crew, including cabin staff, is given much greater prominence in training and operating procedures so that the chances of a similar catastrophe happening should be very much reduced.

7 Washington, USA, 1982
Air Florida Boeing 727-222

Michael Sharpe

By mid-January of 1982, the Atlantic seaboard of the US was wrapped in the icy cloak of one of the bitterest winters on record. It was cold, even by the harsh standards of the north-eastern states. At this time of year, in a bid to escape the chilly winter weather, many of Washington's citizens journey south for breaks in the sunnier climes of Florida and on the morning of January 13, Washington National Airport was thronging with sun-seekers, plus the usual complement of business travelers and government officials.

A dense blanket of snow fell steadily throughout the morning. Cloud ceilings were 400ft with visibility limited to just over half a mile in snow showers. By the early afternoon the ambient temperature had increased a little, reaching minus five degrees Celsius. Just before 13.40hrs, the airport management decided to halt operations while the taxi ways and single instrument runway were cleared of snow. Washington was well-equipped for such an eventuality and a team of specialized snow-clearance operatives swung into action. At just before 15.00hrs, only ten minutes behind schedule, the airport reopened. The delay had thrown schedules into disarray however, and a backlog of departing aircraft had built up on the ramp, adding pressure to an already tight schedule.

During the snow clearance operations Air Florida had elected to begin boarding the 74 passengers booked on Flight 90, the scheduled 14.15hrs service to Fort Lauderdale, Florida, and given the call sign Palm 90 for the short flight south. By 14.30hrs, all of the passengers had safely boarded their aircraft, a Boeing 737-222 registered as N62AF.

The 737 is the archetypal short-haul jetliner and was first introduced in February 1968. Seen as the perfect tool for airlines who make their business in shuttling passengers along the commuter routes that criss-cross North America and Europe, sales of the "pocket rocket" escalated after US airlines were deregulated in the mid-1970s, and rapidly over hauled sales of its chief rival, the McDonnell Douglas DC-9. By mid-1983, 1,083 of all types had been ordered.

Right: *Coast Guard recovering crash victim.* CORBIS-Bettmann/UPI

Above: *A body is transferred to a Coast Guard tug boat.* CORBIS/Bettmann

Above Right: *Diagram showing crash site.*

Below: *Air Florida Boeing 737.* Austin Brown/Aviation Picture Library

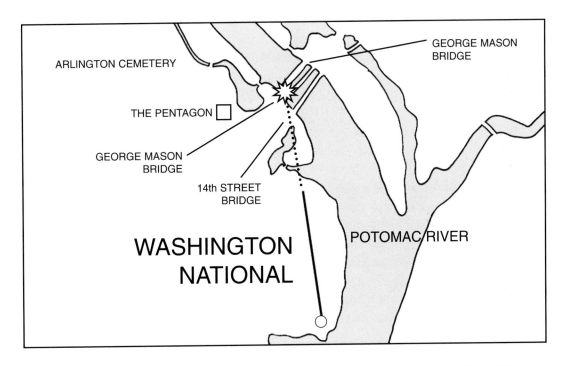

Air Florida was typical of the successful inter-state operators in the United States, and had operated a large number of Boeing 737s since the early 1970s. Originally selected for its notable fuel efficiency on the airline's short-route network, the type provided the backbone of the Air Florida fleet. N6A2F was a -200 series aircraft, a stretched series 115 version of the original mid-1960s design that had accommodation for 103 passengers. After enduring the industry-wide slump of the early 1970s the airline had steadily expanded and enlarged its number of scheduled services.

Up to this time the airline had a blemish free accident record. Indeed, no major accident had been recorded across the whole of the US in the 24 months preceding January 13, 1982, a new record for national air safety.

Piloting that day's 14.15hrs flight were Captain Larry Wheaton and First Officer Roger Pettit, both fairly young pilots enjoying their new jobs with Air Florida.

During passenger embarkation, Wheaton asked for Palm 90 to be de-iced in preparation for departure. The tower told the aircraft that there would be further delay and that Palm 90 was number 11 in priority when the airport did reopen. Wheaton then instructed the de-icing to be discontinued, the port side having just been started. Half an hour later, Wheaton again called for de-icing as the airport was about to reopen. By 15.10hrs, de-icing was complete and ground personnel reported to Wheaton that there was only a "light dusting" of snow on the wings although snow was still falling. At 15.23hrs, Palm 90 was cleared to push from the gate, but when the tug driver tried to push the 737 back, snow that had accumulated on the ground caused the tractor's tires to spin. Wheaton then suggested that, contrary to policy, they would use the aircraft's reverse thrust to assist in the push. The reversers were engaged for about a minute and a half, but only served to throw up more slush and snow. Chains were then attached to the main wheel legs and, finally, the aircraft was pulled back. Wheaton maneuvered Palm 90 into position behind the last of 16 aircraft waiting for take-off. Fifteen minutes later the New York Air DC-9 that had been parked immediately in front was cleared for take-off and Palm 90 was instructed to taxi into position and hold. The controller asked for no delay on departure, as landing traffic was heavy. At 15.59hrs, Palm 90 was cleared for take-off as it was still positioning itself on the runway. Visibility was now down to a quarter of a mile.

The departure from runway 36 requires aircraft to make a 40° turn to the left shortly after becoming airborne so as to follow the Potomac River and avoid flying over the Washington monument and the White House. The tower lost sight of Palm 90 during its roll due to the reduced visibility, but radar showed it airborne and the tower controller instructed Palm 90 to contact the departure controller. Less than 60 seconds after taking off, with its undercarriage and flaps still extended and with the nose in a 30-40° nose-high altitude, Palm 90 descended at low airspeed into the northbound span of the Rochambeau (14th Street) bridge, which connects Virginia with the district of Columbia. The aircraft skimmed the road, which was heavily congested with slow-moving vehicles, destroying six occupied cars and a truck and tearing away a 30m section of railing, before breaking into two parts. The aft end broke off and went into the icy waters of the Potomac River while the forward section impacted a little further on. Both sections sank quickly leaving only the tip of the tail fin exposed.

Given the nature of the impact only those passengers seated in the rear of the cabin stood any real chance of survival. The ice prevented rescue boats from approaching the scene and it was not until some 20 minutes after the crash that a Bell LongRanger helicopter of the US Park Police arrived on the scene and began searching the ice-strewn surface for signs of life. A few of the passengers had struggled clear of the wreckage and were clinging to ice floes. The helicopter pilot showed great skill and bravery by hovering just above the surface so that they could be plucked from the freezing water by his crew. Two bystanders, one of them a US Congressional Office clerk by the name of Lenny Skutnik, pitched into the river to aid a woman who had lost her grip on the rescue line proffered by the helicopter crew. Perhaps the most selfless act of bravery, though, was that of Arland D. Williams Jr., a passenger on the aircraft.

From "A Hero—Passenger Aids Others, Then Dies," *The Washington Post*, January 14, 1982.

"He was about 50 years old, one of half a dozen survivors clinging to twisted wreckage bobbing in the icy Potomac when the first helicopter arrived. To the copter's two-man Park Police crew he seemed the most alert. Life vests were dropped, then a flotation ball. The man passed them to the others. On two occasions, the crew recalled last night, he handed away a life line from the hovering machine that could have dragged him to safety. The helicopter crew—who rescued five people, the only persons who survived from the jetliner—lifted a woman to the riverbank, then dragged three more persons across the ice to safety. Then the life line saved a woman who was trying to swim away from the sinking wreckage, and the helicopter pilot, Donald W. Usher, returned to the scene, but the man was gone."

Above: *Rescue workers put a rescued survivor into a helicopter for swift delivery to hospital.*
CORBIS/Bettmann

Below: *Dramatic rescue of survivor from the icy river.* CORBIS/Bettmann/UPI

Four passengers and one stewardess were the only survivors of the crash, which also killed four others in vehicles on the bridge.

The waters of the Potomac were only 25–30ft deep where the plane crashed, about 150ft from the south shoreline, but the sub-freezing weather and heavy ice cover on the river prolonged the operation to retrieve the victim's bodies and aircraft wreckage until early February. The crash scene was close to the offices of the National Transportation Safety Board, which appointed Rudi Kapustin and Ron Schleede to lead the investigation. Both men knew that they would have to work under the intense scrutiny of the media and their bosses in Congress—the fact that the aircraft had crashed while flying out of Washington National, which is used by the White House, the Congress, and all the senior government officials, generated a high level of interest. Questions were immediately raised about the ability of Washington National to cope with the current volume of traffic, and measures were taken to safeguard the VIPs who frequented the airport. Allegations of sabotage by airport maintenance staff were also batted around in the media, prompting Kapustin to bring in the FBI, but its agents were soon able to discount criminal involvement. There was to be no quick and easy answer to the crash of Palm 90.

The NTSB gathered evidence from as wide a range of sources as they could conceive. Tapping into his own knowledge, and that of his colleagues, of operating aircraft in hostile weather conditions, Kapustin ordered the de-icing equipment that had been used on Palm 90 to be impounded. Samples were taken of the chemical de-icing fluid, but these came up clean in tests. "Icing" refers to an accumulation of a ice on the airframe, either during flight or on the ground. For icing to occur on the ground, as in the case of Palm 90, the outside temperature must have fallen to below 0°C. If ice accumulates on the wings, it will have a significant affect on the air flow over them, which in turn will result in a higher stalling speed and a reduction in the amount of lift that the wing produces.

In his preparations for take-off Wheaton had allowed nearly an hour to elapse between his final anti-icing operation and take-off, and in this period snow and ice had accumulated on the upper surface of the wings to a depth of between one quarter and one half of an inch. By using the reverse thrusters when backing the aircraft away from the ramp, the captain undoubtedly aggravated the problem and caused more slush to be deposited. It seems that both Wheaton and his First Officer were aware of this problem, and made an attempt to rectify the situation while waiting in the queue for take-off by positioning their aircraft close behind the New York Air DC-9 parked in front and using the warm exhaust gases from the DC-9 engines to try and melt the ice on the wings. They probably succeeded only in melting the snow, which may have blown off during the take-off anyway, allowing it to freeze on the wing leading edges.

Intriguingly, a passenger on another flight that was parked on the ramp next to N6A2F came forward with pictures that he had taken of the aircraft from his seat; as a former US Navy pilot, with knowledge of these matters, he expressed his concern at the fact that at no time did he see either of the pilots making the required external ground checks. The pictures that he produced revealed unmarked snow on the wing upper surfaces, lending weight to this allegation. All the evidence pointed to icing

Above: *Rescue workers on the banks of the Potomac.* CORBIS/Bettmann/UPI

on the wings as the cause. Had the black boxes not been recovered, it is likely that the cause of the accident would have been attributed solely to this.

As it transpired, the truth was rather more complex. Only after a detailed examination of the CVR and FDR equipment, which was recovered with great difficulty from the silted river bed, was Kapustin able to gain a true picture of what had gone so tragically wrong with Palm 90.

McDermott Associates, an established company that deals in expert analysis of CVR tapes, were given the task of analysing the engine sounds revealed as background noise on the CVR. From this it was possible to establish that the engines were producing only 80% of the required thrust at take-off, irrespective of the fact that the snow and ice on the wings had added to the overall weight of an aircraft that was already heavily loaded with baggage and passengers. Again, ice had seriously degraded the performance of the aircraft, but in a rather different and unexpected way.

The wet, slushy mixture created by using the thrust reversers while moving the aircraft off the ramp was also deposited in the engine air intakes, thereby narrowing the inlet tube. Situated in the exhaust of the twin Pratt & Whitney JT8D-9 engines that were developed to power the 737 is a discharge probe which provides a constant measure of the amount of thrust generated. An obstruction to the inlet of the probe or the inlet tube will produce a false reading, higher than the amount that is actually being developed. This knowledge prompted the development of engine anti-icing equipment, which commonly works by circulating a heated fluid around the intake and induction areas, and the PTT probes. N6A2F had this equipment, yet mystifyingly it seems that the crew failed to turn it on during their routine take-off procedures. Their mistake sealed the fate of the aircraft. As is standard procedure in air accident investigations, the NTSB pieced together the flight check procedures list from the CVR, but even with the expert analysis of McDermott Associates and by FBI voice experts, who spent months picking through the background noise, it was difficult to say for sure whether the co-pilot had responded with the word "off" or "on" to the question regarding the status of the engine de-icing equipment.

Roger Pettit was a former US Air Force pilot with rather more experience of flying than his captain. Perhaps Wheaton was self-conscious of this, and felt a need to establish his authority over his junior officer. This is pure conjecture, and lacks any clear evidence, yet it is very clear that Wheaton had only recently qualified to fly jets, having transferred from a company that flew nothing more complex than Douglas DC-3s, and did not fully understand the turbine-engine. The CVR revealed a certain amount of jocularity during taxiing that is common on any flight-deck, but in this instance the NTSB investigating team saw this as indicative of the nervousness of Wheaton and Pettit, neither of who had much experience at cold-weather flying.

It was also suggested that the crew may have conducted their checks somewhat hurriedly after the tower request for "no delay on departure."

Right: *Fuselage recovery; note icy surface of river.* CORBIS/Bettmann

Shortly before take-off, the crew had a brief discussion concerning anomalies in the engine instrument readings. Pettit suggested that the hot (less dense) exhaust from the DC-9 ahead was causing a lower than normal reading on one of the EPR gauges. The indications seemed to return to near normal as Palm 90 got closer to take-off. Just before take-off, Pettit began the brief, calling out take-off power as EPR 2.04, V1 (last point where captain can decide to abort take-off) as 138kts, VR (rotation speed—ie when the aircraft actually takes off) as 140kts, and V2 (take-off safety speed and initial climb-out speed) as 144kts.

From the transcript of the CVR it is clear that during the take-off run Pettit, who was flying the aircraft, became aware of the apparent anomaly between the Engine Pressure Ratio reading and the relative position of the thrust levers, which were not advanced sufficiently to produce an EPR of that magnitude.

Pettit's instincts told him something was wrong, and the CVR recorded him saying "This sure doesn't look right" moments before rotation. However, his military training had probably instilled in him a natural reluctance to disobey the orders of a senior officer even though he clearly felt that something was amiss, and he proceeded with take-off as quickly as possible. After they had established that the de-icing equipment was switched off, the investigating team were able to conclude from tests on other JT8D-9 engines that the engines were only producing 1.70, rather than the required 2.04 (EPR). In response to Pettit's statement Wheaton replied "Yeah, here's 120," which can only mean that he was looking at the airspeed indicator, and did not respond to further comments from his first officer.

Forty-five seconds into the take-off roll, Palm 90 reached its rotation speed and pitched up abruptly, due to the extra weight of the accumulated snow and the disruption of the airfoil. Investigators found that ice build-up on the wing leading edge and slats of the 737 could cause an abrupt nose up pitch on take-off, and that this was a well established characteristic of the aircraft. The sudden movement caused Captain Wheaton to exclaim "Easy!" to Pettit and then, as the stick-shaker stall warning device was activated, "Forward! Forward!" indicating to Pettit to lower the nose to prevent the stall. Pettit tried to lower the nose to gain airspeed, but with the reduced power setting the aircraft had staggered to an altitude of only 300ft and he was forced to pull the nose up to avoid the ground. It was in this attitude that the aircraft struck the bridge. Pettit apparently believed that the engines were producing maximum thrust because at no time during the 30-second flight were the throttles advanced to provide more power to prevent stalling.

The CVR transcript tells the story of the last moments of Palm 90:

Capt: "Forward, forward. Easy. We only want five hundred."
Capt: "Come on, forward."
Capt: "Forward. Just barely climb."
Cap: "[Stalling] we're [falling]."
F/O: "Larry, we're going down, Larry . . ."
Captain: "I know it." [Sound of initial impact]

In their final report, the NTSB attributed the cause of the accident to pilot error.

Above: *Salvaging the tail from the Potomac.* CORBIS/Bettmann

8 Sakhalin Island, USSR, 1983
Korean Airlines Boeing 747-200B

Stan Stewart

On a wet and windy summer evening at New York's JFK Airport, passengers began checking-in for Tuesday's late night departure of Korean Air Lines flight KE007 to Kimpo Airport, Seoul, via Anchorage in Alaska. The date was August 30, 1983. The South Korean airline was handled in New York by American Airlines whose terminal building was also made available for their use. The passengers waiting to board Flight KE007, a Boeing 747-200B, registration HL7442, faced a long and tiring journey. The scheduled departure of near midnight out of Kennedy led to a seven-hour flight through the darkness with an arrival in Anchorage the next day. After a short transit the Boeing 747 would then proceed to Seoul, arriving, after another eight-hour journey under the stars, on the following morning. This routing avoided overflying the airspace of the USSR, although it lay very close to its eastern border.

On the Anchorage—Seoul sector Flight 007 would cross the international date line and the travelers would jump one day ahead. The flight path of the Korean 747 from New York (local time GMT-4) to the transit at Anchorage (-8) and on to Seoul (+9) was along the shortest route, passing over the top of the earth on a course which lay close to the Great Circle track, the line joining the shortest distance on a globe between departure point and final destination. Such a northerly track traversed a large number of time zones. The time changes resulted in both sectors being flown through the hours of darkness, with each long leg beginning late at night, and was a tiring ordeal for the crews as well as the passengers.

The Korean Boeing 747 lifted off from JFK at about 00.20hrs local New York time (04.20hrs GMT) after a 30 minute delay and arrived at Anchorage at 03.30hrs local Alaskan time (11.30hrs GMT). Scheduled departure for Seoul was 04.20hrs local (12.20hrs GMT), which allowed just sufficient time for the passengers to stretch their legs in the spacious airport transit lounge and to browse through the many shops. As the weary travelers relaxed in the terminal building the 747 was cleaned, replenished, and refueled for the next stage of the journey. The crew which had operated from New York disembarked for a period of rest in Anchorage while a fresh crew of three flightdeck personnel and 20 cabin staff prepared to board the flight. About 15 minutes after KE007's arrival another Korean Air Lines flight, KE015 from Los Angeles, also bound for Seoul, parked at the terminal and its passengers swelled the numbers mingling in the transit area.

Flight KE007 was now to be commanded by Captain Chun Byung In who, with his co-pilot, First Officer Sohn Dong Hui, and Flight Engineer Kim Eui Dong checked the flight details in the operations room before proceeding to the flightdeck. Continental Airlines prepared the paperwork, the flight plan of which had been telexed earlier from Los Angeles. All the information was carefully examined and the fuel uplift approved by Captain Chun. Only one item on the notices to airmen (Notams) was of any relevance and that was the unserviceability of the VOR radio beacon at Anchorage. The flight time, however, required some attention. The scheduled Anchorage to Kimpo journey time was 8 hours 20minutes, but because of favorable forecast winds the computer flight plans indicated a flight time of only 7 hours 35 minutes. A quick mental calculation in round figures revealed the problem. Departing from the gate at 04.20hrs Anchorage local time gave an airborne time of about 04.30hrs which, when the eight hours in flight were added, resulted in an estimated arrival time at Seoul of 05.30hrs local Korean time, 30min earlier than planned. South Korea, in keeping with other countries such as Japan and Australia, had a policy of closing their airports at night. No jet air traffic movements were permitted. Kimpo airport was not due to open until 06.00hrs local, so the simplest solution was to delay departure of KE007 by 30 minutes.

Meanwhile, Captain Chun and his crew boarded the aircraft and commenced their pre-flight checks. Among the flight crew's tasks was programing of the Inertial Navigation System (INS) which would navigate the Boeing 747 on the next leg of the flight to Kimpo airport. In the last decade civil aviation had witnessed the demise of the navigator and all major intercontinental routes were flown using such electronic navigation devices, or similar equipment. INS is a spin-off from American space projects and is a self-contained airborne unit completely independent of ground-based navigation aids. The system consists of a gyro-stabilized platform on which are placed accelerometers which detect movement of the aircraft in all directions. These movements are processed by the computer and used to compile navigational data. Since the INS always knows where it is, and the computer program contains details of earth shape and movement and direction of true north, the system is able continuously to display actual position as the flight progresses, as well as navigate the aircraft to a distant point. Other data such as speed, distance, track, and wind are also available. In addition, signals from the INS supply stable reference datums for certain flight instruments and for autopilot function. With autopilot engagement, INS mode can then be selected for automatic navigation.

On the arrival of KE007 in Anchorage, the INS computers on board would retain in their memory the position of the aircraft at the terminal ramp and would even compensate for earth movement during the time on the ground. After long journeys, however, small errors can creep in, and, extremely accurate although the system may

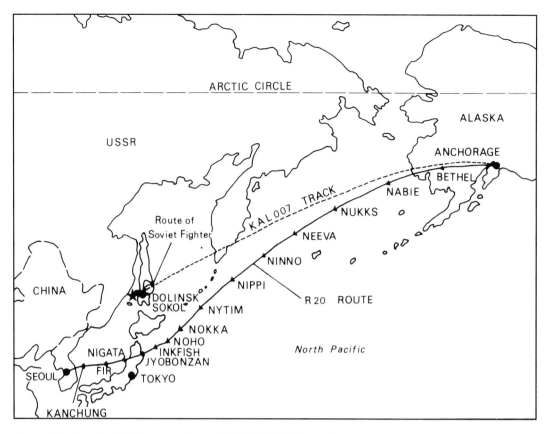

Above: *The intended, R20, route and actual KAL007 (KE007) track.*

be, the computer may "think" it is a mile or two away from its actual position. This is resolved by selecting the INS to an "alignment" mode and by informing the machine exactly where it is. The precise latitude and longitude of the aircraft's position, given to the nearest tenth of an angular minute in the Anchorage Airport booklet (eg Anchorage 61° 10.7′N, 149° 59.2′W) is inserted into the computer via a numbered keyboard. The INS then compares the actual position inserted by the pilot with where it "thinks" it is and corrects itself accordingly. It also works the other way, and can detect a ramp position incorrectly inserted by the pilot—known in the trade as "finger trouble"—by illumination of a red warning light. If the error is significant the pilot can then recheck his figures and reset the correct position. In the align mode, by the simple expediency of sensing earth rotation, the computer recalculates true north from the "corrected" position and adjusts for its previous errors in an attempt to eliminate them on the next flight. The alignment process can take up to 13 minutes and during this period the aircraft must not be moved. A green "ready" light illuminates when the process is completed and the selector must then be positioned to navigation mode before the aircraft moves from the ramp. Checking and setting of the INS to align, and inserting the ramp positions, is normally the function of the co-pilot. All big jets such as the Boeing 747 normally carry three completely independent inertial navigation systems, so the insertion of the ramp position for the alignment process has to be undertaken three times. If only two INSs were on board—like someone wearing two watches—and one malfunctioned, it would be impossible to tell which was operating normally. With three systems it can be reasonably assumed that with any two in agreement the third one must be incorrect. Whilst navigating the systems are electronically mixed, and a compromise position is obtained from the mid-latitude and mid-longitude of the three INSs. By such an arrangement any malfunction of one system does not give a large navigational error. The INS has been proven in service to be an extremely accurate device and an American study has shown that problems associated with pilot insertion of incorrect data occur only once in every 19,600 flights. The INS had also been demonstrated to be remarkably reliable and on no occasion has a triple failure of the system been recorded. INS is a most impressive navigational tool.

With the pre-flight checks completed and the aircraft prepared for service the passengers were finally called from the transit lounge for the delayed departure. As the travelers filed aboard, "clearance delivery" was called on the radio for the departure routing. KE007 was cleared for departure from runway 32 and the crew checked the details from the airport booklet: climb on runway heading as rapidly as practicable to 400ft then turn left on to track 300° magnetic and expect vectors to assigned route or depicted fix. Climb through 3,000ft as rapidly as possible. The initial routing would direct Flight 007 on to airway Victor 319/Jet 501 to Bethel, or on a direct routing assigned by radar to any point on the way, and then on route Romeo 20 (R20) over the Bering Sea along the line of the Aleutian Island chain. The route would then pass over the north Pacific Ocean and south of the Sea of Okhotsk, skirting just outside the edge of airspace controlled by the Tilichiki and Petropavlovsk-Kainchatskiy Soviet air traffic control centers, on through the northern Japanese airways network, and across the Sea of Japan to South Korea. The total flight distance from Anchorage to Seoul was 3,566 nautical miles.

Once aboard, the 246 passengers, mostly Korean, Taiwanese, and Japanese, including some Korean Air Lines crew returning to base, settled down for the long trip ahead. Among the sprinkling of other nationalities on the flight, including American, Canadian, and British, was one gentleman of note, Congressman Lawrence McDonnald, national chairman of the right wing conservative John Birch Society. Almost all the passengers had commenced their journey in New York. The crew of 23 on KE007 brought the total head count on the Boeing 747 to 269 people. With the boarding completed, the doors were shut and the engines were started in sequence. KE007 was cleared to push back and taxi to runway 32 and, with the start checks completed, the aircraft was soon on its way.

The big jet took-off at exactly 05.00hrs local Anchorage time (13.00hrs GMT—now used for convenience throughout) and soon turned left on to the assigned heading of 300°. One minute after becoming airborne, as the 747 climbed quickly as per instructions, First Officer Sohn switched the radio from "tower" to 118.6MHz and called "departure." The radar controller replied with further instructions.

Chun turned the large 747 in the direction of Bethel using the autopilot heading control knob, then, it is assumed, switched the autopilot mode selector from heading to INS. The INS would now be coupled to the autopilot and the navigation system would automatically fly KE007 on a direct track to Bethel.

At Bethel, First Officer Sohn reported KE007's position as overhead, and passed an estimated time for Nabie, the first of the imaginary position reporting points out over the Bering Sea. The other oceanic reporting points were Neeva, Nippi, and Nokka, leading onto the coast of Japan. By now KE007 was outside civil radar cover, but an American military radar station at King Salmon, 220 miles southwest of Anchorage, spotted the 747 flying 12 miles to the north of Bethel. The military installation was part of a chain of radar stations monitoring the approaches to Alaska from the east and was not concerned with flight planned civil traffic departing the region to the west. At that time there was little or no liaison between civil and military aviation organizations, a situation which was not satisfactory but was understandable. The capabilities of military radar installations are classified and any intervention on behalf of civil flights could compromise security. KE007, for all the King Salmon military observer knew, was following civil air traffic control instructions.

On the 747 flightdeck all seemed well as the INS appeared automatically to guide the aircraft along the 239°, magnetic track towards Nabie, 312 miles to the west. But the situation was far from well. The 747 had not only passed 12 miles north of Bethel but was still diverging from course. The track, in fact, led to the north of Romeo 20, on a route to danger which passed over the sensitive Kamchatka Peninsula in Soviet territory. The area was under constant military radar surveillance, and that night Soviet vigilance was to be tested. Meanwhile, the Korean flight crew, apparently unaware of their predicament, settled down to the familiar procedure of monitoring progress and passing position reports where required. At one minute before each waypoint an amber "alert" light illuminated on the INS (it also functioned in the same manner when passing abeam a position up to 200 nautical miles away) to warn the crew of approach to the next position. The INS could then be checked as it turned on to the next track, and the times recorded for transmission to the relevant air traffic control. At about 14.30hrs, KE007 passed abeam Nabie and First Officer Sohn attempted contact with Anchorage on very high frequency (VHF) radio. Although outside normal VHF cover, an automatic VHF link along the Aleutian chain of islands relayed the calls. Korean Air 007, however, was not at Nabie, but was by now 40 miles north of track and was just outside VHF range of the nearest relay station to the south. Fortunately the other Korean Air Lines flight at Anchorage, KE015 from Los Angeles to Seoul, which had departed 20 minutes later, heard the call and relayed the details. KE007's estimate for Neeva was transmitted at 16.00hrs. No indication was given of any problem and every impression was imparted that the Romeo 20 route was being flown. As a check KE007 established high frequency (HF) long range communications with Anchorage at 14.44hrs, but at Neeva, at 15.58hrs, Sohn again relayed his position on VHF via KE015. The estimate given for Nippi, 561 miles away, was 17.08hrs. At Nippi, control would change from Anchorage to Tokyo and the instruction was given to call Tokyo on en route radio at that point. Passing Neeva, KE007 had strayed 150 miles off track.

At 16.06hrs First Officer Sohn requested clearance to climb to 33,000ft, and Anchorage control relayed their approval. The big jet ascended 2,000ft to the next height and cruised on towards danger at flight level 330. If the crew were aware of their actual position they remained remarkably calm, for just under 400 miles away

Above: *INS control/display unit.*

lay the coast of the hostile Kamchatka Peninsula. The Korean 747 was, by now, flying unannounced in an area supervised by Soviet civil controllers but was still well outside Russian airspace. It did not, however, proceed unnoticed. Already Soviet military observers were tracking KE007 on their radar screens.

Captain Chun would also likely have been using radar, in this case to pick up weather, with the scanner tilted down about one degree to detect isolated thunder clouds. The moon, by now, had risen and shone almost half full in the southeast giving some light to the sky, so he may also have been able to see cloud formations. Some ground returns would have been visible on the weather radar screen, but low cloud was expected on the route and may have confused the picture. Had Captain Chun found the need to select mapping mode, it is likely that a clearer outline of the Kamchatka Peninsula would at this stage have been coming into view.

The Soviet radar operators, observing KE007, now noticed another unidentified target appear on the screens about 75 miles ahead of the 747. As the Russians may have suspected, this was a US Air Force RC-135, an adapted Boeing 707 on an intelligence gathering mission. Its presence in the area was not unexpected as such aircraft patrolled the region on up to 20 days per month and sometimes a relay of aircraft remained on station for 24 hours a day. The behavior of the RC-135 did not give cause for concern to the Soviets, but by now they were becoming extremely disturbed by the approach of the unidentified Korean 747. First Officer Sohn's radio reports may have conveyed an air of calm on KE007's flightdeck, but on the ground there was a great deal of consternation. As the 747 approached the Kamchatka Peninsula with its early warning radar systems, missile testing sites and the port facilities at Petropavlovsk, a base for nuclear armed submarines, the Russians could no longer exercise restraint. Six MiG-23 all-weather fighters were scrambled. KE007 took 24 minutes to overfly the Kamchatka Peninsula with the MiGs in hot pursuit, but in spite of being tracked by radar the interceptors were unable to locate their prey. As the Korean flight left Russian airspace over the Sea of Okhotsk the MiGs broke off the chase and ignominiously returned to their stations. The Soviet defence system had been found somewhat lacking.

KE007 passed abeam Nippi at 17.07hrs and should at that moment have been entering Japanese controlled airspace. The aircraft was, in fact, 185 miles off track. First Officer Sohn reported his position as Nippi to Tokyo on HF radio and transmitted the estimate for Nokka, another imaginary reporting point lying 660 miles away, about 100 miles south of the Kuril Islands.

The Korean 747 cruised over the Sea of Okhotsk, now back in international airspace, and continued on a heading towards the southern tip of Sakhalin Island. The island was another Soviet hot spot, controlling the approach to the Sea of Japan and the important naval base of Vladivostok. On the south coast of Sakhalin, by the Soya or La Perouse Strait, is situated the strategic naval establishment of Koraskov, surrounded by a number of airforce bomber and fighter stations and a major missile site. It was a highly sensitive area, second only to the submarine base at Petropavlovsk.

The embarrassment felt by the Soviet defence commander at the failure to intercept the unidentified aircraft could not go unchecked, and every effort was being made to prevent the escape of the intruder. As far as the Russians were concerned the aircraft was probably a US RC-135, although its speed seemed too fast. Perhaps it was a converted Boeing 747—an E-4A or E-4B intelligence gathering aircraft. It might even have been a civilian aircraft pretending to be off track; their own airline Aeroflot was suspected of indulging in such practices. Whatever it was it could only be on a spying mission and it had to be intercepted and forced to land. Soviet fighters on the Kuril Islands were scrambled to block any escape route to the south. Japanese and American intelligence officers, unaware of the situation, simply assumed the Russians were involved in an air defence exercise. On Sakhalin Island, at the Dolinsk-Sokol air base, crews were briefed and more fighters were placed on alert. As the 747 continued on its course, they too were scrambled to intercept.

Time was now running short for the Russians. The south of Sakhalin Island is at its widest only 80 miles across and the 747 would traverse Soviet airspace in less than ten minutes. Just a few miles southwest of the island at the far side of the Soya Strait, lay the northern Japanese Island of Hokkaido and the forbidden area of Japanese airspace. If KE007 was allowed to proceed beyond the shores of Sakhalin Island it could not be followed. It had to be intercepted before that point.

The Soviet fighters climbed rapidly from their Sakhalin base to 33,000ft, and under radar control flew out across the Sea of Okhotsk to meet the intruder. With radar guidance the interceptors turned behind the approaching 747 and took up positions on its tail. Japanese military radar stations observed the scene and saw what

Above: *Sukhoi Su-15.*

appeared to be a Russian transport aircraft being escorted by some fighters. Electronic ears were also listening to the activity and air-to-ground transmissions between the fighters and their control centers were recorded. Three fighters were apparently involved, with callsigns 805, 163, and 121, conducting communications between control centers codenamed Deputat, Karnaval, and Trikotazh.

Ground-to-air radio instructions between these stations and the interceptors were also believed to be recorded, but were not released. Aircraft 805, identified as a Sukhoi Su-15, and ground control station Deputat, played dominant roles in the events which were about to unfold.

After being radar vectored onto the intruder's tail, 805 picked up the target on his own radar and moved in for a closer look. KE007 was flying on course 240° at 33,000ft and at a ground speed of about 500kts. At just before 18.06hrs, as the Su-15 closed the gap on the 747, fighter pilot 805 made a jubilant call to his ground control station, "I see it!" Deputat responded with further directions to which the Su-15 pilot replied at 18.08hrs, "805, Roger. Understood. I'm flying behind."

The Su-15 fighter turned slightly right and pulled almost abreast of the 747's right side, but some way off. Mistakenly KE007 was reported as changing course:

18.09:00: "805, yes, it has turned. The target is 80° to my left."
18.10:35: "805, course two two zero."
18.11:20: "805, 8,000 meters, Roger."
18.12:10: "805, I see it visually and on radar."

The moon was still visible and should have given sufficient light to identify the aircraft in the clear sky. It must have been obvious by now that the aircraft was not an RC-135, but it perhaps could have been identified as an E-4B. If KE007 was recognized by the Su-15 pilot as a civilian aircraft the information was never transmitted to ground control. It was not 805's responsibility to identify the target; he was simply obeying instructions. 805 then activated an identification procedure known as IFF—identification friend or foe—but with inevitable results. Soviet systems are obviously not compatible with other equipment.

On the flightdeck of the 747, the Korean crew seemed oblivious of the activity and were more interested in climbing to the next suitable flight level. The co-pilot radioed Tokyo on HF for approval. Meanwhile the Su-15 pilot continued with his transmissions, confirming the navigation lights (as stipulated in the Air Navigation Order) were lit and that the flashing red anti-collision light was operating. 805 then verified that his ZG indicator was illuminated, which confirmed his radar guided missiles were locked on target. He remained at lock-on for only a short period then called back, perhaps following further instructions.

At about this moment KE007 received a call from Tokyo with approval to climb to flight level 350, to which First Officer Sohn replied "Roger, Korean Air 007, climb and maintain flight level three five zero, leaving three three zero this time."

There was no indication of anything untoward occurring, although at this point the 747 was 365 miles off track. Captain Chun selected vertical speed mode on the autopilot and began the ascent to 35,000ft, with the aircraft slowing slightly as it did so. As the climb clearance was being received the Su-15 pilot fired 120 rounds from his cannons in four bursts, ostensibly as a warning to 007. If any shells did strike the aircraft the incident was not reported. The Korean crew, busy with the climb procedure, did not appear to see any tracers, if that was 805's intentions. The Su-15 pilot, increasing speed to close the gap between the two aircraft, was caught off-balance with the 747 climb maneuver.

18.22:02: "805, the target is decreasing speed."

18.22:17: "805, I am going around it. I'm already moving in front of the target."

18.22:23: "805, I have increased speed."

18.22:29: "805, no. It is decreasing speed."

18.22:42: "805, it should have been earlier. How can I chase it? I am already abeam of the target."

18.22:55: "805, now I have to fall back a bit from the target."

The Su-15 pilot received more instructions from Deputat to which there was a constant stream of replies.

18.23:18: "805, from me it is located 70° to the left."

18.23:37: "805, I am dropping back. Now I will try rockets."

18.24:22: "805, Roger. I am in lock-on."

18.25:11: "805, I am closing on the target. Am in lock-on. Distance to target is eight kilometers."

The Sukhoi Su-15 pilot fired his missiles and the two AA-3 "Anab" rockets streaked toward the 747. A couple of seconds later they struck the tail of the target and probably an inboard engine. The big airliner instantly broke up and spiraled toward the ground. The interceptor pilot watched as the 747 exploded in the darkness, then matter-of-factly called ground control.

18.26:22: "805, the target is destroyed. I'm breaking off the attack."

In the 747 cockpit, the flight crew, surviving the initial strike, were taken completely by surprise. Desperately the co-pilot transmitted a few garbled words to Tokyo Control.

18.27 F/O Sohn: "Korean Air 007. . . all engines. . . rapid decompression. . . one zero one. . . two delta. . ."

Nothing more was heard from KE007. The time was 18.28hrs GMT on August 31, 03.28hrs local Japanese and Korean time on September 1. Japanese military radar operators witnessed the 747 spiraling from the sky and a few minutes later at about 18.30hrs saw the target strike the sea off the west coast of Sakhalin Island, just outside Soviet territorial waters. All 269 aboard the Korean 747 perished.

News of the shoot-down broke upon a stunned world and provoked an international outcry. Angry retorts from leaders of the free world denounced the Soviet Union and demands were made for retaliatory action. The Canadians were the first to stop Aeroflot flights into their country and other nations followed suit. President Reagan closed Aeroflot's offices in New York and Washington and a worldwide 60-day ban was called on all flights to Russia. The Soviet reaction to the fury was predictable. At first they refused to admit the act, but after a few days eventually confessed to the shooting down of KE0071 in mistake for a US RC-135 spy flight. As far as they were concerned, however, the intruder was on a spying mission and they had every justification in shooting it from the skies. An impressive propaganda exercise was mounted by the Soviets to support their claim and they openly condemned the United States for their "deliberately-planned provocations." In an unprecedented move, the chief of the Soviet general staff, Marshal Nikolai Ogarkov, held a press conference in Moscow to present their case. A large chart displayed how, in the Soviet opinion, the Korean 747 had rendezvoused with the US RC-135 before proceeding deliberately to violate Russian airspace. Marshal Ogarkov, giving almost a repeat account of the shooting down of the Korean 707 south of Murmansk in 1978, claimed that the 747 had been tracked by military radar for several hours, that the aircraft was flying without lights, that the crew did not respond to attempts at contact, and that warning shots were ignored. "There was no doubt that it was a reconnaissance plane" and "the aircraft's destruction and the loss of life should be blamed on the US." In the words of the *New York Times*, Marshal Ogarkov gave a "spellbinding performance." The incident soured US-Soviet relations and injured efforts at detente. One year later, however, both sides had greatly modified their stance: Washington no longer maintained that the shooting was a deliberate and callous act and Moscow openly admitted that the shooting was a grave error.

But why was KE007 so far off track? Was the Korean 747 on a spying mission? The Russians made accusations that KE007 was carrying sophisticated electronic eavesdropping equipment, but this is difficult to accept. How this aircraft was supposed to be serviced by other airlines at distant stations without the mechanics' knowledge that such devices were on board was not explained. The array of antennas required would have been obvious to all. The so-called "rendezvous" with the RC-135 can only be dismissed as coincidental. At that time these aircraft were in the region almost every day and at no point were the two flights closer than 75 miles. The RC-135 was back at its Shemya base at the end of the Aleutian Island chain about one hour before the shoot-down of the 747. The Soviets, it was suspected, were preparing to test a new weapon that night, but why should the Koreans take such risks when intelligence-gathering aircraft could patrol effectively at a safe distance and spy satellites could effectively gather intelligence from afar? The Soviet claims of spying are unlikely.

There were plenty of other rumors, however, some originating in the West, that the 747 intrusion had an equally sinister purpose. It was suggested by some that the Korean 747 carried no eavesdropping equipment, but its violation of Russian airspace was arranged simply to provoke a response from the Soviets which could be monitored by the West. It was claimed that the delay of KE007 from Anchorage was arranged in order to maintain VHF radio contact with KE015 who transmitted fake radio calls, that a rendezvous with the RC-135 did take place, and that the intrusion was timed to coincide with the passage of the US Ferret spy satellite and the space shuttle *Challenger*, which had been launched the day before. There is no doubt that the Soviet activity resulting from the Korean 747's demise provided a windfall for US intelligence, but the suggestion that the infringement was planned is totally unfounded. The insinuations that a civilian airliner pretended to be off track either to gather intelligence or to provoke a defence response for monitoring purposes are both based on the premise that the Russians would not shoot down a civilian aircraft. Yet only five years earlier the Soviets had demonstrated quite clearly that they would not tolerate infringement of their borders. If any air carrier was aware of the consequences of inadvertent violation of Russian airspace, it was Korean Air Lines — they had lost an passenger jet in similar circumstances a decade previously. The accusations of spying in this manner are also unlikely.

The same can be said for the charges of deliberate corner-cutting. All pilots, at some time, take short cuts, perhaps following the central line of a twisting airway, but an attempt to cut a corner on this scale is unimaginable. Even had Captain Chun deliberately tried to follow the shortest distance along the Great Circle track from Anchorage to Seoul and had avoided the Soviet interceptors, how was he going to fool the Japanese authorities? Sending "fake" position reports on HF radio over remote areas is one thing, but trying the same trick on VHF through a congested radar controlled airways system is another matter. In most radar controlled areas position reports are not even required, and after initial contact aircraft progress is simply monitored by radar. Since KE007 would have passed to the north of Japan instead of approaching the east coast, it would have been well outside VHF range of the airway sector controller situated 350 miles to the south. Even if First Officer Sohn had been able to establish contact, the controller would hardly accept position reports from a flight he couldn't even see on his radar screen. Yet this is exactly what has been suggested in some quarters. The Japanese would more than likely have scrambled their own fighters if the unidentified 747 had appeared in their airspace in the north, and with the failure of KE007 to appear as planned on the airway system they would immediately have alerted the search and rescue services. Even had Captain Chun managed to outwit the Japanese defence systems he would have had to cross a north bound airway unannounced, pass through a high altitude training area, and breach the Korean air identification zone before reaching Kimpo Airport.

The suggested intention of Captain Chun's corner-cutting was, of course, to save on costs, but this argument does not stand up to scrutiny. Simulated flights of both the Romeo 20 and Great Circle routes have shown that by going direct the total distances would have been reduced by only 178 miles and the flight time by 20 minutes. Since the departure time from Anchorage was delayed by 30 minutes to co-ordinate KE007's arrival at Seoul with Kimpo Airport's opening time of 06.00hrs, what would be the point in making up time just to waste fuel holding over destination? In this respect alone the accusations of corner-cutting seem inconceivable.

Other suggestions as to the demise of KE007 concern incorrect INS and autopilot procedures. One theory is that after Captain Chun turned the aircraft toward Bethel using the autopilot heading control knob, he omitted to switch to INS and the selector was left in the magnetic heading mode. The selection of INS is accomplished by turning an autopilot switch anti-clockwise one notch from heading to INS. In front of both pilots green lights then illuminate on a flight mode annunciator to indicate that the navigation track has been captured. The insinuation that Captain Chun forgot to rotate this mode selector one division is unlikely in this case although there are some arguments in favor of the theory. There is no doubt that similar incidents had occurred. As recently as November 1985, a Japan Air Lines Boeing 747, en route from Tokyo to Moscow, strayed 60 miles off course for that very reason and flew close to the same spot near Sakhalin Island where KE007 went down. The captain had switched from INS to magnetic heading to fly around a thundercloud but had forgotten to reselect INS mode after negotiating the weather. Strong winds had blown the 747 westward. The crew discovered the error when completing a regular INS reporting point check and after repeated attempts managed to contact Khabarovsk air traffic control center. In the meantime two Soviet MiG fighters were scrambled. Fortunately the situation was sorted out in time and the 747 allowed to continue unhindered. The argument in Captain Chun's case is that after establishing on the airway center line from Anchorage to Bethel he omitted to select INS mode on the autopilot and continued on in magnetic heading mode. The wind at the time resulted in a left drift of only one degree so a magnetic heading of 246°, corresponding to the initial magnetic airway track, would lead the aircraft close to Bethel. If the aircraft then continued on a magnetic heading of 246° following an extension of the straight Anchorage to Bethel airway, it has been demonstrated that the course flown by KE007, that is, taking account of the wind and magnetic variation (the difference between true and magnetic north), leads to the shoot-down point over Sakhalin Island. Another convincing fact is that the course of 240° as reported by the Su-15 fighter pilot corresponds with KE007's. The wind aloft in that area resulted in a left drift of 5° and on a heading of 246° the 747 would fly a track of 241°. This implies, however, that the flight crew must have sat for five hours with the selector in heading mode and with no illumination of the green navigation capture lights without anyone noticing. It also indicates that no crew member checked any of the INS sets at any reporting point. It is almost impossible to imagine that an entire crew could be this irresponsible and on these facts alone this theory is unlikely. There are, however, more compelling reasons to indicate that INS was selected.

On initial departure KE007 was cleared to "proceed direct to Bethel when able." This instruction means, quite simply, that the flight was cleared from the aircraft's present position direct to the assigned point. There was no requirement for the Korean flight to proceed along the airway. The addition of "when able" normally applies to non-INS equipped aircraft which can proceed direct to a distant VOR radio beacon only when within range of the signal. The skies of Alaska are full of such aircraft and the controller said 'when able' out of habit, even to the 747 which could proceed direct at the push of a button. It has been suggested, however, that "when able" was added to the clearance because of mountains to the north and west and that it was necessary for Captain Chun to fly the airway route between Anchorage and Bethel to avoid the high ground. At the time Captain Chun received the instruction to proceed direct to Bethel, KE007 was heading southwest over the low lying coastal area, well clear of the 5,500ft mountainous terrain lying 25 miles to the northwest and known locally as the Sleeping Lady. To the west the high ground stood at 5,000ft and lay 45 miles distant. Proceeding direct to Bethel at that moment would not infringe minimum safe altitudes. The only way the 747 could proceed on a straight line from its present position north of the airway to the out-of-range VOR radio beacon at Bethel was by use of the INS, which is standard procedure, and it is most likely that Captain Chun would have programmed the INS and autopilot to fly direct to Bethel. This is the strongest argument in favor of the INS being engaged and narrows the fault to a programming error or unit failures.

Whatever the error or fault in the INS the problem must have occurred before departure, or very soon afterward, for almost immediately the flight began to go wrong. The insertion of incorrect waypoints can be discounted for it is impossible to imagine them all being wrong, but it is possible that the initial ramp position at Anchorage was incorrectly inserted. Analysis of data has shown that a 10° easterly error in longitude, results in a flight path which also leads to the shoot-down point. The theory is also in keeping with the 240° course indicated by the Su-15 pilot. Although the INS position over the earth was incorrect, the directions of waypoints relative to each other would be retained correctly in the INS memory. The true track between Nippi and Nokka was 229°, and with the addition of the magnetic variation in the region of 9°, a magnetic course of 238° results. To achieve the ramp position error, however, the pilot inserting the data would have to key the longitude incorrectly three times as he separately loaded each INS. If this alleged error did occur it seems strange that one digit should be incorrectly entered in such a way and that it was not picked up by the crew. The entry of 139° 59.2′ W instead of 149° 59.2′ W appears an unlikely discrepancy and one that would be sufficiently outstanding to be visually detectable. The transposing of two numbers is more likely ie 159° 49.2′ W instead of 149° 59.2′ W, thus displaying the same digits but in a slightly different sequence. Such a mistake is also more difficult to detect, but in this case results in a 10° (to be exact 9.8°) westerly error. Assuming an error did occur, however, three red warning lights would then be illuminated. The incorrect ramp positions would then have to be inserted once more into each system before the INS would accept the error and the red warning light would extinguish. Had the error been of similar significance in latitude it would not have been accepted, for the INS can detect peripheral velocity of the earth as a cross check. The aircraft's longitude, however, is held only in the memory with no means of cross-check, and a second insertion of an incorrect longitude can override the data. Each flight crew member, though, would then be required independently to check the ramp position at a later stage and, if the theory is correct, would have to fail to recognize the error. Once the aircraft moved off, there would be no way of re-checking the ramp position. Incidents of this nature, although extremely rare, had occurred in the past. Captain Chun and his crew boarded fresh in Anchorage, although "fresh" on that route is only relative bearing in mind the large time changes and journeys through the night. The flight crew, however, were not in a rush, gave no indication of being anything but alert, and such a sequence of errors, although possible, does not seem probable.

So what of INS failure? A simultaneous failure of all three systems is unknown although two have been known to break down on the same flight! INS has also been recorded as suffering from a number of isolated faults. Could an insidious series of events have resulted in the 747 going astray? As has been demonstrated in the 1979 Chicago incident involving the DC-10 engine pylon detachment, if something can happen in aviation, no matter how improbable, the chances are it will. Since no complete investigation of multiple INS failures was conducted it is possible only to speculate about such theories. Let us suggest, for argument's sake, that the number one INS begins to go wrong immediately after take-off. Since Captain Chun was the operating pilot this INS would be coupled to the autopilot to navigate the aircraft. Let us also suggest that before Nabie, where the first check of INS performance would be conducted independent of ground radio aids, the number two INS fails completely. Such incidents have been known to occur. A switch on the INS mode selector is simply set to "attitude" to supply a stable reference for the co-pilot's instruments. The flight is free to continue in this condition although no navigational data would be available from the number two INS. INS position mixing is now lost and the captain is in the position of the man with two watches; if they are at different times which one is correct? If, in the meantime, number three INS becomes faulty, then with two malfunctioning units and no means of cross-checking it would not be long before the pilot would unwittingly fly off track. It must be stressed that this is only speculation, although it has been shown repeatedly within this book that accidents are, more often than not, the result of such an unfortunate sequence of events. On the other hand, INS has proved itself over the years to be a remarkably reliable piece of equipment and, although an insidious sequence of errors is possible, it also does not seem probable.

So what happened to KE007? The CVR and FDR boxes were not recovered from the depths, so it will never be known. In the end, as with the Trident crash at Staines, none of the theories seems likely and it is possible only to speculate. Fortunately, some good has emerged from the incident. Communications between military and civilian controllers have been improved and plans are proceeding to link by telephone the air traffic control centers at Anchorage, Khabarovsk and Tokyo. Whether the international situation will improve as well is another matter.

9 North Atlantic, off Irish Coast, 1985
Air India Boeing 747-237B

Leo Marriott

Determining the reason why an aircraft has crashed is a complex process involving many specialist investigators backed up by the resources of various commercial, national, and international agencies. The most important evidence is usually derived from the wreckage itself with valuable information often forthcoming from witnesses and survivors. However, when an airliner disappears over the vastness of the world's oceans, then these sources are almost non-existent and investigators find themselves involved in pure detective work, unless the accident site can be located and at least some wreckage recovered. This was very much the case when an Air India Boeing 747 suddenly and inexplicably went down over the North Atlantic on Sunday June 23, 1985.

That morning, the scheduled weekly service AI182 from Montreal via London and then onto New Delhi and Bombay was to be flown by a Boeing 747-237B (VT-EFO) named *Kanishka* after the Emperor Kanishka who ruled an Indian state during the second century. After some delay it had eventually taxied out from gate 107, terminal two at Montreal's L.N. Pearson International Airport, and took-off at 00.16hrs local (very early morning in Canada) to cruise across the Atlantic at 31,000ft. The delay of just over an hour and a half was for technical reasons, connected with carrying an extra engine pod under the port wing between the number two engine and the fuselage. This was a common method of ferrying unserviceable engines back to a maintenance base for overhaul and repair and was of no significance in what was to happen later. Otherwise, there were no further problems, and a little under seven hours later, with the Atlantic receding behind the aircraft, Flight 182 was approaching within VHF communication range of Ireland. At 07.05hrs the crew had passed a position report of 50°N 15°W on the HF radio frequency and had then been instructed to call Shannon on 131.15MHz VHF frequency. Their initial call was made at 07.08hrs after a slight pause because of other aircraft also calling. The Oceanic controller then passed routing instructions that would, via Airway Upper Blue 40 to Merley and Upper Red 37 to Ibsley VOR beacon, take the flight to London Heathrow. There was then a momentary confusion before the crew acknowledged and set their allocated transponder code 2005. This was observed on

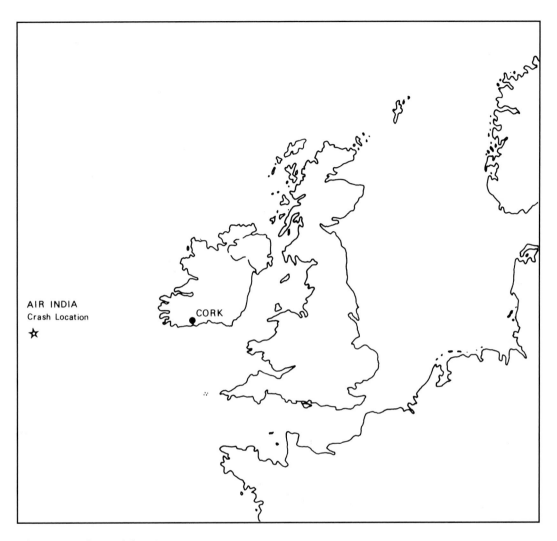

Above: *Air India crash location.*

Below: *Diagram showing the parts of the Air India Boeing 747 that were discovered on the ocean floor.*

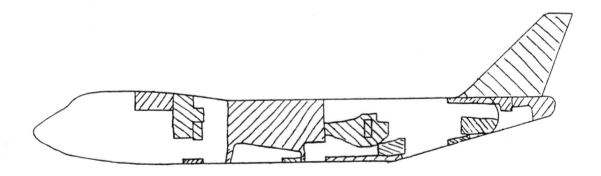

Above: *An Air India Boeing 747-200 in landing configuration at Heathrow, destination of the fatal flight AI182 from Montreal.* Robbie Shaw

the radar screens at the Shannon Air Traffic Control Centre and controllers M. Quinn and T. Lane monitored the progress of AI182 as *Kanishka* flew eastward, sped on by westerly winds, with a ground speed of 519kts. The time was 07.10hrs.

At 07.14hrs both controllers heard the brief clicking sound of a transmit button, and then—without warning and without making a "Mayday" call—the Air India radar return vanished from their screen. Other flights were immediately asked to contact AI182 but there was no reply to any call. The 747, with her 307 passengers and 22 crew, had simply disappeared. By 07.30hrs there was little doubt in anyone's mind that a very serious problem had arisen. The controllers informed the Shannon Marine Co-ordination Centre (MRCC) that AI182 had disappeared from radar at 07.13hrs at position 51°N 12°W and requested emergency action. At 07.40hrs MRCC Shannon telephoned Valentia Coast Radio Station to explain the emergency, requesting an urgent PAN Broadcast asking shipping in the area to keep a sharp lookout and report anything to Valentia Radio. This transmission was made at 07.46hrs and was then repeated, quickly gaining a response (at 07.50hrs) from the Irish Navy vessel *Aisling*, which reported that she was 54 miles from 51°N 12°W and was proceeding there at once. In the ten-minute period 07.40hrs to 07.50hrs, MRCC Shannon briefed the Irish Naval Service, the British Marine Rescue Co-ordination Centre at Swansea, Rescue Co-ordination Centre Plymouth, and the Irish Air Corps, all of which shows how quickly the search and rescue organizations responded to the initial report and how wide the net is spread in such circumstances.

Valentia Radio broadcast the PAN message again at 08.03hrs and at 08.40hrs received a report from a cargo vessel MV *Laurentian Forest* at position 51.09°N

12.18°W stating she was 22 miles from the distress area and proceeding to the site. A further call was received at 08.42hrs from the cargo vessel *Ali Baba* reporting that she was in the vicinity and listening out on 121.5MHz. and at 08.57hrs the cable vessel *Western Arctic* also announced she would proceed to the distress area in about 20 minutes after hoisting in cable. Finally, a call offering assistance was received at that time from *High Seas Driller*. In the hours that followed many other vessels contacted Valentia Radio in a typical response from the world's professional mariners who are prepared to offer assistance, regardless of individual operational penalties, whenever an emergency is declared.

While Valentia Radio was gathering offers of assistance, MRCC Shannon had been in further discussions with RCC Plymouth in the period 08.15–08.20hrs and were informed that Sea King helicopters had been dispatched to Cork Airport. In addition an RAF Nimrod maritime patrol aircraft would shortly take-off to commence a search of the distress area, with a second being brought to operational readiness. It was at this time that reports were received by Shanwick Oceanic Control that aircraft were receiving ELT (Emergency Locator Beacon) signals from two positions, namely 51°N 15°W, and 51°N 08°W. By 09.05hrs the *Laurentian Forest* was reporting that she was five miles from the distress position and had not yet sighted anything but a few minutes later, at 09.13hrs, she reporting seeing two liferaft. This first positive confirmation of a major disaster was followed by an amplifying report saying that the liferaft were not inflated and that some wreckage had also been spotted at position 51°01.9'N 12°42.5'W. While Valentia and Baltimore lifeboats reported to Valentia Radio that they were now proceeding to the position of the wreckage the *Laurentian Forest* made a further call at 09.37hrs to say she had sighted three bodies in the water. Over the next few hours many more bodies were found and the Sea King helicopter arrived to assist with the search. It quickly became apparent that there was little or no likelihood of finding any survivors and the search and rescue operation was eventually terminated as darkness fell over the Atlantic on the evening of the 24th. By then *Laurentian Forest* had picked up 66 bodies, the Valentia Lifeboat had picked up five, and *Aisling* 56 bodies. Subsequently, only one more body was recovered, although numerous pieces of wreckage were found. The final count was 131 bodies including five cabin staff, but none of the flightdeck crew.

The most urgent task facing investigators of the tragedy was the recovery of the cockpit voice and digital flight data recorders. Both were fitted with submersible beacons as an aid to recovery but the wreckage lay at a depth of about 6,700ft, although the ocean bed in the area is relatively flat. However, recovery of the recorders from this depth would be a unique achievement, and it would not be possible to raise the main wreckage. The attempt to recover the recorders was made using a remotely controlled submersible vehicle, *Scarab I*, launched from the French ship *Leon Thevenin*. This was designed to operate to a maximum depth of 6,000ft only but, in the circumstances, the risk of exceeding the design limitation was accepted. In fact, the operation was outstandingly successful and the two units were recovered on the 10th and 11th of July. Prior to these dives, the UK Accident Investigation Branch vessel *Gardline Locator* and the Irish Navy's *Le Aiofe* used side scanning sonar equipment to survey the area where the wreckage had come to rest. This spadework was then followed up by the Canadian Coast Guard ship *John Cabot* and her submersible craft *Scarab II* which, whilst also designed to operate only to depths of 6,000ft, was equipped with manipulators, a complete optical suite, and sonar, and could be used to locate and recover some elements of the aircraft.

The transcript from the recovered DFDR showed that the aircraft had been cruising normally at 31,000ft at an airspeed of 340mph until there was an abrupt loss of power to both recorders (DFDR and CVR) at 07.14:35hrs. Some 30 seconds before the loss of power, the CVR recorded a loud noise which the British Air Accidents Investigation Branch considered was caused by an explosive decompression. Further research into the recordings was undertaken in India at the Bhabha Atomic Research Centre (BARC), whilst a copy of the Shannon Air Traffic Control tape (which contained the short series of unusual sounds that had occurred about the time of the accident) was also made available to the Indian authorities. These sounds, the BARC concluded, were probably generated during the in-flight break-up of *Kanishka*.

Even while recovery of the wreckage continued, some possible causes could be investigated and eliminated. One such item was the unserviceable engine being transported under the wing in an enclosed pod. When flying in this configuration the aircraft's operating manual stipulated a speed limit of 290kts (0.81 Mach) and the DFDR showed that the aircraft speed had actually varied from 287 to 296kts. However this speed variation was ruled out as a contributory factor when Boeing reported that flight tests of a model in the five pod configuration had been done at speeds up to 386kts (0.92 Mach) without any adverse effects. It was also known that loading of the pallet containing the inlet cowl of the unserviceable engine had encountered difficulties that made it necessary to remove the door stop fittings from the aft cargo compartment door cut-out. The removal of the stops and their subsequent installation had been carried out under approved procedures, and these were vindicated when it was seen on the video films of the wreckage that the aft cargo door was intact and in position. The door had come slightly adrift, but was latched at the bottom and was found in the wreckage of the aft portion of the aircraft, a clear indication that it could not have caused flight problems.

Kanishka had been acquired by Air India in June 1978 and had been maintained following approved maintenance schedules. It had logged 23,634:49 hours in 7,525 cycles and had undergone a maintenance check "B" (which was valid for 200 hours) only a short time earlier (on June 17) at 23,564:14 hours. On the pre-flight check at Montreal the flight engineer had noted that the rear latch handle of the fifth pod engine fan cowl was loose. This had been faired and had high speed tape applied to it by a technician, and there had been no other snags. The group that investigated the six incidents involving the aircraft since its last Certificate of Airworthiness concluded that all work had been correctly carried out to approved schedules. Another group investigated the possibility of aircraft structure failure following corrosion but was able to report that no significant corrosion was found in the fleet which had been maintained in accordance with Boeing's recommended corrosion prevention measures. Among the nine 747 aircraft checked, five aircraft had logged more hours than *Kanishka*, and three of those aircraft had flown nearly twice as many. Corrosion, therefore, was ruled out as a cause of the crash.

Above: *Air India Boeing 747-200 (VT-EGA) taxying at Heathrow. Air India is a major user of 747s as befits her status as a world airline with an excellent safety record.* Robbie Shaw

Below: *A Boeing 747-237B operated by Air India. It was an identical aircraft which fell victim to the terrorist bomb over the North Atlantic on June 23, 1985.* Leo Marriott

While the investigators were obliged to look at every possible mechanical cause of the accident, there were early suspicions that the disaster was caused by an act of sabotage, possibly achieved by placing an explosive device in the aircraft. However, checks to eliminate other possible causes were important as they could also provide clues that might confirm that an explosion had occurred. With no pre-existing defect discovered, and no indication of structural failure, evidence obtained from the recovered wreckage pointed to an explosion in the forward cargo hold. One large piece was a section of skin panel which would have been located near the compartment, and in this were small puncture holes. Also, there were tiny "moon craters" in a piece of alloy filled with foam, and there was damage to the bottom of some recovered seat cushions. It was concluded that other wreckage showed signs of being distorted, prior to failure, by an outward force from within the aircraft. It was subsequently determined that the aircraft spoilers had been deployed and it was also noted that the horizontal tail stabilizer jackscrew ballnut was located at the upper jackscrew stop, the fully nose-up trim condition. It seemed unlikely that it would have moved there under the influence of gravity, and with no indication of a trim malfunction given by the flight recorder, the indications of nose-up trim and deployment of spoilers suggested that the crew had started an emergency descent before being overcome by lack of oxygen. Lack of oxygen could well have happened as a result of the emergency oxygen supply lines being severed, as was the power supply to the recorders, by an explosion in the cargo hold. At 31,000ft consciousness would be lost in seconds, resulting in loss of control and the aircraft breaking up soon afterward.

The possibility of a sabotage attempt was also given credence by an apparently related event which had occurred on the other side of the world. At Narita Airport in Japan, about an hour before the *Kanishka* disaster, a suitcase bomb went off in the transit area, killing two and injuring four airport workers. Enquiries revealed that the suitcase had been off-loaded from Canadian Pacific Air Flight 003 from Vancouver, Canada, and was to have been placed aboard Air India Flight 301 bound for Bangkok, Thailand. As Canada appeared to be the linking factor between the two explosions, the Royal Canadian Mounted Police and their Japanese counterparts began full-scale investigations. The bomb which destroyed *Kanishka* could have originated in Montreal or Toronto, while the bomb at Narita might have originated in Vancouver. As investigations continued through July a confusing picture of bookings and changed bookings was brought to light. On June 19, a call had been made to a CP Air reservations agent by a man with a slight Indian accent. He, Mr. Singh, was making bookings for one Jaswand Singh flying on Flight CP086 from Vancouver to Montreal Dorval Airport on June 22, to link with Air India Flight 182 out of Montreal Mirabel Airport. The second booking was for Mohinderbel Singh to fly from Vancouver to Tokyo Narita Airport on Flight CP003 and then Flight AI301 from Tokyo to Bangkok. An hour and 20 minutes later another reservations agent was contacted and asked to change the booking for Jaswand Singh. He would now travel on Flight CP060 from Vancouver to Toronto and there be wait-listed on Flight AI181/182 from Toronto through Montreal to London and Delhi.

The next day, soon after midday, an Indian man paid, in cash, for the tickets from the CP Air ticket office in Vancouver, and further changes were made. The booking in the name of Mohinderbel Singh was changed to "L. Singh," and the booking for Jaswand Singh changed to "M. Singh." On the following Saturday, June 22, a passenger agent working at the CP Air ticket counter at Vancouver International Airport began dealing with a passenger of Indian origin who was boarding Flight CP060 with one piece of baggage which he wanted tagged right through to Delhi. Despite being told that this interlining was not permitted because he was wait-listed at Toronto, the passenger continued to insist that his case be interlined. Conscious of the delay to a long line-up that the argument was causing, the agent relented and interlined the suitcase. The flight manifest for CP003 to Tokyo shows that L. Singh also checked through the same counter, and also checked one piece of baggage. When CP Air's records were checked and other passengers of flights CP003 and CP060 interviewed, it was clear that the passengers identifying them-selves as M. Singh and L. Singh never boarded their respective flights. The suitcase bombs had, however, begun their journeys and in due course completed their deadly work. *Kanishka* was brought down west of Ireland, whilst the bomb that exploded at Narita had been intended to destroy Air India Flight 301, but the timer had been incorrectly set.

The vast majority of the Sikhs in Canada, and indeed Vancouver, are hard working and law-abiding, but suspicion focused increasingly on the Vancouver community. Singh, meaning "Lion" is the given middle name for all Sikh men, just as Kaur, meaning "Princess" is given to the sect's womenfolk, so the use of the name for registration as a passenger gave some anonymity. Both "Mr. M. Singh" and "Mr. L. Singh" failed to board their aircraft, yet a considerable amount of money had been paid for the tickets. No-one had tried to reclaim the baggage because of a "no show" at departure, and the names used for the final booking of tickets were the names of Sikhs wanted by the FBI in connection with a recent plot to assassinate Rajiv Gandhi while visiting the US. It was as if the booking names had been deliberately chosen to advertise the actions of a Sikh terrorist group, yet no such group claimed respon-sibility. The questions that followed were why had the suitcases been stowed on board aircraft when unaccompanied, and why had the bombs not been detected by security screening? Here, system failures aided the sabotage plot. Despite the pres-sure to which the booking agent had been subjected by "Mr. M. Singh" (who insist-ed he had just phoned Air India and been confirmed to board the flight), "his" suit-case should never have been interlined onto AI182 when the confirmation details could not be verified. At Toronto, the regular X-ray machine had gone unserviceable during checking, and subsequent baggage checking had to be done with hand-held PD-4 "sniffers." The effectiveness of these was considered by the court of inquiry as doubtful, particularly as the staff concerned had not been properly trained in their use. The correlation of baggage with the check-in of passengers did not include interlining passengers, and M. Singh's absence was not detected. While Toronto—Delhi baggage pallets were spread through the aircraft holds, it was known that two were placed in the forward cargo hold just behind the electronics bay, and it seemed all too probable that it was here that the suitcase of explosives came to rest.

The bomb which exploded at Narita airport had been concealed in the frame of an AM/FM stereo tuner identified by forensic experts as a Sanyo model FMT 611K, all of which had been shipped to Vancouver. Bigger than later models, it was suitable for the explosive charge and timer assemblies. The RCMP even located the store where a tuner had been sold to two Sikhs three weeks earlier, and it was considered probable that a second tuner had already been in possession of the terrorists who assembled the two bombs. One reason why no terrorist group claimed responsibility for the disaster can be deduced from the airline timetables. Timetables state arrival and departure times in *local time*. Canada and the UK advance their clocks by an hour for daylight saving in the summer, which Japan does not. The one hour discrepancy could have resulted when synchronizing the timing devices. AI182 should have been on the ground at Heathrow when the bomb exploded, whilst the Narita bomb should have exploded at the same time, but on board the Air India aircraft. The simultaneous destruction of two Air India aircraft on the ground at opposite ends of the world close to the first anniversary of the bloody storming of the sacred Golden Temple at Amritsar in the Punjab in June 1984 would have been a dire warning to the Indian Government that Sikhs had the ability to strike at Indian interests anywhere, any time, at will. When the plot went wrong and claimed so many innocent lives, no organization wished to be associated with it. Police work continued long after the media interest in the tragedy had waned. Several years later an Indian Sikh was sentenced in Canada to ten years' imprisonment for his involvement in the explosion that had occurred at Narita Airport, and in July 1992 the case of *Kanishka*'s destruction was finally closed when a 30 year old Sikh terrorist who was believed responsible was arrested by Indian Authorities in Bombay.

The inquiry into the loss of Flight AI182 made a number of recommendations to the International Civil Aviation Organization, International Air Transport Association, and to state authorities. These were aimed at securing significant improvements and checks in airport security to ensure that systems, equipment, and staff training were improved and adequately backed up. IATA was urged to develop practical procedures for reconciliation of interline passengers and their baggage at intermediate airports and to ensure that interlining of checked-in baggage could not happen in the absence of a confirmed reservation. Governments and airlines, it was recommended, should alert airlines if they became aware of a particularly high risk security threat so that extra precautions could be introduced at potential points of introduction of interline baggage. Where passengers did not check in for the flight, their baggage should be off-loaded, and all baggage should not only be screened properly but should be matched with passengers boarding the aircraft. The inquiry also pointed out that explosives could be hidden in innocent looking or shaped containers and thus not always discovered by security equipment. It also recommended that aircraft manufacturers take steps to protect sensitive parts of the aircraft from explosive damage, and examine the feasibility of separating the avionics bay and emergency oxygen systems from cargo areas as well as ensuring that emergency oxygen for the flight crew be provided from two different sources. Following this incident, and with the added impetus resulting from the destruction of the Pan American 747 over Lockerbie, much work has been done to design containers for use in aircraft holds that will be capable of containing and damping out an explosion within, at least to the point where the aircraft structure will not be fatally damaged.

Above: Air India had lost a Boeing 747 previously. This 747-237B (VT-EBD) was lost on New Year's Day 1978 following the failure of one of the captain's main flight instruments. The pilot became disorientated and the 747 crashed into the sea shortly after take-off from Bombay. Boeing

10 Gunma Prefecture, Japan, 1985 Japan Airlines Boeing 747-100(SR)

Leo Marriott

O ne of the most successful airliners ever produced—the mighty Boeing 747—
has become a large and familiar sight dominating the skies at all major
airports around the world while maintaining a good accident record. Sound
failsafe design together with duplication of control systems and flying control
surfaces are intended to ensure that the aircraft can continue safe flight even after
suffering a series of failures, while frequent and detailed inspections are scheduled
to spot signs of potential trouble as soon as they appear. Even so, the very repair and
maintenance programs which should ensure safety can themselves be the cause of an
accident if not correctly performed and applied. It was just such a failure which led
to the world's worst single aircraft accident on August 12, 1985, when a Japanese
Airlines Boeing 747SR-100 went out of control and eventually crashed in mountainous terrain, killing all but four of the 524 occupants.

The unusually high number of people on board this aircraft reflects the fact that
Japan Airlines was one of only two airlines (the other was All Nippon Airlines—
ANA) to fly the Short Range SR version of the Boeing 747 optimized for high
density short haul domestic routes instead of the normal long haul intercontinental
flights on which most airlines operated the aircraft. The original 747-100(SR) first
flew in 1973 and provided accommodation for up to 498 passengers in a high density configuration. It also featured a strengthened structure and undercarriage to cope
with an estimated 52,000 landings over a 20-year lifetime, a figure considerably in
excess of that likely to be achieved in normal long haul operations. JAL took
delivery of 12 747-100(SR) between 1973 and 1986, and this total included a number of 747-100B(SR) capable of operating at higher gross weights. Once in service,
some aircraft were modified to carry up to 550 passengers—still a world record for
an aircraft in regular airline service.

The aircraft involved in the 1985 accident was JA8119, a 747-100(SR) which had
been delivered to JAL in February 1974. On that fateful Monday it had already operated four uneventful short haul flights and had landed as Flight JAL366 at Tokyo
International Airport (Haneda), parking at Stand 18 and undergoing inspection and
preparation for departure as Flight JAL123 for the routine one hour journey from

124

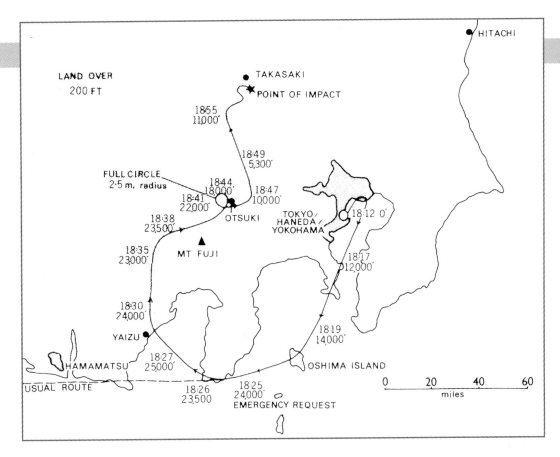

HITACHI

LAND OVER
200 FT

TAKASAKI

★ POINT OF IMPACT

18:55
11,000'

18:49
5,300'

FULL CIRCLE
2·5 m. radius

18:44
18,000'

18:47
10,000'

18:41
22,000'

18:38
23,500'

OTSUKI

TOKYO/
HANEDA/
YOKOHAMA

18:12 0'

18:35
23,000'

▲
MT FUJI

18:17
12,000'

18:30
24,000'

YAIZU ●

18:19
14,000'

HAMAMATSU

18:27
25,000'

OSHIMA ISLAND

0   20   40   60

miles

USUAL ROUTE

18:26
23,500

18:25
24,000'

EMERGENCY REQUEST

JAL123 flight route.

Tokyo to Osaka, some 250 miles to the west on the Japanese mainland. With the exception of the flight engineer, who had been on board for the previous two flights, a new crew took over the aircraft at Tokyo. Flight 123 was fully booked for the scheduled 18.00hrs departure to Osaka, with many travelers and families with children intending to enjoy the three-day observance of the Bon festival, due to begin the next day. When the aircraft eventually taxied out, it had on board a crew of 15 and 509 passengers, all but 21 of whom were Japanese. Training Captain Masami Takahama was in the right hand seat, supervising the co-pilot who was under training for command, therefore occupying the left-hand seat as acting captain.

JAL123 was airborne at 18.12hrs local time and made a normal departure, tracking south and then south-west to cross the island of Oshima, south-west of Tokyo, in a climb to the cruising level of 24,000ft. Expected flight time to Osaka was 54 minutes. During this climb the aircraft requested a direct route to the non-compulsory reporting point SEAPERCH in order to shorten the flight distance while still flying over coastal areas and avoiding the mountainous interior. This was approved by ATC. At 18.24hrs, just as the aircraft was reaching 24,000ft over Sagami Bay and approaching the eastern coast of the Izu peninsula, a loud bang was heard from the rear of the aircraft. The cabin pressure warning horn in the cockpit sounded briefly, then was silent. The passenger cabin had suffered a loss of pressurization, the alarming incident causing the atmosphere to mist, oxygen masks to drop from the cabin

Above: *Japan Airlines is the world's largest operator of the Boeing 747. Three aircraft from its fleet are shown here at Tokyo's Narita airport.* Robbie Shaw

ceiling and triggering the automatic announcement instructing passengers on the use of the masks. Twenty-six-year-old off-duty JAL stewardess Yumi Ochiai, one of the only four survivors, witnessed the scene and explained, "There was a sudden bang. It was overhead in the rear. My ears hurt. Immediately the inside of the cabin became white. The ceiling above the rear lavatory came off." On the flightdeck it was clear that a severe emergency was rapidly developing. The emergency code 7700 was selected on the radar transponder to alert air traffic control, while the flight engineer reported falling hydraulic pressure (which would operate the flight controls). Then the first officer announced that the controls were having little effect when he tried to follow Captain Takahama's instruction to start a right turn. Whatever had happened at the rear of the aircraft, the four hydraulic lines had apparently been fractured, losing all fluid and causing failure of any systems dependent on hydraulic controls.

Whilst air traffic control could see from the transponder code that an emergency existed, they had no idea of the nature of the problem, and received only a garbled message requesting permission to return to Haneda Airport. Subsequent messages were also garbled and infrequent, even when it was agreed to switch to the Japanese language while dealing with the emergency. Surprisingly, and shortly before the final moments of the flight, the aircraft was advised to change radio frequency (to Tokyo Approach Control), which suggests that ATC, despite being told that the aircraft was out of control, had not understood just how severe the emergency had become. A change of frequency was yet another distracting task for an aircrew who already had their hands more than full.

Captain Takahama's requested return to Haneda Airport, with a descent to 22,000ft and a radar vector to Oshima was made at 18.25hrs, and in that short time the flying controls had become ineffective. The aircraft began to oscillate in phugoid (longitudinal) and "Dutch roll" (lateral roll and yaw) motions, an extremely uncomfortable, corkscrew-like flight motion (and a terrifying experience for the alarmed passengers). The loss of the hydraulic systems meant that all the aerodynamic surfaces were inoperable and the only method of attempting to control the aircraft was by varying the power of the engines. In theory an increase of power to all four engines would cause the aircraft to pitch up and climb, while a reduction would result in a pitch down and descent. Gentle turns could be accomplished by differential application of power to the port and starboard engines. All very well in theory, but almost impossible to achieve in practice as the captain and first officer found as they attempted to turn back toward Tokyo. In fact they initially drifted north and then north-west, heading towards the mountainous interior where turbulence and updrafts only made matters worse. When ATC gave Captain Takahama his vector, "Fly heading Zero Nine Zero" at 18.28hrs the aircraft was struggling over Suruga Bay, and he replied that the aircraft was "Now uncontrol." To add to the pilots' problems, the warning light on door five right (on the right-hand side of the aircraft) came on to indicate that the door was unlocked, and a cabin crew report on the interphone to the flight engineer appeared to confirm failure of the door window.

By 18.35hrs, some ten minutes into the emergency, the aircraft had been brought onto an easterly heading, flying to the north-west of Mount Fuji, and here the crew tried gingerly to carry out a descent. Speed would build up quickly under these circumstances, so the landing gear was lowered to act as a brake. With no hydraulic power, this had to be done by releasing the up-locks and letting the gear fall into place through gravity. The lowered gear did seem to dampen the motion, and the aircraft descended to 22,000ft as it flew toward Otsuki City. Soon after reaching 22,000ft, control appeared to be lost because the aircraft swung into a sharp right-hand turn, completing a full circle in less than three minutes before again rolling out on an easterly track. By 18.44hrs the aircraft was at 18,000ft, and a mere three minutes later it was down at 10,000ft as the rate of descent increased. Here the crew could see the approaching high ground, with Captain Takahama calling, "Turn right. Up. We'll crash into a mountain." The aircraft almost stalled in the ensuing maneuver, flaps were lowered to five degrees (a four-minute process under electric power) to aid recovery and the aircraft climbed from 5,300ft at 18.49hrs to 11,000ft at 18.55hrs. Here the aircraft again began to descend, the rate of descent increasing to 1,350ft per minute. Flap setting was increased to 10° in an effort to raise the nose, then the crew tried to raise the flaps and apply full power.

Their strenuous efforts were in vain. Just over one minute later the agonies of the flight ended as JA8119 crashed into the side of Mt. Osutaka at 4,780ft. The accident report comments laconically that the shock force of impact "estimated as much as hundreds of G" would have killed the majority of crew and passengers almost instantly. Even the four survivors, who had been seated in the center seats of row 56, had been subjected to a force of "tens of G," but were probably sheltered from much of the cabin equipment, locker contents and other debris that would have ripped around the cabin during the moments of the crash. Twelve-year-old Keiko Kawakami, Hiroko Yoshizaki, and her eight-year-old daughter Mikiko, together with stewardess Yumi Ochiai were the only ones who survived this worst single accident in aviation history. The horror endured by the passengers during their 30-minute ordeal can be easily imagined, because many of them wrote notes of farewell, certain that disaster was imminent. These tattered fragments of paper were later found by the rescue teams.

As often happens when there is a major aircraft accident, fate conspires to obstruct rescue attempts in every way possible, and the crash of JA8119 was no exception to this. The accident had occurred in a remote mountain forest, in an area where even helicopters could not land with safety. Darkness was gathering and rain set in. Units of the Self-Defence Force that flew passes over the site could see no signs of life, but a team of local firemen set out on the difficult climb to the wreckage and reached it around 09.00hrs the following morning, some 14 hours after the crash had occurred. They were joined by paratroopers who slid down ropes from helicopters which hovered overhead, and so began both the search for survivors and the grim task of clearing bodies from the wreckage. The aircraft had brushed into trees near the top of the ridge which had torn away the tail and the port outboard engine before the aircraft had collided with the ridge itself. The port wing had been torn away and the port inner engine had been flung over the ridge and into the valley beyond. The aircraft had disintegrated on impact, bursting into flames as fuel tanks ignited. This was the scene of desolation that greeted the rescuers, and they can have had little expectation of finding anyone alive. Fortunately a fireman who was searching a gully noticed a movement in the debris and found Yumi Ochiai trapped in wreckage but alive despite suffering a broken arm and pelvis. Mother and daughter Hiroko and Mikiko Yoshizaki had broken bones, whilst 12-year-old Keiko Kawakami, thrown clear into the branches of a tree, had miraculously sustained only cuts and bruises.

News of the disaster shocked not only the Japanese nation, but the aviation world too, as this was the second accident in two months where the seemingly reliable Boeing 747 had apparently suffered from a structural failure of some kind and then crashed. The other accident had been the Air India Boeing 747 which had disappeared on a trans-Atlantic flight on June 23, and for which, at that time, no cause had been established. Commentators and media sources wondered if there was some fatal flaw in the 747, only now being revealed and echoing the fatigue cracking which had proved so disastrous for the de Havilland Comet.

As the accident investigators began their melancholy task, an obvious point of interest was the cabin door which had been mentioned by the flight engineer. Fortunately this was in that part of the wreckage which had been least damaged, and was found in the correctly closed and locked position. Inevitably the possibility of some form of terrorist attack had to be considered, especially following claims that a bomb had been placed on board, but there was no evidence to support any such explosion. It was an indistinct photograph which had been taken by a witness on the

128

Above: *Japan Airlines Boeing 747-146 on final approach to Nagoya.* Robbie Shaw

Below: *The 747 layout and pressure bulkhead details showing, (a) correctly mended section; (b) incorrectly mended section (note gap of doubler plate between top two rivets) and (c) the original bulkhead.*

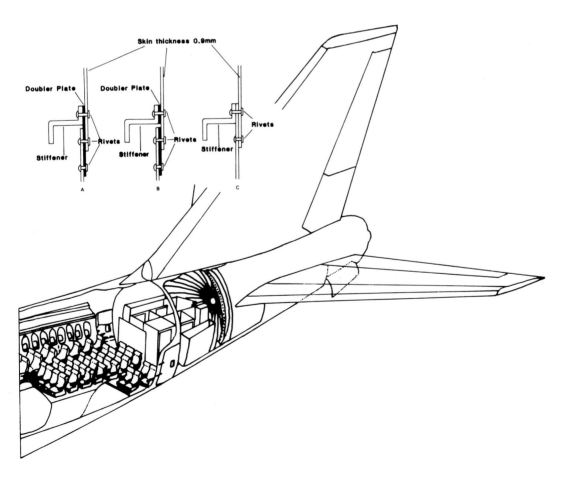

ground while the aircraft passed overhead that provided the first definite clue for investigators. When the blurred and small image was enlarged it apparently showed that the vertical fin and rudder, such a prominent feature of the 747, was missing. Confirmation of this came almost immediately, when a Japanese naval destroyer reported finding wreckage in Sagami Bay. This was found to include a large section of a 747 tailfin, a piece of rudder, and part of the aircraft's auxiliary power unit (which is housed in the tail assembly of the 747). Almost half the tail fin had become detached in flight and, significantly, the wreckage had been found in the Bay close to the position at which the aircraft had first reported the emergency.

Evidence from Yumi Ochiai, the stewardess, pointed toward a sudden cabin depressurization. She denied that there had been an explosion, speaking instead of a sudden loud noise above and behind her, of the cabin filling with white mist, and papers and light articles being blown back through the cabin. Later, the cockpit voice recorder and flight data recorder, both recovered from the crash site, were to provide further evidence which pointed to cabin decompression and loss of hydraulic systems. As evidence was gathered, it pointed increasingly toward failure of the pressure bulkhead, and when this was discovered in the wreckage it was indeed found to be holed. The bulkhead is circular and dome shaped, its purpose being to hold within the cabin the higher pressures that, at altitude, are used to keep the cabin at atmospheric pressures which allow normal passenger comfort. Behind the pressure bulkhead, the airframe is subject to the prevailing, much lower pressures that exist at altitude. The question now to be answered was whether the damage had occurred in flight or in the crash impact. Positioned as it is under the fin and rudder of the 747 series, failure of the bulkhead during the flight could have directed the powerful blast of escaping air upward into the fin and blown it apart from the inside. The loss of control surfaces, and the severing of hydraulic lines which in turn would drain the whole hydraulic system and lead to further control failures, would seal the fate of the aircraft. But why would a bulkhead, designed in a failsafe manner for a life of 20 years and subject to regular checks, fail with such catastrophic results? Until an answer was found, the entire fleet of 747s was under suspicion.

An examination of the aircraft's maintenance records showed that this tragedy had its beginning almost seven years earlier, on June 2, 1978, at Osaka Airport. During its landing, which may have been heavy and with an excessive nose-high attitude, the rear fuselage had struck the runway and received substantial airframe damage which included deformation of the rear pressure bulkhead. It now appeared possible that the subsequent repairs to this bulkhead had led directly to the loss of the aircraft on August 12, 1985 A detailed and exhaustive examination of the bulkhead fitting, which was in several pieces, showed that all edges were saw-toothed, consistent with it being torn away from the rivets that held it in place. In one section, however, there was a straight failure of one of the seams holding together the different sections of the bulkhead, and this was at the point where the repairs had been made after the tail strike on the runway at Osaka in 1978.

Right: *Troops sifting through the wreckage on Mt. Osutaka.* CORBIS/Reuters

At the inspection which had followed that earlier accident, it was found that, apart from other structural damage, the lower half of the pressure bulkhead had been deformed. Instead of replacing the complete bulkhead, the airline engineers (under supervision from Boeing engineers) fitted a new lower half, with the intent of splicing this to the upper half using what is known as a doubler plate. Three lines of rivets were used, one of which was used to hold in place a stiffening bar to keep the bulkhead in its correct shape. The doubler plate should have been a single plate extending across the join line between the bulkhead sections, picking up all three rivet lines to create a really strong sandwich section. In this repair, two narrow plates had been used instead. One was positioned under the stiffening bar and another plate was positioned onto the other half of the bulkhead where, unfortunately, it connected to the mating bulkhead surface through only one rivet line instead of the two lines called for in the correct plan. With only one row of rivets holding upper and lower bulkhead halves together, the intended sturdy sandwich did not exist. Flexing along the gap between the two plates was both possible and likely, and this in turn would lead to metal fatigue cracking (as is achieved when a piece of wire is flexed and counter-flexed until it breaks) as the number of flight cycles increased.

The incorrect repair affected the pressure bulkhead in two serious ways. Firstly, the overall strength of the bulkhead section was reduced by about 30% (increasing the likelihood of flexing along the join). Secondly, it destroyed the failsafe concept of the design. The bulkhead design ensured that if a fatigue crack was to appear, it could only extend for a limited distance before the stiffening straps forced a change of direction on it. Any such failure would therefore lead only to a small gap through which air would escape at a restricted rate that would not cause damage to the tail structure of the aircraft. However, the actual repair applied, permitted any fatigue crack to run the whole length of the seam between the bulkhead halves. Fatigue cracks had indeed occurred, most originating at the one rivet row connection points, during the 12,319 flights which had followed the repair work, but none had been noticed at the six "C" maintenance (3,000 hour) inspections. When the failure finally occurred, it blew out a hole of size estimated at two or three square meters. The surge of air from the cabin, like the waters from a breached dam, swept away obstructions in its path; in this instance smashing through the auxiliary power unit wall, then rushing upward through the opening in the fin torque box and into the vertical fin, blowing it apart.

In these circumstances it is amazing that the crew managed to sustain flight for as long as they did. The pilots must have been all too aware that the chances of making a successful landing either on land or on sea were minimal but nevertheless made a very creditable attempt until the aircraft became totally uncontrollable in the landing configuration. It is relevant to compare their actions with the crew of the United Airlines DC-10 at Sioux City in 1989 (see Chapter 13). Here all control was lost when the hydraulic system failed after the tail engine disintegrated, but the crew managed to control the aircraft using only the power of the wing engines long enough to make an approach and land at Sioux City airport. It was only in the final seconds that the aircraft dropped a wing just before touchdown and it cartwheeled to a halt, breaking up and catching fire. The Americans had an advantage over their

Japanese counterparts in that, entirely by chance, there was a senior DC-10 training captain riding as a passenger on the flightdeck when the incident occurred and he was to be of great assistance to the two pilots attempting to actually fly the aircraft. In the Japanese accident, the two pilots did not have this extra assistance but put up a magnificent performance which ended in tragedy despite their best efforts.

As a result of this accident, the US Federal Aviation Agency ordered the installation on 747s of a cover for the opening into the vertical fin so as to prevent an increase of pressure in the rear section of the aircraft from reaching the fin and causing internal damage. Added to this was a requirement for security in the hydraulic system lines to prevent a total loss of fluid if all four lines were to be severed as had happened on board JA8119. Boeing were also asked to evaluate again the failsafe validity of the rear pressure bulkhead.

In Japan, other repercussions followed in the wake of the tragic loss. Yasumoto Tankage resigned the presidency of JAL, a gesture of corporate guilt as he shouldered full responsibility for the crash, and a JAL maintenance engineer at Haneda committed suicide as an apology for the disaster. The airline itself suffered a drastic reduction in passenger traffic and revenue following the crash, and it is noteworthy that some two years later, when it was anticipating and preparing for privatization, the company adopted a new logo as part of its effort to rebuild its high reputation for aviation safety.

Above: *Another view of the wreckage.* CORBIS /Reuters

11 Straits of Hormuz, Persian Gulf, 1988
Iran Air Airbus A300B2

Leo Marriott

Most aircraft disasters are genuine accidents in which the cause is in some way related to the aircraft or its crew. Unfortunately there have also been a number of innocent civil aircraft which have been lost as the result of unjustified or mistaken military action and two of these are described in this book. The first occurred in 1983 when a Boeing 747 belonging to Korean Airlines was shot down by a Soviet fighter over Sakhalin Island, north of Japan. This incident brought bitter condemnation from other governments, particularly that of the United States. However, they in turn proved not to be infallible and America suffered a humiliating embarrassment when one of its warships accidentally shot down an Airbus A300-B2 over the Persian Gulf on July 3, 1988. The origins of this incident lay in the long running Iran–Iraq war which dragged on through the 1980s. Due to significant military operations in the area, Western nations including the United States deployed warships to the Persian Gulf with the object of providing security to the movement of non belligerent shipping. From 1984 onward the United States Navy had notified air operators that any aircraft approaching within five nautical miles of any of their warships and below 2,000ft would risk unspecified defensive action. In May 1987, the US Navy began to provide specific protection to Kuwaiti oil tankers in the Gulf Area but within days the seriousness of the situation was brought home when the frigate *Stark* was hit by an Exocet missile launched from an Iraqi Mirage jet fighter and 37 sailors were killed. As a direct response, the United States Navy immediately increased its readiness levels and, by means of a NOTAM (Notice to Airman, promulgated through the international aeronautical teleprinter network), issued warnings to all aircraft operators in the area. This stated that aircraft approaching US warships would be contacted and challenged on frequencies 121.5 MHz (VHF) and 243 MHz (UHF). Failure to respond to requests to confirm identification and intentions on these frequencies could place the aircraft at risk from defensive measures. Aircraft and helicopters were also requested to remain well clear of US warships, while any illumination of warships by fire control radars would be taken as evidence of hostile intent. It should be noted that the two frequencies nominated were those used for international distress purposes and that

Above: *Satellite photograph of the Straits of Hormuz.* CORBIS

Above: *The U.S.S.* Vincennes. CORBIS

243MHz was a military frequency not normally carried by civil aircraft. Also it was not standard practice for civil aircraft to maintain a listening watch on 121.5 MHz.

The operation of naval forces in the Gulf caused problems for legitimate civil air traffic in the area and there were many instances of challenges to aircraft engaged on routine flights along established airways, or flying standard approach and departure procedures. In addition there had been at least one incident where a civil aircraft was in imminent danger of being engaged by a ship before ATC was able to intervene. Despite this there appeared to have been little attempt to set up formal co-ordination procedures between the naval air defence systems and the shore based ATC network. One of the American ships assigned to the Gulf was the guided missile cruiser USS *Vincennes*. Displacing some 9,000 tons, this large ship was equipped with the state of the art Aegis air defence weapon system which could engage multiple targets simultaneously using a battery of SM-2 Standard surface to air missiles directed by a sophisticated array of radars. In addition the ship carried Link 11 and 14 datalink systems which enabled real time information on all targets to be instantly shared with other ships and aircraft. The *Vincennes* carried a crew of around 400 officers and men and had arrived in the Gulf area at the end of May. On the fateful July 3, 1988, she became involved in operations against hostile forces for the first time.

In company with the frigates USS *Sides* and USS *Elmer Montgomery*, the *Vincennes* was operating at the entrance to the Straits of Hormuz where the distance between Oman and Iran narrows to just over 30 miles. A number of Iranian gunboats had been reported as threatening merchant ships in the area and a helicopter from the *Vincennes* was fired upon as it approached to investigate. Following this a short but inconclusive engagement with the gunboats ensued but while this was in progress an aircraft was observed on radar as departing from Bandar Abbas airport on the Iranian coast, only a few miles from the scene of the naval action. Although a civil airport, it was known that American supplied Iranian Air Force F-14 Tomcat fighters were also based there. As the radar contact was first observed, the ship's Electronic Surveillance Measures (ESM) system briefly picked up a Mode 2 SSR emission from an aircraft transponder. Mode 2 is used exclusively by military aircraft while civil aircraft use the longer pulsed Mode 3. The combination of an ongoing naval engagement, the known proximity of potentially hostile F-14s, the appearance of a radar contact heading toward the ship and the receipt of the Mode 2 emission led to the radar target being labeled on the Aegis display in the ship's Combat Information System as a possible fighter. The contact was also observed aboard the frigate USS *Sides* but, interestingly, was not classified as hostile by that ship whose captain recognized it as a possible civil aircraft and did not consider that it offered any threat.

Three minutes after the contact was first observed, the *Vincennes* began transmitting a series of seven radio messages to the "Iranian Fighter" or "Iranian F-14" on the UHF frequency, demonstrating that it was still believed to a hostile target. A further four transmissions were made on VHF (121.5 MHz) requesting the

Above: *Camouflaged Iranian F-14 Tomcat.* CORBIS/Bettmann

"Unknown Aircraft" to "Remain Clear" and "Alter Course to 270°." No replies were received as the radar contact appeared to continue heading out over the sea, almost directly towards the *Vincennes*. Although there was a known airway route, Alpha Five Nine, originating from Bandar Abbas, the target appeared to be deviating slightly from that track. In addition, there were no apparent emissions from radar altimeters and weather radar that might have indicated that the target was a civil aircraft. The atmosphere in the ship's CIC, already at a high pitch of anticipation due to the surface action, was extremely tense as Captain Will Rogers III and his air warfare team attempted to determine the nature and intentions of this unidentified target which could be a very real threat to the ship itself. As long as it appeared to climb steadily there was room for doubt but suddenly the anti-air warfare officer, in response to unverified reports from radar operators who had made incorrect deductions from their information displays, reported to the captain that the target had begun to descend and accelerate. Throughout the seven minutes which had elapsed since the contact had first been observed, it had been monitored by the ship's Aegis SPY-1 and SPS-49 search radars, and followed by the SPG-62 target illuminators which provided tracking data for the SM-2 Standard missiles mounted on twin launchers fore and aft.

With tension almost at breaking point, the anti-air warfare officer's report was enough to convince the captain that his ship was under attack and in immediate danger. Without further hesitation he ordered the missiles to be launched. Two Standard missiles leapt off their rails, achieving Mach 3 within seconds and tracked unerringly towards the target which was now some ten miles away at an altitude of 13,500ft. It was a textbook engagement and the target was hit and destroyed. The missile impact was witnessed from the USS *Montgomery* and subsequently an aircraft with a wing and part of the tail missing was observed spiraling down into the sea, although the type was not identified. Unfortunately, it was not an F-14. It was an Airbus A300B2 civilian jet airliner operated by Iran Air on a scheduled flight from Bandar Abbas to Dubai and all 290 persons aboard had perished.

The Airbus, registration EP-IBU, was operating four sectors of a regular scheduled flight which originated from Tehran as flight IR451, went on to Dubai and back as flights IR655 and IR654, and finally was due to fly the Bandar Abbas–Tehran sector as IR452. It was on departure from Bandar Abbas as IR655 that the fatal engagement took place. The flight plan for this sector had been filed earlier from Tehran and before take-off ATC issued a clearance for the aircraft to route to Dubai via airways Alpha Five Nine and Alpha Five Nine West at 14,000ft. Take-off was at 06.47hrs from runway 21, which meant that after departure the Airbus could climb more or less straight ahead without having to turn to establish itself on track. Two minutes after take-off, while passing 3,500ft, the pilot contacted Bandar Abbas approach control and reported estimating MOBET at 06.52hrs, DARAX at 06.58hrs, and Dubai at 07.15hrs. MOBET and DARAX were navigational reporting points along the way, although the crew were not to know that the *Vincennes* was stationed

Right: *Combat Information Center aboard U.S.S.* Vincennes. CORBIS

approximately 20 miles south of MOBET. While one pilot was engaged in passing this information to ATC and Bandar Abbas, the other contacted Tehran Area Control Center, which controlled flights along the airways and had issued the original clearance, and repeated the details. Tehran told IR655 to report reaching 14,000ft and to confirm that transponder was squawking the allocated SSR code 6760. At 06.54hrs, Bandar Abbas approach instructed the flight to continue with Tehran ACC. This call was acknowledged and no further transmissions were received. Thirty seconds later the Airbus was hit by two Standard missiles whilst within the limits of Airway Alpha Five Nine and some ten miles south of MOBET. On board were 274 passengers, mostly Iranian nationals but also including several Indians, Pakistanis, Arabs, and six Yugoslavs. There were also 16 crew members, also Iranian. All were killed either by the blast of the missile explosions or in the impact with the sea.

Despite these dramatic events, controllers at Tehran center were not initially concerned about the loss of contact with the aircraft, assuming that it had contacted Dubai. It was only at 07.15hrs, when the Emirates ACC contacted Tehran to request the position of IR655, that it was realized that the aircraft was not in contact with Emirates or Dubai and enquiries were directed to other ATC units and airfields. As the negative replies began to come in, Tehran contacted the Emirates Rescue Coordination Center (RCC) at 08.00hrs and advised them that the Airbus was missing, having been last observed on radar just south of DARAX. In response a search and rescue mission was mounted involving four aircraft and helicopters from the United Arab Emirates and vessels and aircraft of the Iran Navy, Islamic Revolutionary Guard, and the National Iran Oil Company. Bodies and floating wreckage were eventually located some 20 miles north of DARAX, the Emirates ACC being informed of this at 09.25hrs. There were no survivors and the major sections of the aircraft which had sunk to seabed were not recovered.

It did not take long to link the loss of the Airbus with the missile engagement reported by the *Vincennes* and the recriminations and investigations began. It soon became apparent that the measures designed to protect US warships had been insufficiently thought out and that an accident of this sort was almost inevitable in the heightened state of tension following the attack on the *Stark*. Flight IR655 was a regular scheduled passenger service which normally operated twice a week on Tuesdays and Sundays and in the month prior to the incident there had been 28 other Iran Air flights between Bandar Abbas and Dubai or Sharjah. In the same period a further 30 flights had followed airway Alpha Five Nine to cross the Straits of Hormuz en route to other destinations. On the days when IR655 had operated, it had taken-off reasonably close to its scheduled departure time. The Iranian ATC authorities had introduced a "Red Alert" procedure under which civil aircraft were notified of any military activity which might endanger them. Under this system instances had already occurred when aircraft in flight had been recalled or diverted. However, on the fateful July 3, there was no alert in progress and both Tehran and Bandar Abbas were unaware of the naval engagement just offshore. Aboard the *Vincennes*, the civil airways route structure, locations of major airfields, and associated arrival and departure procedures were overlaid on the large screen Aegis displays in the CIC. Actual flights could be monitored in real time but there was no way in which the

Above: *Launch of a surface-to-air missile from an Aegis class cruiser.* CORBIS

identity of a particular civil aircraft could be established. Its SSR code could be seen and this might indicate from where the flight had originated, but there was no established procedure whereby the warship could communicate directly with any shore based ATC unit in order to correlate an observed SSR squawk with a specific civil flight. Inexplicably, the *Vincennes* was unable to monitor civil VHF frequencies other than 121.5 MHz and so could not even derive information by listing in to routine ATC transmissions. The only information available on board was a list of flight schedules but this was nowhere near enough to be of any use in identifying aircraft as routes and times could vary quite substantially in practice (as any seasoned air traveler will vouchsafe!).

It was unfortunate that the crew of the Airbus did not respond to the challenges from the USS *Vincennes* on the VHF frequency 121.5 MHz. Although company instructions required the crew to maintain a listening watch on this frequency, it was not possible to prove that they had complied with this. However, even if they had, they might well have been distracted by their other tasks immediately after take-off, including several calls on other frequencies. The warnings on 243 MHz can be discounted as the Iran Air aircraft did not carry military UHF equipment and, even if they had heard the warnings on 121.5, it would not have been immediately obvious that the transmissions were directed at them.

Nevertheless, the critical events in the chain which led to the identification of the innocent civil A300 as a probable military threat were the emission of a military Mode 2 SSR squawk and the perception that the target being tracked on radar had suddenly started to maneuver towards the ship. The Mode 2 emission had been picked up by the ship's ESM system just as the Airbus had taken off. Although not positively linked with the observed target on the radar screens, it caused the air warfare team to label it as a possible fighter. Consequently all those who subsequently followed the progress of the symbol on the Aegis and other displays saw it designated as such and this helped to create an atmosphere that a military target was actually there. The source of the Mode 2 emission has never been established. It was recorded only briefly and could well have come from an another aircraft on the ground at Bandar Abbas or from an Iranian Lockheed P-3 Orion patrol aircraft which was known to be airborne at the time (although some 70 miles away and actually in radio contact with the *Vincennes* at the time). Whatever the cause, no further Mode 2 emissions were recorded during the tracking and engagement of the Airbus and that aircraft was consistently transmitting its civil Mode 3 code, 6760. Despite this, no steps were taken to change the designation of the radar target.

With the ship already fighting a surface action, firing its guns and heeling as it maneuvered, there was an air of tension amongst the untried CIC crew and their captain. Loose gear crashed to the floor as the ship turned and the loud reports of the gun reverberated through the ship's structure causing lights to flicker. Instructions, information, and challenges were being shouted across the compartment. In the confusion, the anti-air warfare officer received a report from one of the Aegis operators indicating that the air target was descending and accelerating. Without checking his own display, which would have shown the true situation, he allowed these reports to reinforce his own preconception and advised the captain that the target was now maneuvering in a manner which threatened the ship. Conscious of the US Navy's already stated rules of engagement and certain that his ship, and the lives of the 400 crew, were in imminent danger, he ordered the firing of the missiles.

In fact, post incident analysis of the Aegis radar data showed that correct indications had been given throughout and the question therefore arose as to why that information had been misinterpreted and relayed incorrectly. After an exhaustive investigation, the most likely explanation was that one or more of the Aegis operators responsible for monitoring the height and range information of the various target tracks had been distracted by the events and atmosphere in the CIC and had then inadvertently transposed or misread the complex data presented on their displays. The tracking appears to begin as the Airbus passed 2,000ft in its climb to 14,000ft and at that point it was approximately 47 nautical miles from the ship. As it climbed, altitude increased and range decreased. Thus at 40 nautical miles range it

Above: *Admiral W. Fogarty testifying before the Senate Committee.* CORBIS/John H. Clark

was passing 4,000ft, and at 30 nautical miles it was passing 7,000ft; this occurring at time 06.51:11hrs. At 06.52:44hrs further reports indicated a range of 20 miles and a height just above 10,000ft. Significantly there was some gunfire at this point and shortly afterward there were some confusing position reports putting the aircraft at around 15 miles and 7,500ft. The report that triggered the missile firing at 06.54:22hrs gave a range of ten miles and a height of around 7,500ft. At the time the Airbus was actually climbing through approximately 13,000ft altitude, its rate of climb having been steady throughout.

The incident caused considerable embarrassment to the US Government and Navy and naturally they attempted to justify their actions and while admitting that it was a tragic and regrettable accident, sought to imply that Iran should not have allowed the flight to have operated in a "war zone." In fact of course, despite the warnings issued by the US Navy about its intention to take defensive measures if its ships were threatened, the area was not a war zone in the internationally accepted and legal sense. It also subsequently became clear that there was some dissension within US Navy circles as to whether the captain of the *Vincennes* had acted appropriately. Wherever the blame really lay, the US Government accepted the moral responsibility when, in 1996, it agreed to pay the sum of $62 million to the relatives and dependents of the 290 victims of this sorry incident.

12 Lockerbie, Scotland, 1988 Pan American Airways Boeing 747-121

Leo Marriott

Lockerbie has become synonymous with the devastation and horror that is created when an aircraft and innocent lives are ruthlessly destroyed in a cold-blooded act of vindictive terrorism. Unfortunately it also served as an indictment of government and administration complacency because a warning to the US embassy in Helsinki, dismissed as a hoax by some authorities, was given limited circulation and not made known to the general public. The anonymous telephone message, 16 days before the tragedy, predicted that a sabotage attack would be made at some point during the coming two weeks and specifically pointed to its occurrence on a flight from Frankfurt in West Germany to the United States. There was other evidence at the time which lent credence to the warning, unlike so many hoax calls that have to be evaluated, and had greater security measures been in place then the outcome of Flight PA103 might have been entirely different—just another routine flight.

The Frankfurt to New York flight was actually scheduled over two legs, of which the first, from Frankfurt to London's Heathrow Airport, was flown by a Boeing 727 and carried 109 passengers and their baggage. On landing at Heathrow the 727 was then parked at stand Kilo 16, next to the ill-fated N739PA "Maid of the Seas" which had been allocated stand Kilo 14 following its inbound flight from San Francisco. The Boeing 747-121 was being prepared for the scheduled flight to New York Kennedy airport, operated as PA103, and some 49 passengers were transferred directly from the Frankfurt 727, joining the 194 passengers departing from London. Nearly all of the passengers were Americans returning home for the Christmas holidays, no doubt looking forward to seeing their families and preparing for the season's festivities. None of them would have had any inkling of the disaster which was about to occur. Significantly, their baggage, which had already been screened at Frankfurt, was transferred to the Boeing 747 with no further checks. Altogether N739PA was on the ground at Heathrow for some six hours but the passengers were boarded on time and after a slight delay pushback from stand Kilo 14 was at

Right: *The cockpit of PA103.* CORBIS/Bryn Colton

Above: The unfortunate Pan American lost two Boeing 747s in exceptionally tragic circumstances. One was lost in aviation's worst disaster in which a Pan Am 747 collided with another 747 belonging to KLM on the runway at Tenerife in 1977. The other was Pan Am 103 over Lockerbie in December 1988, destroyed by a callous terrorist bomb. Boeing

18.04hrs. Due to congestion on the ground, it was another 20 minutes before PA103 lined up on runway 27R and was cleared for take-off. Carrying 16 crew and 243 passengers the big 747 made an uneventful take-off that Wednesday evening at 18.25hrs and followed a normal departure profile, being instructed to level off at 6,000ft while being vectored under radar control below the Bovingdon holding stack. Subsequently it was cleared to climb to flight level 12,000ft and then to its initial cruising level, 31,000ft. The aircraft passed Pole Hill VOR on its north-westerly track and leveled off at 18.56hrs. By now the passengers would have been settling down to the routine of a long haul flight and the cabin crew would have been serving drinks and handing out menus and information of the in-flight films.

At 18.58hrs co-pilot Ray Wagner requested his Oceanic Clearance from Prestwick Air Traffic Control Centre, and at about 19.03hrs Oceanic Control transmitted details for the aircraft's clearance to cross the Atlantic. This transmission was never acknowledged and even as the controller was talking the secondary radar return from Flight PA103 disappeared from the radar screen and in its place multiple primary radar returns were observed by controller Alan Topp. These rapidly began to to fan out downwind for a considerable distance before fading from view. His immediate efforts to alert the watch supervisor were frustrated because the supervisor was taking a telephone call from Eskdalemuir Earthquake Monitoring Centre reporting a seismograph jump at 19.03hrs that had recorded an earth tremor of 1.6 on the Richter Scale. Unknown to both of them at that very instant, Pan American Clipper "Maid of the Seas" had just been blown apart by a massive explosion in a baggage container positioned on the left side of the forward cargo

146

hold, and her severed remains had plummeted instantly to earth. One part appeared to witnesses below as a meteor-like object which trailed flame and made a rumbling noise like thunder which swiftly increased to the deafening roar of a jet engine under full power, before slamming into the north-eastern part of Lockerbie, creating a 15ft deep crater. This was identified as one of the 747's Pratt & Whitney engines, in this instance the starboard inner engine. A large, dark, delta shaped object resembling an aircraft wing landed in the Sherwood area of the town at about the same time. This was not on fire in the air, but a very large fireball ensued when it struck the ground, blew out an even bigger crater, and severed a gas main. The fireball explosion, although of short duration, hurled large amounts of debris into the air, while other less well-defined objects were seen also to land in the area.

The force of the explosion on board the 747, and the ensuing depressurization which shattered the aircraft, caused the human cargo to be flung into the blackness of the night five miles above the ground. As passengers and crew, some alone, some together, some still strapped in their seats, fell through the void to the earth below, the force of the air stream ripped away clothing and even stripped flesh from human anatomy already shattered by the explosion. Bodies that thudded into the fields around Lockerbie were, upon impact, driven inches into ground softened by recent rain. In the space of a few seconds, 270 human beings—mothers, fathers, families relaxing into the early stages of a long trans-Atlantic flight—had all been wiped out. It was not the end of the tragedy.

The wings and connecting section of fuselage that crashed into Sherwood Crescent and gouged out a 155ft long crater contained most of the almost full load of aviation fuel for the 3,000 mile journey to New York. The impact created the huge fireball that lit up the town, the weight of material displaced being estimated as well in excess of 1,500 tons, and the crater volume some 560 cubic meters. Neighboring houses were set on fire and the debris carried aloft in the explosion was blown down-wind for several miles. Three houses were destroyed when the fireball crater was blasted out, and fire or impact so damaged surrounding properties that 21 had to be demolished while many other homes required substantial repairs. To all this was added the toll of human life among residents of Lockerbie. Thomas and Kathleen Flannigan and their daughter Joanne aged ten; John and Rosaleen Somerville together with children Paul aged 13 and Lyndsey aged ten; of those who died, only Joanne's body was found, the others had vaporized in the inferno. Others who perished were Maurice and Dora Henry; and two ladies in their eighties, Jean Murray and Mary Lancaster. Two other people had serious injuries, and three cases of minor injuries were recorded. In retrospect it was nothing short of miraculous that there were not more casualties on the ground.

Like a cannonade, other major portions of the aircraft hit the town and its surroundings in quick succession. The remaining three engines fell within the Lockerbie town boundaries, and the rear section of the fuselage, together with a shower of baggage, fell onto the Rosebank housing estate a third of a mile from the initial sites of impact. This wreckage formed the beginning of a trail stretching some 80 miles to the east coast of England and included more fragments from the rear fuselage, wings, and tail of the aircraft. Other large parts, including the flightdeck and forward fuselage section, landed in the countryside two-and-a-half miles to the east of the town. The flightdeck, where searchers found bodies of the crew still strapped in their seats, and that of an air hostess who had perhaps been making a report when the explosion occurred, marked the start of a second, southerly wreckage trail. Smaller pieces of wreckage, baggage, letters from the mail containers, bodies, and fragments of bodies were scattered over the town and its vicinity; in all a truly terrible spectacle.

Police forces have contingency plans to cope with foreseeable disasters appropriate to their area of responsibility, and the small Dumfries and Galloway force was no exception. The consequences of a jumbo jet falling on a small community in the border country might not have seemed likely enough to warrant such a plan, and it would in any case have severely stretched a much larger force, so it is not surprising that Chief Constable John Boyd was quick to request assistance from neighboring regions Lothian and Strathclyde. It proved hard, however, to deploy and effectively co-ordinate the assistance that was promptly given to his force. The disaster had occurred at night in cold and unpleasant weather, covering, as the initial reports came in, an estimated 10 square miles around Lockerbie. Search parties were being asked to cover unfamiliar countryside, often coping with poor visibility, and with little in the way of radio communication available. By the early hours of December 22, almost 1,100 police were on the task, assisted by some 600 service personnel and many civilians. Messages had to be carried by human carrier between the police incident room at the school and the search parties, and such messengers frequently lost their way in the darkness and chaos. A 02.00hrs meeting that morning was used to thrash out a strategy to deal, not only with the search for survivors and bodies, but the painstaking preservation and gathering of evidence that would be needed to prepare for criminal proceedings should these be instigated at a later date. The necessary delays that this would cause before bodies and possessions could be released to next-of-kin was to create much bitterness among grieving relatives in the days that followed. When the meeting broke up, senior officers knew what was wanted, but had little comprehension of what was actually on their hands. Initial search reports quickly confirmed that no-one in the aircraft could have survived, so the rest of the night could only be used for checking and re-checking the Sherwood area of the town to try to find anyone still alive in the rubble, and for planning the next day's tasks.

That day saw the arrival of the investigating team from the Aircraft Accident Investigation Board (AAIB), flown in to Carlisle Airport aboard a special Pan American Boeing 727. Their investigation began at the forward fuselage and flightdeck. This section of the fuselage, forward from station 480 (left side) to station 380 (right side) incorporating the flightdeck and nose landing gear, had fallen almost flat on its left side in a slight nose-down attitude with no discernible horizontal velocity, almost completely crushing the left-hand side structure. The radome and right nose landing gear door had detached in the air and were found further back along the southern trail. Their examination of the torn edges of the fuselage skin did not indicate the presence of any pre-existing structural or material defects that could have accounted for the separation of this section. There were no signs of explosive

Below: *Pan Am 103 crash location.*

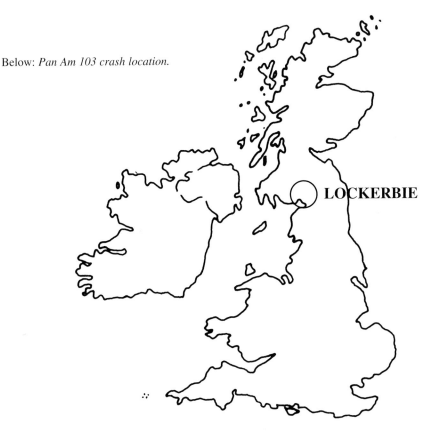

LOCKERBIE

blast damage or sooting on any part of the structure or the interior fittings, but there was a semi-elliptical scuff mark on the lower right side of the fuselage near station 360 which was later matched to the intake profile of the number three engine. They also found that the status of the controls and switches on the flightdeck was consistent with normal cruising flight operations, and there were no indications that the crew had attempted to react to rapid decompression or loss of control, or that any emergency preparations had begun prior to the catastrophic disintegration of the aircraft.

The northern trail of wreckage, narrow and clearly defined, began close to the main impact crater (where the wings and center section struck Sherwood Crescent) and extended eastward, aligned with the mean wind direction between sea level and 20,000ft. It included the lower rear fuselage at Rosebank Crescent, and the group of numbers one, two, and four engines. Items of structure were distributed over the trail out to ten miles, with items of low weight but high drag, such as interior trim and paper found out to 16 miles. Found on this trail was wreckage from the rear fuse-lage, fin, and inner regions of both tailplanes, as well as structure and skin from the upper half of the fuselage. Here, too, lay the three starboard Kruger flaps, much of the port Kreuger flap components, the aft ends of the flap-track fairings (one of which had a slide raft wrapped around it), both HF antennae, and a number of pieces of the engine cowlings.

The southern trail extended across southern Scotland and northern England in a straight band out to the North Sea, with most of the significant items of wreckage within 19 miles of the main crater. Numerous large items from the forward fuselage, fragments of the left tailplane, and the outboard portion of the right tailplane had landed along this trail, and either side of Langholm, between 13 and 17 miles from the main impact point, substantial sections of tailplane skin came to rest. Many of these bore distinctive signs of contact with debris moving outward and backwards relative to the fuselage. Isolated sections of fuselage frame which had originated from the crown region above the forward upper deck were also found in this area.

The next task was to collect every item of wreckage for analysis and to reconstruct the aircraft in two dimensions so far as was possible. This work was carried out at the Army Central Ammunition Depot Longtown, 20 miles from Lockerbie, and about 90% of the hull wreckage was recovered, identified, and laid out on the floor in its correct position, while baggage container material was sorted into a three-dimensional construction. Even as this evidence was being collected and collated, significant facts were emerging. While pieces of the rear cargo hold fell within the town boundaries, equivalent parts of the forward hold were spread over miles of the southern trail. The reconstruction revealed the presence of damage consistent with an explosion on the lower fuselage left side in the forward cargo bay area. Two cargo containers which had been positioned here, one made of metal, the other of fibreglass, were identified as exhibiting damage caused by the explosion. The bomb had been detonated inside the metal container (serial number AVE 4041PA), particles being blasted into the forward face of the fiberglass container and into the adjacent skin paneling of the aircraft in the region of station 700. It was during this work that an inspector found, trapped within the folds of a buckled section of the metal container, a tiny portion of printed circuit board which was later traced by forensic scientists to a Toshiba radio/cassette player which, they were able to establish, had been fitted with an improvised explosive device.

More detailed analysis was needed, however, to establish the mechanisms by which the failure process had developed from local damage in the immediate vicinity of the explosion to the complete structural break-up and separation of the forward fuselage section. A 65ft section (to cover some 30ft either side of the explosion) was transported to AAIB Farnborough where a full three-dimensional reconstruction was made so that the investigating team could determine the sequence by which the initial explosive damage had led to the 747 breaking up. The Cockpit Voice Recorder (CVR) and Flight Data Recorder (FDR) were retrieved 15 hours after the accident and examined, as were the airliner's four engines when these were recovered. Decoding of the data from the FDR showed that only normal behavior of the data sensors had been recorded; recording had simply stopped at 19.02:50hrs. The CVR tape had recorded nothing out of the ordinary until, also at 19.02:50hrs, there was a sudden loud sound followed abruptly by the cessation of recording while the crew were copying their trans-Atlantic clearance from Shanwick ATC. This was almost certainly the sound of the bomb detonation at the port side of the forward baggage area and, linked to damaged fan blades on number two engine (the port inner), was consistent with the results of a major airflow disturbance while delivering power. (This "shingling" effect on the turbine blades is produced when random bending and torsional deflection occurs, permitting the mid-span shrouds to disengage and repeatedly strike the adjacent aerofoil surface of the blades). There were also paint

Above: *Part of PA103's cockpit. The name* Maid of the Seas *is just visible on the side.* CORBIS/AFP

smears and other evidence in the air intake indicating the passage of debris. Number three engine (the inner starboard) showed no such shingling, confirming that blast effects had occurred out to port. There was another kind of damage which all four engines had in common. All had evidence of blade tip rubs on the fan cases to a greater extent than previously seen on any investigation concerning Boeing 747 aircraft by Pratt & Whitney. Data supplied by that company indicated that the damage was consistent with a marked nose-down change of pitch combined with a sharp roll to port.

The further reconstruction also showed that the initial explosion had blown a small hole in the port side of the fuselage, ahead of the wing leading edge. This had twisted the edges of the fuselage which were then stripped backward by the 430kts slipstream, thus enlarging the hole and starting secondary cracks which lengthened quickly and weakened still further the aircraft structure. There is little doubt that separation of the forward fuselage was complete within two to three seconds of the explosion. Part of the blast was, however, also reflected back into the fuselage where it buckled upward the cabin floor and this may well have applied forces to the flying control cables which caused the main portion of the aircraft immediately to enter a maneuver involving the marked nose down and left roll attitude change which was confirmed by the engine damage. The forward fuselage deflected to the right, pivoting about the starboard window belt before peeling away and striking the inner starboard (number three) engine which detached from its pylon and fell away in turn. The remains of the aircraft entered a steepening dive until, by the time it had fallen through 12,000ft it was plummeting vertically whilst shedding more of its structure all the time. After falling a further 10,000ft the remains fell progressively apart to form the more compact northern wreckage trail. When the fin and rudder were torn away at about 19,000ft above the final impact point it caused the remains to yaw sufficiently sharply to cause side-load separation of numbers one, two, and four engines, complete with their pylons, and these then fell separately to earth within the town perimeter. Break-up of the rear fuselage continued during the vertical descent, leaving a section of cabin floor and baggage hold which together with three landing gear units, fell into Rosebank Terrace.

A one-kilogram charge of Semtex had taken just over a minute and a half to utterly destroy a 300-ton airliner and kill 270 people.

This was a terrorist outrage and not a failure of the aircraft or the ATC system, so the work of the accident investigators ended and the task of unraveling the full story fell to the Royal Armament Research and Development Establishment (RARDE), based near Sevenoaks in Kent. The criminal investigations remained with the police and other counter-intelligence organizations such as the FBI, but these services needed proven information upon which to base their work. RARDE research showed that the case which contained the explosives must have been loaded above the bottom layer of baggage in the pallet, and that meant that it must have traveled to London from Frankfurt on board the Boeing 727. At London, the case had been transferred to "Maid of the Seas" with the rest of the New York-bound baggage. The forensic experts also identified clothing fibers found in the fragments of the bomb suitcase. These were traced to articles bought in Malta and flown to Frankfurt on the day of the flight, though no 727 passenger was identified as coming from Malta. Police later traced the purchase of the clothes to an unknown Libyan. The inference was that the destruction of Flight PA103 four days before Christmas was a carefully timed revenge attack, a retaliation for an earlier air tragedy on July 3, that year when the US Navy cruiser *Vincennes*, mistaking an Iran Air Airbus with its cargo of pilgrims for an attacking F-14 fighter, shot it down just four days before the Muslim festival of Id Al-Adha. Some two and a half years after the tragedy over Lockerbie, a joint American/British investigation had shifted its focus to Libya as the perpetrator of the massacre, carrying out a reprisal for the US bombing of its capital in April 1986. That bombing had itself been aimed at Colonel Gaddafi because of an earlier terrorist attack perpetrated by Libya.

In November 1991, America indicted two Libyans suspected of being intelligence agents, claiming that they had planted the explosive device in a suitcase which was carried from Malta to Frankfurt and then interlined onto Flight PA103. Embedded in a piece of the luggage container was a minute piece of a timer which had been manufactured in Switzerland and sold to Libya in 1985. If Flight PA103 had not been delayed at London, the aircraft would have crashed into the Atlantic, possibly blotting out for ever any evidence that it had been destroyed by a bomb. Libya refused to allow the extradition of the accused men on the grounds that they would not receive a fair trial, and for some years there was an impasse. However the passage of time and the effect of US and UN sanctions eventually resulted in Libya agreeing that the men should stand trial under Scottish Law, but proceedings should take place on neutral ground in Holland, at the Hague, and they were duly handed over to the Dutch authorities in 1999. The trial of Abdel-Baset Ali Mohmed Al-Megrahi and Al-Amin Khalifa Fhima is now scheduled to begin on February 3, 2000, and so the final act of this tragedy is yet to be played out.

Above Left: *Scottish prosecutors Norman McFayden and Jim Brisbane at Schipol Airport.* CORBIS/AFP

Above Right: *Colonel Gadaffi, Libya's controversial leader, who has always been linked to state terrorism by Western governments.* CORBIS/AFP

Below: *The two men handed over by Libya to stand trial—Abdel Baset Ali (Left) and Al-Amin Khalifa (Right).* Both CORBIS/AFP.

13 Sioux City, USA, 1989
United Airlines McDonnell Douglas
DC-10-10

Michael Sharpe

All man-made machines are fallible and aircraft are no exception to this rule. Despite the multitude of checks that are undertaken at every stage in the life of an airframe and its engines, which together constitute an airplane, airlines have to balance out the cost of guarding against the risk of systems failures with the maximum cost that the traveling public will pay for the convenience of flying from A to B. In the process of risk reduction, manufacturers incorporate duplicate and triplicate systems into modern jetliners that offer ever higher levels of safety. The chance of all systems failing simultaneously is further reduced by the addition of every duplicate back-up, making for a more secure aircraft, but the safeguards are accompanied by penalties of higher weight and higher cost. Of course, engineers could design aircraft that incorporate ever greater back ups in aircraft systems but the expense of guarding against the million-to-one occurrence may not necessarily make for a cost-effective aircraft. In a competitive market place with airlines seeking to maximize profits this is a key issue.

On July 19, 1989, that million-to-one chance struck United Airlines Flight 232 while en route from Denver, Colorado to Chicago, Illinois, the first leg of a domestic service to Philadelphia. Aircraft commander that day was Captain Al Haynes, an ex-Marine Corps flight instructor and a United employee since 1956 with 7,000 hours experience on the DC-10, nine years as co-pilot. First Officer Bill Records had flown the Lockheed L011 Tristar for many years before switching to DC-10s, and therefore had considerable experience of three-engine jetliners. However, Flight Engineer Dudley Dvorak, the Second Officer, was on his first scheduled flight in the DC-10 since his initial operating experience flight.

Just before 15.15hrs, as the crew began to turn toward Debuke, Iowa, they heard a loud bang, loud enough to make people on the ground 37,000ft below look up, quickly followed by vibration and a shuddering of the airframe. In the rear of the aircraft the senior flight attendant was thrown to the cabin floor by the force of an explosion. Almost immediately Dvorak's instruments registered an almost complete loss of hydraulic fluid, and the crew began to experience problems with controlling the aircraft.

Left: *A United Airlines 727 carrying survivors takes-off over the crashed DC-10.* CORBIS-Bettmann/UPI

Above: *Police guard the wreckage of UNITED AIRLINES flight 200. This is the rear fuselage and tail section of the crashed aircraft.* CORBIS-Bettmann/UPI

At 15.16hrs Records reported the loss of No. 2 engine to Minneapolis ATC, called for a lower altitude, announced that he was turning off the airway, and in line with procedure, deployed the air driven generator (ADG) that powered the No. 1 auxiliary hydraulic pump. However, hydraulic power could not be restored, leaving Haynes, his crew of 11, and 284 passengers trapped in an aircraft over which he had virtually no control and which showed a marked tendency to turn right. Neither the elevators, ailerons, or rudder would respond to control inputs. To compound the problem he had no leading edge flaps or slats to slow the airplane, no trailing edge flaps for landing, and no spoilers on the wing to get the plane down or slow it. The only option was to try and control the airplane using the thrust from the two wing-mounted engines. Having cut off the fuel supply to the No. 2 unit and with the aircraft in a right bank, Haynes and Records fought to stabilize against uncontrolled pitch oscillations using the little influence over the aircraft that remained to them.

At 15.20hrs a full-scale emergency was declared. By this time the aircraft was proceeding on a southwesterly heading back toward Sioux City and Minneapolis ARTCC handed control over to a young ATC, Kevin Bockman, who was on the radar station at approach control.

Meantime, Dvorak ran through the checklist of emergency procedures and made radio contact with the airline's maintenance facility at San Francisco, where the experts began trawling through their computer databases trying to find information that would be of any use in dealing with the crisis. At this point Haynes called Dennis Fitch to the flightdeck. Fitch, an off-duty DC-10 check captain who made himself known to the cabin crew when the emergency was first declared, provided a much-needed extra pair of hands. Although Haynes and Records were aware that their efforts were achieving very little, both men had a pilot's natural desire to "fly"

156

the aircraft through the yoke and were reluctant to release their two-handed grip. The problem was that the aircraft could only be controlled in pitch and roll through the asymmetrical No. 1 and 3 throttles. With the No. 2 (central) throttle jammed, this was a two-handed operation. With Fitch standing between the two seats controlling the throttles , the crew were able to synchronize their movements and regain some degree of control.

15.23, Center: "Sioux City, got an emergency for you. Got a United aircraft, coming in, lost #2 engine, having a hard time controlling the aircraft right now, he's out of 29,000 right now, descending to Sioux City right now. He's ?? VOR but he wants the equipment standing by right now."

15.25, Sioux City: "Radar contact."

UAL232: "So you know we have almost no controllability. Very little elevator, and almost no ailerons, we're controlling the turns by power. I don't think we can turn right, I think we can only make left turns. ?? We can only turn right, we can't turn left."

15.26, Sioux City: "United 232 heavy, understand, sir, you can only make right turns?"

UAL232: "That's affirmative."

15.29, Sioux City: "32 heavy, say souls on board, and fuel remaining."

UAL232: We have 376, fuel ?

15.32, Sioux City: "United 232 heavy, Sioux City."

UAL232: "Confirm we have no hydraulic fluid, which means we have no elevator control, almost none, and very little aileron control. I have serious doubts about making the airport. Have you got someplace near there, that we might be able to ditch? Unless we get control of this airplane, we're going to put it down wherever it happens to be."

Sioux City: "United 232 heavy, roger, standby."

In the passenger cabin the flight attendants calmly began to prepare the passengers for an emergency landing and the undercarriage was extended manually to help slow the aircraft. Emergency services at Sioux City assembled in preparation. Fortunately, the Air National Guard's 185th Tactical Fighter Group were on exercise, effectively doubling the number of trained emergency staff at the airport.

15.40, Sioux City: "United 232 heavy, say again. 232 heavy, think you'll be able to hold about a 240 heading?"

UAL232: "We're going to turn into it about right now."

Sioux City: "When you turn to that 240 heading, sir, the airport will be about oh, 12 o'clock and 38 miles."

UAL232: "Okay, we're trying to control it just by power alone, we have no hydraulics at all, sir, we're doing our best, here."

Sioux City: "Roger, and we've notified the equipment out in that area too, sir. The equipment's here on the airport, standing by, and they're sending some out to that area."

15.46, UAL232: "232, we're going to have to continue in a right turn. We've got the elevators pretty much under control, but that's three or four hundred feet, but still can't get much ** steering."

Sioux City: "United 232 heavy, roger, understand you do have the elevators possibly under control, will you be able to hold altitude?"

UAL232: "Negative, we don't have it. We're better, that's all."

Sioux City: "Roger."

Sioux City: "United 232 heavy, there's a small airport 12 o'clock and seven miles. The runway's 4,000 feet long, there."

UAL232: "Control, ** myself right now, soon as the captain gets back on, he'll give me a hand here. He's talking on the PA."

Sioux City: "Roger."

At Sioux City airport fire crews began preparing for a crash-landing.

UAL232: "United 232, we're starting a left turn back to the airport. Since we have no hydraulics, braking is going to really be a problem. I would suggest the equipment be ** toward the far end of the runway. And I think under the circumstances, regardless of the condition of the airplane when we stop, we're going to evacuate, so you might notify the ground crew that we're going to do that."

Sioux City: "United 232 heavy, wilco, sir, and if you can continue that left turn, to about a 220 heading, sir, that'll take you right to the airport."

15.47, Sioux City: "United 232 heavy, you're going to have to widen out just slightly to your left sir, to make the turn to final, and also to take you away from the city."

15.51, UAL232: Whatever you do, keep us away from the city.

15.53, Sioux City: "232 heavy, be advised, there is a four-lane highway up in that area, sir, if you can pick that up."

UAL232: "Okay, we'll see what we can do, here. We've already put the gear down, and we're going to have to be putting on something solid, if we can."

15.59, Sioux City: "United 232 heavy, roger, airport's currently at your one o'clock position, ten miles."

Sioux City: "United 232 heavy, if you can't make the airport, sir, there's an interstate that runs north to south to the east side of the airport, it's a four-lane interstate."

UAL232: "We're just passing it right now. We're going to try for the airport."

Sioux City: "United 232 heavy, roger, and advise me when you get the airport in sight."

UAL232: "We have the runway in sight, and will be with you shortly. Thanks a lot for your help."

Sioux City: "United 232 heavy, winds currently 360 at 11, three sixty at eleven, you're cleared to land on any runway."

UAL232: "You don't want to be particular and make it a runway, huh?"

Sioux City: ". . .010 at 11, and there's a runway that closed, sir, that could probably work too, it runs northeast to southwest. "

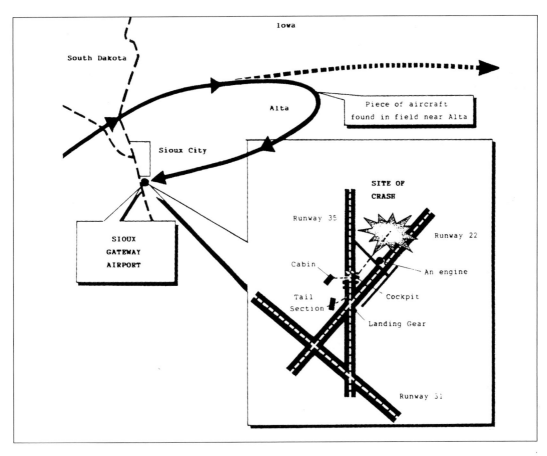

Above: *The path of flight 232 into Sioux City and the site of the crash.*

Below: *DC-10 hydraulic systems' detail.*

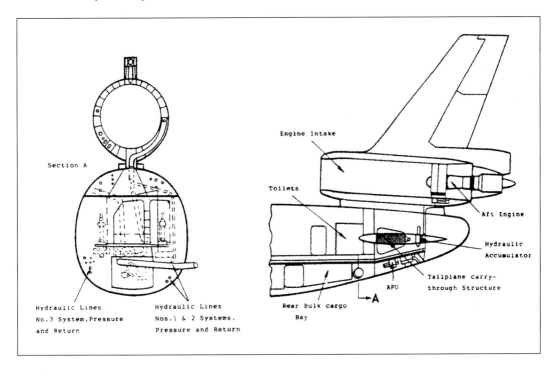

UAL232: "We're pretty much lined up on this one, here, I think we will be."

Sioux City: "United 232 heavy, roger sir, that's a closed runway, that'll work, sir. We're getting the equipment off the runway, and they'll line up to that one."

UAL232: "How long is it?"

16.00, Sioux City: "At the end of the runway is just a wide open field, sir, so the length won't be a problem."

UAL232: "OK."

Haynes and the crew were hoping that they could stay on the gear, go off the end of the runway, shear the gear and go onto the belly of the aircraft. The aircraft approached with a high sink rate (1,620ft per minute for the last 20 seconds) and an airspeed of 215kts, with a quartering tail wind turning the plane from left to right. Normal approach speed in the DC-10 is 140 knots, and rate of descent is about 200-300ft per minute.

At about 100ft above the ground the nose began to pitch downward and the right wing dropped. The right wingtip touched the centerline followed almost simultaneously by the right mainwheel leg, No. 3 engine and the nose wheel. The force of the impact drove an 18ft hole through the 12in thick concrete tearing both the right wing and entire tail section off. The aircraft then skidded to the right on the intact left gear and right wing stub for 2,000ft before it lifted off, bounced onto the nose, and flipped upside down before coming to rest at a point across runway 17/35. Fire then engulfed the aircraft, overcoming many, though mainly due to the fact that it had separated into three sections some of the passengers were able to walk away from the wreckage unaided and at least another 200 were pulled out before the fire intensified. Haynes came round after losing consciousness at the initial impact, amazed to discover that he and the three-man flight crew were still alive. Thirty-five minutes after the crash rescue crews began the delicate operation to extract them from the mangled cockpit.

Others were not so lucky; 102 people died, overcome by the effects of smoke and trauma, as the aircraft burned on the ground. Another ten unfortunate victims succumbed to their injuries in hospital. Of the 184 survivors, 171 suffered injuries, many serious.

Recovery of the FDR and CVR presented no problem and after preliminary examination of the wreckage it was confirmed that the aircraft had suffered a massive hydraulic failure. Fortunately, the tail section had been severed in virtually one piece during the initial impact, and this showed extensive impact damage to the skin and hydraulic lines.

As investigators reconstructed the DC-10's tail in a Sioux City hangar the reasons became clear. In normal circumstances localized damage to the No. 2 engine, mounted on the centerline, would not have been a serious problem and would have not presented any great threat to safety. But after examining the wreckage it was discovered that the entire fan unit was missing. After the second-stage disk had been recovered suspicion fell on the first-stage, which was discovered in a farmer's field near the flight path after an intensive two month search across rural Iowa. Six months later a section of the booster disk was also found.

Above: *Flight investigators examine the wreckage.* CORBIS-Bettmann/UPI

Below: *The DC-10's tail section is lifted carefully onto a truck to be taken for examination at the NTSB hangar.* CORBIS

Investigators were able to deduce that the first-stage compressor disk had torn through the containment ring, shattered the No. 2 accessory drive section and No. 2 hydraulics before disintegrating into at least 70 pieces of shrapnel that penetrated the horizontal stabilizer, and sliced through the Nos. 2 and 3 hydraulic system lines resulting in total loss of hydraulic power. Nothing in the training or experience of the crew could have prepared them for this eventuality. The DC-10, of course, has no manual reversion on the flying controls. The cables go to the servos that drive the flying surfaces, and hydraulic pressure does the work. The aircraft has three completely independent hydraulic systems each driven by two pumps that are powered by Nos. 1, 2, and 3 engines respectively. Should any of these systems fail because of fluid loss, the others will not fail because they are not connected together and as all of the major flight controls have two and sometimes three of the hydraulic systems providing power it is still quite easy to land the aircraft safely. Loss of hydraulic pressure is not an uncommon event. Even if two of the systems are lost, it is possible to fly the airplane—although the controls will be rather sluggish.

The problem was eventually traced back to an error in the manufacture of the titanium ingot from which the titanium disk was forged by the Alcoa Company. At an early stage in the process, before the disk had been cast, excessive nitrogen was introduced into the molten metal, creating a bubble that became a cavity when the disk was finished with aggressive cleaning techniques. Over 18 years the disk was routinely subjected to enormous stresses generated by an engine working at full thrust, exacerbating the cracking. Finally at 37,000ft over Iowa, the disk fractured in two places, causing one third of the rim to separate. A series of inspections at the foundry and at General Electric's assembly plant had failed to pick up on the casting fault, before the disk was installed into the CF6-6 engine. GEAE immediately recalled disks from six other engines that had been forged from the same ingot. In its report, the NTSB determined that the probable cause "was the inadequate consideration given to human factor limitations in the inspection and quality control procedures used by United Airlines' engine overhaul facility which resulted in the failure to detect a fatigue crack originating from a previously undetected metallurgical defect located in a critical area of the stage 1 fan disk that was manufactured by General Electric Aircraft Engines. The subsequent catastrophic disintegration of the disk resulted in the liberation of debris in a pattern of distribution and with energy levels that exceeded the level of protection provided by design features of the hydraulic systems that operate the DC-10's flight controls."

Three months after the crash Al Haynes was back at work. He subsequently embarked on a tour of the US, talking about his experiences and advising aviation industry professionals and community safety staff about the lessons to be learned from the incident. In his speech to the staff of the Dryden Flight Research Facility on May 24, 1991, Haynes identified a number of factors that allowed 184 people to survive an accident that on paper should have killed them all. He pointed to the excellent communication between the flight crew, which he felt was the product of United's pioneering Cockpit Resource Management Training program. This program, which was developed by NASA in the 1970s to meet the growing demands of multi-engine jetliner operations, enabled all of the crew to make a positive contri-

Above: *A man consoles his daughter after learning the fate of a loved one following the Sioux City crash.*
CORBIS-Bettmann/UPI

bution to the decision making process on the flightdeck; a solution was arrived at by common consent, without Haynes imposing his authority as commander over the others. The prompt actions, cool thinking and efficient organization of the staff at Sioux City airport was another important factor. Fifteen minutes before crash, at 15.45hrs, the tower changed the alert status from Level 2 to Level 3. Alert 3 means "an aircraft has crashed," signaling to local hospitals and relevant support facilities to prepare for an influx of casualties. Even before the aircraft had crashed-landed, back-up medical supplies were being flown from nearby Des Moines.

Haynes also made special reference to the cool-headedness of ATC Kevin Bockman, who kept up a constant dialogue with Flight 232 in the 40 minutes prior to the crash, providing them with selective, relevant information. Nevertheless, Haynes has no doubts that luck played a role. The engine exploded over land, whereas it might so easily have been mid-way across the Pacific, and the weather was unusually kind for the time of year, with good visibility and virtually no wind shear across the runway. Also, the emergency was called at a time when staff at Marion and St. Luke's hospitals were changing over shifts and so twice as many medical staff were available to care for the injured. But although luck helped to get them on to the ground, it was the efficiency of the Sioux City emergency services, who had prepared an organized, up-to-date disaster plan for that million-to-one chance, that saved Flight 232 from total catastrophe.

14 Bijlmermeer, Amsterdam, 1992
El Al Boeing 747-258F

Leo Marriott

Most people living close to busy airports give little thought to the aircraft which pass over their heads every day. True, noise and environmental pollution issues now have a higher profile than they ever did in the past, but it is often a vociferous minority who register the greatest proportion of comment and complaint. Other people may express apprehension as to the possibility of an approaching or departing aircraft crashing into residential areas but, statistically, such accidents are rare. Despite vague misgivings, everyday life goes on and the possibility of an horrific disaster is almost completely forgotten amid the more immediate problems of life. Nevertheless, the potential is always there as was graphically illustrated on the night of October 4, 1992, when a Boeing 747 freighter flown by El Al, the Israeli national airline, sliced through a crowded block of apartments in a suburb of Amsterdam, some eight miles east of the city's Schipol Airport.

In this dreadful accident, the devastation on the ground caused by the impact of the heavily laden 747 with the 11 storey apartment block was almost beyond imagination and no less than 43 people on the ground were killed as well as the four occupants of the aircraft. The accident happened at night but in the cold light of the following dawn, as a pall of smoke from the smouldering ruins and wreckage pervaded the melancholy scene, it was apparent that the 747 must have been banked at almost 90° as it carved through the apex of the two connected and angled apartment blocks.

Compared to some accidents, the investigators of this particular event had a relatively easy task as the origins and subsequent course of this drama were quickly determined. The actual aircraft was a Boeing 747-258F(SCD), a dedicated cargo version of the popular wide-bodied airliner. The SCD designation indicated a side cargo door. Registered 4X-AXG, it had been delivered new from Boeing in March 1979 and had served continually with El Al from that time. Earlier that day it had arrived at Amsterdam from JFK Airport, New York, and had landed at 13.40hrs, It was refueled and a routine maintenance check carried out as the cargo load was processed. By the time that all of this had been done, the 747's take-off weight was calculated to have been 338.3 metric tons of which cargo accounted for 114.7 tons,

Above: Rescue workers sift through the debris of the apartment block in Amsterdam. The nine-story hole is a somber reminder of the people killed in the block.
Association Press Photograph

Above: *El Al 747 freighter (4X-AXK) displaying the all-white livery common to many of the airline's cargo aircraft.* Robbie Shaw

and fuel for a further 72 tons. It was this highly volatile mass which was to hit the block of apartments later that evening.

With the turnaround complete, El Al Flight 1862 was ready for departure on schedule at 16.30hrs but ATC delays resulted in a take-off slot of 17.20hrs and the captain called up for push back and start up clearance at 17.04hrs. This was approved and the 747 subsequently taxied and lined up for departure on runway zero one left almost exactly at the appointed time, beginning its take-off roll at 17.21hrs. The initial climb after take-off went quite normally and the heavily laden 747 climbed steadily on a PAMPUS departure which took it on a sweeping right turn over the heart of Amsterdam before settling onto an easterly track. Suddenly, as it was climbing through an altitude of 6,500ft some six minutes after take-off, the 747 yawed violently and all power readings for the number three and four engines on the starboard wing fell to zero. In addition there was an indication of a fire in number three engine.

On the ground, the progress of the El Al flight was being monitored by the sector two controller at the Amsterdam Air Traffic Control Center. The calm interchanges on the sector frequency, 124.87 MHz, were suddenly interrupted by the call from the captain, "El Al one eight six two, Mayday, Mayday, we have an emergency!"

The sector controller acknowledged the call and asked if the crew wished to return to Schipol, observing at the same time from his radar display that the 747 was turning right and descending. The reply from the aircraft left no doubt as to the urgency of the situation, "Affirmative, Mayday, Mayday." The controller instructed the aircraft to turn right onto a heading of 260° with the intention of positioning it downwind right hand for a landing on runway 06. This course of action would have entailed bringing the 747 back south of the airfield and then some miles out to west before turning back onto a final approach for landing. As the crew struggled to bring the stricken 747 round to the right, they were some 18 miles to the east of the airfield and, believing the indications of a fire, informed the controller that there was a fire in the number three engine. In the circumstances, they were obviously desperate to get the aircraft back on the ground as soon as possible, and were therefore disconcerted when advised that they were being vectored for runway 06. The captain therefore asked if runway 27 was available so that they could make a straight in approach and save valuable minutes. As a result of this request, the crew were instructed to call Schipol Approach on frequency 118.4 MHz so that they could be vectored onto final for that runway.

On contacting approach, they were instructed to turn right onto a heading of 360°. It was now 17.30hrs and the 747 had already descended to around 4,000ft. There then followed an exchange between the captain and the controller concerning the distance required to lose height and make an approach to land on runway 27. As a result of this, the controller gave heading instructions which took the aircraft through the extended centerline and then turned it again to the right with the intention of coming back onto the centerline from the north. The crew complied with these instructions but the rate of turn was not enough and the 747 described a wide loop back through the centerline so that the controllers final instructions were to roll out on a heading of 310° and descend to 1,500ft. In normal circumstances this would have put the aircraft on a closing track from the left to intercept the ILS localizer at around eight miles from touchdown. The controller cleared the El Al aircraft for an ILS approach and also gave a landing clearance. Up to this point (at time 17.35hrs), although the track of the aircraft had been erratic and its speed greater than normal for an approach, it had basically followed ATC instructions and appeared to be under a degree of control. Suddenly the situation changed and the 747 began to turn uncontrollably to the right and the crew reported control problems. Some 25 seconds later a final spine chilling call was received from the co-pilot, "Going down, one eight six two, going down." A subsequent analysis of the tape recordings also picked up the voice of the captain in the background frantically calling for the flaps to be raised and the landing gear to be lowered.

But it was too late. The big 747 now tilted out of control until the wings were almost vertical and it spiraled down in an ever tightening right turn until it smashed into the apartment blocks at Bijlmermeer, eight miles east of the airport and almost exactly on the centerline for the approach to runway 27. The aircraft struck almost exactly dead center at the apex of the two sections of the building, plowing right through it and scattering wreckage over an area some 650 by 400 yards. The damage to the building was compounded by an explosion and a subsequent fierce fire as the tons of fuel ignited. Crash investigators later determined that the angle of bank was just over 90° while the nose down pitch was around 70°. In some ways it might be considered fortunate that the aircraft was so heavily banked as the damage to the building was confined to a relatively narrow vertical section. Had the impact occurred in a wings level attitude, a substantially greater proportion of the building might have been destroyed. Even so, 43 people were killed on the ground and many others seriously injured. The shock experienced by the survivors can only be guessed at. Within the space of a few seconds their ordinary homes and routines had been catastrophically destroyed by, literally, a bolt from the blue. The scenes which greeted the firefighters and rescue services arriving a few minutes later must have been terrible.

The immediate investigation quickly produced the cause of the accident. Reports from witnesses on the ground at around the time of the original Mayday call established that there had been some loud bangs and smoke emanating from the aircraft and that objects had been observed to fall to the ground. At the actual impact site only the number one and two engines were located and it was apparent that the other two must have broken off earlier. Following an analysis of the witness reports, and a search of the Ijsselmeer by the Dutch police and naval authorities, the number four engine was recovered immediately following the accident and the number three engine ten days later. Also in the same area were found several other pieces of wreckage including parts of the starboard wing leading edge and leading edge flaps. Examination of these sections, together with parts of the wing at the actual accident site, enabled investigators to piece together the sequence of events which led to the ultimate loss of control. It quickly became obvious that the pylon supporting the number three engine had failed and the whole assembly had become detached from the aircraft. As it did so, it had swung outboard and impacted on the number four outboard engine, causing this in turn to break away and also causing considerable damage to the leading edge flaps and the fixed wing surfaces as far back as the front main spar. The starboard side hydraulic systems were completely disabled, while the pneumatic system was partly damaged.

As far as the crew were concerned, they had suffered a complete power loss from both engines and the multiple faults indicated to the master warning system triggered the fire alarm for number three engine. Unfortunately, the rearward view from the flightdeck of a 747 is extremely limited and so the co-pilot, seated on the starboard side, would have been unable to see that the engines had actually separated. Although 747 pilots were routinely trained to handle the aircraft in the event of a double engine failure by means of flight simulator exercises, the performance characteristics of the seriously damaged aircraft were totally unlike those which would have been expected if the engines had merely failed. The accident investigators subsequently determined the 747 was in fact only marginally flyable in its damaged condition. However, the crew appeared initially to have some success but, as they attempted to reduce speed and lower flaps on turning in toward runway 27, severe control problems were encountered. The accident report notes that, in its damaged condition, the 747 was barely controllable at 270kts. As the speed was decreased and the pitch angle increased, it became necessary to increase the power on the remaining two engines to overcome increased drag and prevent undue loss of height. This would have produced an asymmetric roll moment which was probably made worse by an asymmetric deployment of the leading edge flaps due to the damage to the starboard wing. Almost certainly, the captain realized what was happening and this would account for his recorded calls to raise the flaps although by that time it was too late and the aircraft went into a steeply banked uncontrollable dive.

Although the general train of events was quickly established, determining the exact cause of the pylon failure was more difficult, especially as not all of the relevant components were recovered. However, exhaustive examination of those parts which were available, together with numerous computer simulations carried out by Boeing, led to a hypothesis which supported all the known facts. Although covered in a streamlined fairing, the engine pylon structure is quite complex and it is attached to the wing at four separate points. A link strut connects the forward part of the pylon to the wing leading edge, but the main weight and dynamic forces are carried by two side by side mid spar fittings, while a diagonal bracing strut connects the lower edge of the pylon to the wing rear spar. As a fail safe feature, the whole pylon structure was designed so that, in the event of abnormal dynamic loads which would otherwise damage the integrity of the wing and fuel tanks, it would break cleanly away from the wing. This objective was achieved by means of fuse pins incorporated in each of the four attachment points. These were designed to shear if specified load conditions were experienced, allowing a clean break away of the whole pylon. This system had proved effective and satisfactory on the earlier Boeing 707, and was simply scaled up and approved by the FAA when the 747 was being built and tested. However subsequent in-service experience showed many problems including cracks and failures of the fuse pins, lugs, and fittings. Over the course of time following the service debut of the 747 in 1970, the American FAA issued a number of airworthiness directives (ADs) requiring modification and inspection of various pylon components. It was also noted that examples had occurred where the fuse pins had deformed under normal operational loads although a subsequent failure had not occurred.

WING LOWER SURFACE

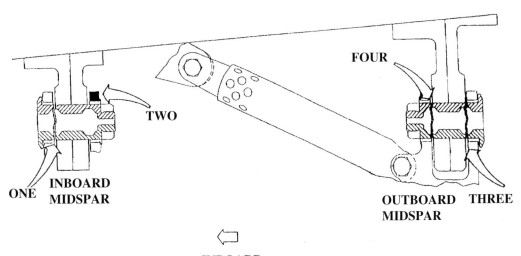

Above: Strut No. 3 fracture detail and sequence.

In fact there was already a substantial case history pointing to defects in the pylon design prior to the El Al accident in November 1992. The problem was first highlighted when the number four engine pylon partially separated on a Boeing 747 freighter landing at London Heathrow on December 27, 1979. This particular aircraft had already flown some 43,615 hours and made 9,505 landings. In addition there was evidence of some previous damage to the pylon which partially explained this incident. A more serious accident, chillingly similar to the Amsterdam disaster and occurring almost exactly 12 months earlier, involved a China Airlines aircraft which again lost the number three and four engines due to a pylon failure as the aircraft climbed through 5,200ft after take-off from Taipei, Taiwan. The aircraft crashed into the sea and all five occupants were killed. Even more coincidentally, this 747 was also a freighter. Accumulated hours and flight cycles were 45,868 and 9,094 respectively. In September 1991, a similar incident was averted when a routine ground check revealed that a 747-200 had an incipient pylon failure with a broken fuse pin in the outboard midspar fitting while only a month later a 747-212B was also found to have a cracked midspar fitting lug. In both of these incidents it was again the number three engine pylon that was affected. As a result of these and other occurrences, all 747 operators, including El Al, had been advised of specific checks and inspections to be carried out and the airline had conformed with these in respect of all aircraft in its fleet. Subsequent to the accident, Boeing had concluded that a detectable crack must have been present in the failed fuse pin at the time it was last inspected—257 cycles prior to the fatal flight. However, El Al strongly disputed this theoretical finding.

As a result of the Amsterdam accident, Boeing embarked on a substantial redesign of the pylon mountings and this was subjected to considerable testing to ensure that it met new failsafe requirements resulting from the accident investigation. However the program of refitting the entire 747 fleet would be a lengthy one and was expected to take up to seven years from 1994 onward as the work involved some 10,000 man hours per aircraft. In the interim, Boeing produced new stainless steel fuse pins for immediate fitting, produced a new inspection schedule at more frequent intervals, and introduced a newly developed ultrasonic sensor capable of detecting smaller cracks. Even so, this was not quite the end of the story as, on March 31, 1993, a Boeing 747-121 freighter operated by Evergreen lost the number two engine and pylon when severe turbulence was experienced shortly after take-off from Anchorage, Alaska. Fortunately the crew were able to retain control and land the aircraft safely. In this case there was evidence of a pre-existing crack in the midspar attachment fittings and the aircraft had previously flown 83,906 hours over 18,387 cycles. Altogether, there had been three instances of the pylon separation in a period of 15 months, but subsequently the modifications introduced by Boeing have prevented any further instances. In addition, it should be noted that all the in-flight separations occurred to freighter variants of the 747 which regularly fly at greater all up weights than the passenger versions. The more modern Boeing 747-400 series aircraft has a completely redesigned wing and current production aircraft incorporate all the lessons of the earlier incidents.

Above: A sister aircraft to the El Al 747 freighter shown taxiing. ASM Photo

15 Nagoya, Japan, 1994
China Airlines Airbus A300B4-600R

Leo Marriott

Pilot error is often cited as a cause of aircraft accidents and usually relates to simple mishandling of the aircraft or misinterpretation of navigation aids. Despite the development of jet airliners and their widespread introduction into service during the 1960s and 70s, the operation of commercial aircraft followed well defined procedures and techniques. If a pilot operated a particular switch or lever, then it would directly operate the associated device. If he pulled back on the control column, the nose of the aircraft would rise, while the power developed by the engines was directly related to the position of the throttle levers. A classic example of an accident in which pilot error was the most significant factor was the crash of a BEA Trident at Staines in 1972, shortly after it had taken off from London's Heathrow Airport. This was caused by the retraction of the leading edge flaps well before the aircraft had reached the required speed for this action, with the result that it stalled and crashed, killing all 118 occupants.

During the 1970s, aircraft designers began to apply new digital computer techniques to aircraft systems with the intention of making them more efficient to operate and safer to fly. The result of such work was seen in the new generation of airliners such as the Boeing 757 and 767 that entered service in the early 1980s. These were equipped with "glass cockpits" in which computer generated graphics on electronic displays replaced conventional instruments, while flight management systems, autopilots, and autothrottles, made flying almost a push button operation. However, it was the European-based Airbus consortium which pushed the new technology to its limits and produced aircraft with automatic flight control systems which were capable of preventing the aircraft being flown outside its safe performance envelope. This was expected to make the aircraft safer to fly and prevent typical pilot error associated accidents, but in doing so it required new skills of pilots and changed the whole nature of professional flying. Instead of directly flying the aircraft, pilots now became systems managers and needed an in-depth knowledge of how they worked, so they could understand and predict the outcome of any of their own actions. Even today, it is a standard joke among pilots that the most commonly heard phrase on the modern flightdeck is, "I wonder why it is doing that!"

Above: Rescue workers at Nagoya. Associated Press Photograph

Above: *The A300 flightdeck was one of the first to be fully automated and fitted with electronic flight displays. The go around button, instrumental in the China Airlines crash at Nagoya, is located just below and to the right of the central power levers.* Airbus Industrie

The first Airbus to enter airline service, in 1974, was the A300 which was also Europe's first wide-bodied aircraft and was relatively conventional in design and operation. It was followed in 1978 by the smaller A310 which introduced the automatic flight control system and the two-pilot electronic flightdeck which did away with the traditional third crew member, the flight engineer. Boeing had not gone that far at the time and the rival 767 retained provision for a flight engineer's position. Airbus applied the new technology to a new version of the A300 known as the 600 series which entered airline service in 1984. Subsequently Airbus won several hard fought sales battles with Boeing and the A300-600 was particularly popular with Middle East and Asian customers. Amongst these was Taiwan-based China Airlines which had already received six A300B4-200s in 1982–83 and followed up with further orders for the new A300-600 for delivery from 1989 onward. It was one of these aircraft that was involved in a major accident at Nagoya Airport in Japan on April 26, 1994 and the subsequent investigation painfully revealed the new and unsuspected problems which modern technology had brought to the flightdeck.

China Airlines' Flight 140 from Taipei International Airport to Nagoya on that day was operated by an Airbus A300B4-622R, registration B1816. It had departed at 17.53hrs (all times quoted in this narrative are Japanese Standard Time unless otherwise specified) carrying a total of 271 persons on board, a figure which included 15 crew members. The flight to Nagoya was completely routine and the aircraft had cruised at 33,000ft before commencing its descent into Nagoya at 19.47hrs.

Subsequently it was vectored by Nagoya Approach for an ILS approach to runway 34 and once established on the ILS, the first officer deselected the autopilots which had been in use since take-off and began to fly the aircraft manually on the approach. This occurred at 20.11:36hrs but the approach continued normally and Nagoya Tower cleared CI140 to land just after it had passed the outer marker, some four miles from touchdown. Although it was dark, the weather was almost ideal with a light westerly wind, a visibility of 12.5 miles and scattered cloud at 3,000ft. The temperature was 66°F. It was at this point that things began to go wrong, the aircraft began to pitch up uncontrollably and the first officer reported to the tower that they were "going around" (aborting the landing). Subsequently, the Airbus climbed steeply before stalling and diving into the ground just to the right of the runway where it broke up and burst into flames. Almost all on board were killed, although seven seriously injured survivors were eventually located and rescued.

What had happened? How had the aircraft got into a position where it had stalled? The automatic flight control system was designed to prevent just such an occurrence but, nevertheless, it appeared that somehow the impossible had taken place. An aircraft accident investigation committee was immediately set up by the Japanese Ministry of Transport and a painstaking examination of the wreckage began as soon as the rescue services had completed their work. As the aircraft had a low forward speed at the time of impact, the wreckage was not spread over a particularly wide area but it was badly broken up with many sections destroyed by fire. In common with most modern commercial aircraft the Airbus was equipped with a Digital Flight Data Recorder (DFDR) and a Cockpit Voice Recorder (CVR). Both of these were found in a badly damaged state but their recording tapes were unaffected and proved to be the prime source of evidence.

It was determined that the initial approach had been completely normal with the first officer acting as the handling pilot or "Pilot Flying" (PF) and the captain monitoring. As the aircraft intercepted the ILS localizer, speed was reduced to 170kts to avoid turbulence from a preceding aircraft and the first stage of flap was deployed. At 20.11:35hrs, the first officer disengaged both autopilots and continued to fly the aircraft manually but set 3,000ft on the ALT SEL autopilot control as the level to which it would climb in the event of a go around. The Airbus passed over the outer marker, some four miles from touchdown, at 20.12:19hrs and subsequently the flaps were lowered to 20° and the undercarriage lowered. At 20.13:14hrs the first officer called "Thirty/forty. Speed vee approach 140, landing checklist please."

In response the captain lowered the flaps to their final setting and, a few seconds later reported, "Landing checklist completed." It was now 20.13:27hrs and the approach continued normally for another half a minute until, as the aircraft passed through an altitude of 1,070ft at time 20.14:05hrs, the DFDR recorded that the first officer triggered the go around lever. The reason for this action could never be determined but it was almost certainly unintentional. However, this action immediately put the aircraft into an automatic mode and it commenced a go around procedure in which the autothrottle system initiated an increase in engine thrust which in turn caused the aircraft's nose to rise and it began to fly above the glideslope. The first officer's immediate and natural action was to push forward on the control column in an attempt to overcome the nose up pitching movement. He also manually reduced power slightly and succeeded in leveling off. An aural warning alerted the pilots to the fact that the go around mode had been triggered and the captain instructed the first officer to deselect it. Although this order was acknowledged, the appropriate action was not taken immediately but both autopilot systems (AP1 and AP2) were selected ON at 20.14:18hrs. With the go around mode still selected, the autopilots immediately attempted to make the aircraft climb and the autothrottles cut in again, increasing power. Again the first officer attempted to correct by pushing forward on the control column, while the captain ordered the autothrottles to be disengaged. Unfortunately, the first officer's actions in pushing forward triggered the autotrim mechanism which started to adjust the setting of the tail horizontal stabilizer (THS) in order to maintain the nose up pitch.

At 20.14:30hrs, the captain noticed that the go around mode was still selected and again instructed the first officer to disengage it, but for some reason this was not achieved and a few seconds later the THS reached its fully nose up position. At this point it was impossible to prevent the nose up pitch by the action of the elevators and the aircraft was effectively "out of trim." It was also descending rapidly through 800ft altitude and speed was falling off dangerously. In a further effort to counteract the situation, the first officer increased power slightly and deselected the autopilots. He almost regained control as he continued to push forward on the control column and the pitch up angle began to decrease. However, he must then have relaxed a little and the pitch up began again while the speed fell to 127kts as the Airbus descended through an altitude of 570ft. This combination of parameters brought the aircraft to a point where its angle of attack (AOA or Alpha) exceeded the safe limit for the 40° flap setting, a situation known in Airbus terminology as the "Alpha Floor:" As a safety device, the autothrottles were programed to cut in at this point and increase thrust in order to sustain flight. In this particular situation, with the aircraft already out of trim, the result was an excessive nose up pitching movement which proved impossible to overcome.

At this point (20.15:03hrs) the captain at last realized that things were going badly wrong and took over control from the first officer although he too continued to push forward on the controls in an effort to lower the nose. He also attempted to reduce power and disengage the autothrottles, probably with the intention of continuing the descent to land. These efforts were in vain and he expressed his puzzlement saying, "What's the matter with this?" A few seconds later, still struggling with the controls, he said, "Damn it, how come it's like this?"

With the approach now going badly astray, the captain attempted to initiate a go around maneuver and reapplied power. The CVR recorded the sounds of the slats/flaps lever being operated to raise the flaps, a standard action in a normal go around situation although inappropriate at the low airspeed now existing. The increase in power again triggered an uncontrollable pitch up movement but the captain was probably reluctant to decrease the power setting as the aircraft was climbing steeply with a decreasing airspeed. However, he was now seriously alarmed and shouted "He . . . if this goes on it will stall." In fact this was exactly what happened a few seconds later, at around 20.15:25hrs. By this time the speed had decayed to a

Above: A China Airlines Airbus A399-600R taxying at Hong Kong's Kai Tak airport in 1994. This shows the airline's livery at the time of the fatal Nagoya crash. Since then a different color scheme, predominantly blue, has been adopted. Robbie Shaw

177

mere 75kts while the maximum pitch angle reached almost 53°. The CVR recorded a cluster of stall warning and system alarms as the aircraft reached a maximum altitude of 1,730ft before beginning to fall uncontrollably towards the ground. There were frantic shouts of "Power, power!" and "Push the nose down!" recorded on the tapes but the aircraft did not respond and hit the ground at 20.15:45hrs, just over a minute and a half from the time that the first officer had inadvertently triggered the go around lever.

The accident investigators were able to compile an amazingly accurate picture of the exact sequence of events during these final minutes by means of the data recovered from the CVR and DFDR. However, although this set out what had happened, they could only surmise at the reasons as to why various actions had been taken. The key question surrounded the operation of the go-around lever and the most likely explanation relied on the fact that it was positioned immediately below the thrust lever knob and operated in the same sense. Thus it was possible that the first officer, while flying the aircraft manually, attempted to reduce power by pulling back the thrust lever and at the same time accidentally caught and operated the go around lever. Another explanation was that he had mistakenly operated it instead of the autothrottle disengage button. Whatever the reason, it set in motion the events which led quickly to the final destruction of the aircraft.

The other major contributory factor was the crew's persistent attempts to lower the nose by pushing forward on the control column in an attempt to override the automatic flight system which was initiating the go around maneuver. In fact Airbus were well aware of the dangers inherent in such a situation following earlier incidents involving an A300 at Helsinki in January 1989, and an A310 at Moscow in February 1991, although neither of these resulted in fatal accidents. However, a caution was added to the Flight Crew Operating Manuals (FCOM) in which pilots were warned that an out of trim condition could occur if the autopilot was overridden in pitch while in the land or go around mode. The caution was confusingly worded though and significantly failed to make clear that selection of some alternative autopilot modes, particularly VS (Vertical Speed), would cause the go around indication to disappear from the flight management display even though it was still operating in that mode. Even so, these ambiguities need not have been important because Airbus had actually produced a modification (SB A300-22-6021) which caused the autopilots to disengage automatically if a force greater than 15kg (32lb) was applied to the control wheel while the aircraft was in the go around mode at a radio altitude greater than 400ft. Unfortunately this modification was only issued as "recommended" and not "mandatory," and it had not been incorporated in this aircraft.

The report also looked at the qualifications and training status of the crew members and concluded that, although China Airlines had basically complied with all the required training and competency checks, it could not be determined if either crew member had actually experienced the effects of attempting to override the autopilot in the go around mode while undergoing their simulator checks. These incidentally were carried out on the Thai International Airways simulators at Bangkok as China Airlines did not have any of their own. The report concluded that as the CVR

Above: *Overall the A300 has sold well to Asian airlines such as JAS (as here) with an excellent safety record.* Airbus Industrie

recording clearly showed the crew's relative lack of understanding of the automatic flight system, then their training was, *de facto*, inadequate.

In the immediate aftermath of the crash, the airport fire and rescue services were alerted and raced to the scene. The accident report goes into some detail concerning the response and notes that over 3,000 personnel were involved together with 144 vehicles and a helicopter. Rather bizarrely, 107 dentists were included in these figures but this is an indication of the later post mortem work done on identifying the many burned bodies rather than an implication that they actually attended at the crash scene. It was not until 21.48hrs that the last of the fires in the wreckage was extinguished, although by then the few survivors had already been located and transported to nearby hospitals.

The repercussions of this accident were widespread and the accident report made many recommendations which were followed up by China Airlines and the Taiwan civil aviation authorities, Airbus Industrie, and various other interested parties. As far as the airline was concerned, its cockpit crew procedures were tightened and additional training for pilots was introduced so that the effects of attempting to override the automatic flight control system when operating in the go around mode were fully understood. Other civil aviation bodies such as the US National Transport Safety Board also recommended similar actions by their own national Airbus operators. Airbus Industrie again notified all A300 and A310 operators of the hazards of this situation and followed up by making the previous SB A300-22-6021 modification mandatory. Had this originally been the case, it is entirely likely that this tragic accident would not have occurred.

16 Everglades, Miami, USA, 1996
ValuJet McDonnell Douglas DC-9-32

Michael Sharpe

The fatal crash of ValuJet Flight 592 in the Everglades in May 1996 was, in the eyes of many industry watchers and NTSB staff, the inevitable result of the progressive deregulation of the US airline industry. A large body of these people believe that deregulation, which has—in theory—created a free market for domestic operations, has also had the negative effect of compromising air safety.

Congress' decision to bow to industry pressure and allow further deregulation in 1978 was supposed to guarantee lower prices for the American consumer and end the monopoly on national air routes. In this respect the policy has been successful, although some analysts argue that in fact a regulated industry would have been able to funnel savings back to the consumer and that deregulation was therefore unnecessary.

Critics argue that by allowing cut-throat profit driven business practices into the air transportation industry, the temptation of small operators working within tight budgetary planning to cut corners on safety has, in some instances, been overwhelming. Before deregulation, air fares gradually became cheaper over time because regulated airlines were guaranteed a profit, which could then fund the purchase of new and more efficient aircraft equipped with the latest in safety equipment. The savings in fuel and maintenance costs could then be passed along to the customer. Since deregulation, airlines have been forced to trim expenses wherever they can. They cut maintenance crews and sub-contract work to unqualified companies, cut the in-flight hot meals (some would see this as a bonus!), reduce the number of flight attendants, and, perhaps most importantly, use older, recycled planes.

The larger and more established carriers operating on international routes employ the best of the pilots, as they can afford to pay the wages that experience and skill command. Start-up airlines tend to opt for second-string pilots with less experience because they are cheaper to hire, and rarely do they employ a large full time maintenance staff. And in a competitive market place, it is only a matter of time before another operator undercuts you, whereupon further savings must be made to maintain profitability. The danger of deregulation is that the path of relentless cost-cutting (rather than steady technical upgrading) yields a competitive race to the bottom.

Above: *Divers search the Everglades for DC-9 wreckage.* Associated Press Photograph

ValuJet Airlines, Inc., a new entrant air carrier (any airline with less than five years history is designated new entrant by the Federal Aviation Administration) based in Atlanta, Georgia, was incorporated on July 10, 1992, under the name Charter Way, Inc. The company name was changed to ValuJet in May 1993, and the airline began flight operations under 14 CFR Part 121 on October 26, 1993, with two Douglas DC-9-32s. ValuJet, as its name implies, competed mainly by offering discounted, no frills air fares along US national trunk routes, operating eight daily flights between Atlanta, Georgia, and Jacksonville, Orlando, and Tampa, Florida.

By March 1994, the fleet size had grown to 10 airplanes and the number of daily scheduled flights had increased to 70, with a new service to Washington's Dulles International Airport. About a year later, the airplane fleet consisted of 14 DC-9s and scheduled service had increased to 92 daily flights, with Chicago and Philadelphia being added to the schedule. By December 1995, ValuJet had increased its fleet size to 22 airplanes, served 17 cities, and operated 124 daily scheduled flights.

In 1996, ValuJet continued its growth with scheduled flights to New York and 31 cities in the East, the South, the Midwest, and the Southwest, and increased its DC-9 fleet to 48. At the time of the accident, ValuJet's fleet consisted of 52 airplanes: 4 DC-9-20s, 44 DC-9-30s, and 4 MD-80s. Of the total fleet, 44 were used for scheduled line operations and 8 were used for maintenance, training, and operational spares. The airline employed 191 captains and 209 first officers.

ValuJet was one of the countless competitors in a marketplace congested with start-up airlines seeking to profit from deregulation. By early 1996 ValuJet's recycled DC-9s were among the oldest in the skies, averaging over 26 years old, compared to 15 years for all domestic airlines, and less than 12 for American, Delta and United. A 25-year-old plane can of course be perfectly airworthy if maintained properly—many of the aircraft in USAF and Navy service are of considerable vintage. However, at the time of the accident, ValuJet was under close scrutiny by the Federal Aviation Administration (FAA) because of its appalling maintenance record. New planes are enormously expensive and it is often the case that the more that airlines undergo cut-throat downsizing, the more they try to squeeze out of ageing aircraft. ValuJet contracted out most of its maintenance work to SabreTech, Incorporated, a Miami subsidiary of St. Louis-based Sabreliner Corp.

SabreTech, Incorporated was an FAA-certificated domestic repair station. Its original Air Agency Certificate, certificate No. RD3R811L, was issued December 3, 1969, when Sabreliner was operating as DynAir Tech of Florida, Inc. It began running as SabreTech, Inc., on February 1, 1996, after Sabreliner Corporation, headquartered in St. Louis, Missouri, purchased DynCorp's DynAir Tech maintenance operations in Texas, Arizona, and Florida. Although DynAir had performed maintenance on ValuJet airplanes as early as 1993, no heavy checks were done until May 1995, and there was no ongoing formal "Aircraft Maintenance Service Agreement" until September 15, 1995. Before this date, a separate maintenance agreement was executed for each individual aircraft.

The log of incidents relating to ValuJet aircraft in the period 1994–96 makes for some startling reading, and raises some pertinent questions about the safety of their aircraft and the quality of maintenance that SabreTech was providing.

During 1995 alone, ValuJet experienced at least 66 aborted take-offs and unscheduled landings, and had four times the number of flight disruptions as TWA, with about the same sized fleet. Nine of the incidents were serious. The worst of them occurred in June 1995, when a DC-9's engine caught fire during take-off from Atlanta. Six crew members and 52 passengers evacuated safely, although one flight attendant was seriously burned. Operations were constantly hampered by aborted take-offs and unscheduled landings, prompted by the failure of warning lights, engine hydraulics, door seals, loose oil caps, dirty switches, malfunctioning bulbs, and a host of other problems indicative of slack maintenance work.

In this period one of ValuJet's DC-9-32s, registered as N904VJ, made seven forced landings, due to a variety of malfunctions. This aircraft was delivered to Delta Air Lines, the launch customer, as N1281L, c/n 47377, on May 27, 1969, and served with this carrier until 1992 when it was reacquired by McDonnell Douglas. In December 1993, ValuJet bought the aircraft.

Douglas' DC-9 went from design to flight in a little over 30 months during the early 1960s, and, like the Boeing 727, was targeted at operators who needed a small jet that could use runways in the 10,000ft range usually only available to slower piston-engine types. The -32 is a stretched version of the original aircraft with accommodation for 105 people and 14,000lb thrust JT8D-7 turbofans. Designed primarily for operations on the US East Coast and in Europe, where runways in the 10,000ft range were generally available, it first became available in January 1967. N904VJ had a revised cabin seating configuration for 113 Economy class passengers and up to the time of the accident had a total flying time of 68,395 hours accumulated over 80,663 cycles (a cycle being defined as a flight involving take-off and landing).

At 14.04hrs on Saturday, May 11, 1996, ValuJet Flight 592, assigned to N904VJ, lifted off Miami International's runway 09L, bound for Atlanta-Hartsfield International Airport, the company's hub. On the DC-9's flightdeck that afternoon was Captain Candalyn Kubeck and First Officer Richard Hazen. The captain, age 35, had experience on the DC-9, B-737, SA-227, and BE-1900. She also held flight instructor, ground instructor, and ATC tower operator certificates. She became an employee of ValuJet on November 25, 1993 and was assigned as a DC-9 captain on May 1, 1994. At the time of the accident she had accumulated 8,928 flight hours, 2,116 of them on the DC-9. On September 23, 1995, while serving as Pilot In Command of a ValuJet flight that departed Dallas Forth Worth, Kubeck experienced an emergency caused by an overheated air conditioning pack. According to the incident report filed by the captain, flight attendants notified the flight crew of smoke in the cabin shortly after take-off. On this occasion the airplane returned safely to DFW.

The first officer, age 52, became an employee of ValuJet on November 13, 1995. He finished his training and successfully completed a PIC (pilot in command) proficiency check in the DC-9 in Atlanta on November 14. According to company records, Hazen had accumulated 6,448 total flight hours as a pilot, and had a further 5,400 hours as a military and civilian flight engineer. He had 2,148 hours of DC-9 experience.

Carrying three other crew members and 105 passengers, Flight 592, callsign Critter 592, climbed northwest over the Florida Everglades on heading 300°. At 14.10hrs, while flying at 10,628ft at 232kts Indicated Air Speed (IAS) the altitude dropped 815ft and the IAS decreased 34kts in three seconds. Shortly thereafter the crew requested permission to return to Miami due to smoke in the cockpit. Flight 592 was vectored for a runway 12 approach. At 7,207ft, descending at 260kts on a 210° heading, the FDR stopped recording. Fifty seconds later ValuJet 592 struck a swamp with the nose pitched down 75–80° and disintegrated.

Rescue crews dispatched to the area had to use air boats to reach the crash site, and were forced to bring in special equipment to protect them from jet fuel. Though the search continued for nearly a month, no survivors were ever found and to date, only 75% of the aircraft and the remains of only 37 passengers have been located. Fortunately, the CVR and FDR were found.

Analysis of the CVR and FDR revealed information that allowed NTSB officials to build a picture of the events. About six minutes after departure, the crew noticed some sort of electrical anomaly and the CVR recorded Captain Kubeck saying "we're losing everything," indicating a possible loss of electrical power on the flightdeck. Just after this, shouts of "fire" were heard on the CVR. First Officer Hazen immediately told Miami departure that 592 needed to return to Miami. At this time, 592 was about 100 miles out of Miami and climbing to 16,000ft. Miami control gave 592 vectors back to the southeast and cleared them to descend to 5,000ft. The senior flight attendant came forward to the flightdeck to tell the crew that there was fire in the cabin and that oxygen needed to be provided. Hazen continued to query Miami for assistance until the aircraft plunged into the swampy Everglades. The CVR transcript sounded like this:

Captain: "We got some electrical problem."

14.10:17hrs, F/O: "Yeah."

14.10:18hrs, F/O: "That battery charger's kickin' in. Ooh, we gotta."

14.10:20hrs, Capt: "We're losing everything."

14.10:21hrs, Miami Controller: "Critter five nine two, contact Miami center on one thirty two forty five, so long."

14.10:22hrs, Capt: "We need, we need to go back to Miami."

14.10:23hrs, CAM [=Unidentified voice(s)]**:** (*Sounds of shouting from passenger cabin.*)

14.10:25hrs, CAM: "Fire, fire, fire, fire" [from female voices in cabin]

14.10:27hrs, CAM: "We're on fire, we're on fire."

14.10:28hrs, CAM: (*sound of tone similar to landing gear warning horn for three seconds.*)

14.10:30hrs, Capt: "** to Miami."

14.10:29hrs, Miami Controller: "Critter five ninety two contact Miami center, one thirty two forty five."

14.10:32hrs, F/O "Uh, five ninety two needs immediate return to Miami."

14.10:35hrs, Miami Controller: "Critter five ninety two uh, roger, turn left heading two seven zero. Descend and maintain 7,000."

14.10:36hrs, CAM: (*Sounds of shouting from passenger cabin subsides.*)

14.10:39hrs, F/O: "Two seven zero, 7,000, five ninety two."

14.10:41hrs, Miami Controller: "What kind of problem are you havin'?"

14.10:42hrs, CAM: (*Sound of horn.*)

14.10:44hrs, Capt: "Fire."

14.10:46hrs, F/O: "Uh, smoke in the cockp . . . smoke in the cabin."

14.10:47hrs, Miami Controller: "Roger."

14.10:49hrs, Captain: "What altitude?"

14.10:49hrs, F/O: "7,000."

14.10:52hrs, CAM: (Sound similar to cockpit door moving.)

14.10:57hrs, CAM [sound of six chimes similar to cabin service interphone]

14.10:58hrs, CAM-3 [=Unidentified cabin crew member]**:** "OK, we need oxygen, we can't get oxygen back there."

14.11:00hrs, Intercom: (*Sound similar to microphone being keyed only on interphone channel.*)

14.11:02hrs, CAM-3: "Ba, is there a way we could test them?" (*Sound of clearing her voice.*)

14.11:07hrs, Miami Controller: "Critter five ninety two uh, when able to turn left heading two five zero. Descend and maintain 5,000."

14.11:08hrs, CAM: (*Sound of chimes similar to cabin service interphone.*)

14.11:10hrs, CAM: (*Sounds of shouting from passenger cabin.*)

14.11:11hrs, F/O: "Two five zero 7,000."

14.11:12hrs, CAM-3: "Completely on fire."

14.11:14hrs, CAM: (*Sounds of shouting from passenger cabin subsides.*)

Above: *An Inex Adria DC-9-32 crashed near Prague on October 30, 1975, while making an approach to land. The crew did not follow the correct instrument procedure and the aircraft hit the ground killing 77 out of the 124 people on board.* ASM Photo

Below: *Map showing crash site.*

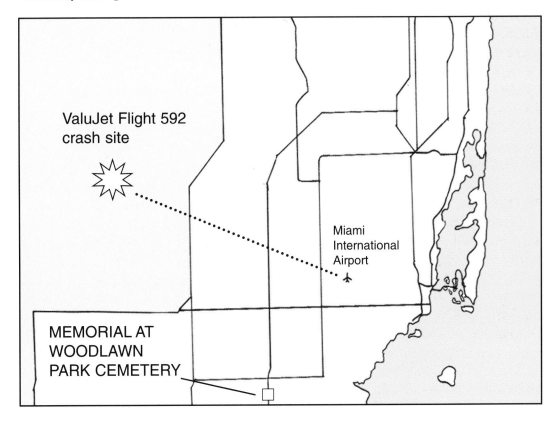

14.11:19hrs, F/O: "Outta nine."

14.11:19hrs, CAM: (*Sound of intermittent horn.*)

14.11:21hrs, CAM (*Sound similar to loud rushing air.*)

14.11:38hrs, F/O: "Critter five ninety two we need the uh, closest airport available."

14.11:42hrs, Miami Controller: "Critter five ninety two, they're gonna be standing by for you. You can plan . . ."

14.11:45hrs, CAM: (*One minute and twelve second interruption in CVR recording.*)

14.12:57hrs, CAM: (*Sound of tone similar to power interruption to CVR.*)

14.12:57hrs, CAM: (*Sound similar to loud rushing air.*)

At the early stages in the investigation, lacking a significant amount of physical evidence, investigators had to rely on clues in the CVR and FDR data. The long gap at the end of the CVR data and various eyewitness accounts suggested that the flight crew was not able to maintain control of the aircraft during the last minutes of flight, possibly because of incapacitation by smoke or the effects of fire. It was clear that there was some sort of fire on board the aircraft during the flight, but until the recovery of key sections of the airframe it was impossible to determine the source.

After the forward cargo section was found the mists began to clear. It was now possible to ascertain that there had been an intense fire in the middle of the forward cargo hold, that burned through the cabin floor at seat rows 5 and 6 on the left-hand side. Arson was ruled out but a check through the flight inventory revealed that Critter 592 had been carrying boxes containing 144 chemical oxygen generators, and two MD-80 main wheel tires in the forward hold. In the course of the recovery efforts, the search crews were able to locate several of these oxygen generators, which were being transported to ValuJet's Atlanta base. They were labeled as empty. Investigators were able to determine that the canisters were not empty and that vital safety rings were not in place. Testing revealed that these canisters could ignite intense fires very rapidly if activated. Although it is impossible to specify the exact time that the fire began, it is thought that it probably started when the boxes containing the generators shifted as the aircraft was rotated at take-off point, activating one or more of them. It was concluded that that the loss of control experienced by the crew was the result of this fire burning through the control linkages.

As is invariably the case in fatal accidents caused by operator negligence, both ValuJet and SabreTech were keen to avoid damaging litigation by relatives of the deceased, and accusations and counter-accusations were traded though the press.

In the week prior to the publication of the NTSB report ValuJet told federal investigators, and the national media, that Sabretech deliberately mislabeled the shipment of oxygen canisters implicated in the Everglades crash. ValuJet claimed that SabreTech was anxious to pass an inspection by a potential client, Continental Airlines, and mislabeled five boxes of hazardous oxygen canisters to get them "off the shop floor" in Miami. SabreTech's attorney responded angrily, calling the charges preposterous, and said federal investigators found that ValuJet had knowingly carried hazardous materials at least six times in 1996.

The NTSB report, published in August 1997, was highly critical of the airline, the FAA, and SabreTech. It directed particular criticism at "the failure of SabreTech to properly prepare, package, identify, and track unexpended chemical oxygen generators before presenting them to ValuJet for carriage," as well as "the failure of ValuJet to properly oversee its contract maintenance program to ensure compliance with maintenance, maintenance training, and hazardous materials requirements and practices," and "the failure of Federal Aviation Administration (FAA) to require smoke detection and fire suppression systems in Class D cargo compartments."

Also contributing to the accident was "the failure of the FAA to adequately monitor ValuJet's heavy maintenance program and responsibilities, including ValuJet's oversight of its contractors, and SabreTech's repair station certificate; the failure of the FAA to adequately respond to prior chemical oxygen generator fires with programs to address the potential hazards; and the failure of ValuJet to ensure that both ValuJet and contract maintenance employees were aware of the carrier's no-carry hazardous materials policy and had received appropriate hazardous materials training."

The report had a pronounced effect on the fortunes of ValuJet. A year after the incident ValuJet was flying to only 24 cities, compared to 31 before the accident. The fleet had been reduced by more than 50% to 24 aircraft, compared to 51 before. Some 2,200 of the 4,200 employees had lost their jobs in the down-sizing. Before the crash of Flight 592, four FAA inspectors were assigned to monitor ValuJet. In the 30 days after the crash, inspectors made an average of 1.2 inspections per day per airplane, the most intense scrutiny in the history of commercial aviation, and 11 full-time inspectors were subsequently assigned to the carrier. In that same year ValuJet aircraft were involved in two minor incidents—less than the current industry average of about three for similarly sized carriers. A plane lost engine oil pressure after take-off and returned to land safely. Another plane also landed safely after a wing-slats' activating motor wouldn't shut off.

On November 17, 1997, shareholders of ValuJet, Inc. approved the merger of the company and AirWays Corporation. Shareholders also voted to rename the holding company AirTran Holdings, Inc. The combined carriers serve 46 cities and operate a fleet of 43 aircraft, comprised of 32 DC-9 aircraft and 11 737s with 239 peak daily departures. AirTran is one of the two launch customers for the new Boeing 717, which can trace its lineage directly back to the DC-9. In the 18 months that it has been operating this new airline has demonstrated a much improved safety record.

In theory, deregulation was supposed to apply to fares and routes; safety was to stay regulated. Anybody could enter the airline business, but the competence of pilots and the rigor of aircraft maintenance would all stay tightly supervised by government. In practice, the economic regulation of airlines has spilled over into the regulation of safety. The regulatory body, the FAA, has fewer people to monitor a whole host of new (and old) aircraft, mechanics, and pilots. Whole categories of management reports are no longer required, leaving government with less information to go on. Price competition in air travel is healthy, but only when operated within a vigorous regulatory presence to prevent that competition from driving out necessary safety outlays and compromising the ability of the industry to invest in better airplanes. Competition can benefit air travelers—but only with a bigger dose of regulation.

17 Charkhi-Dadri, India, 1996 Saudi Arabian Airlines Boeing 747-168B and Kazakhstan Airlines Ilyushin Il-76TD

Leo Marriott

The great increase in commercial air transport in recent decades has put a great strain on the world's air traffic control infrastructures. In general, the United States and Europe have kept pace by a combination of technological innovation, more efficient use of airspace, increasingly complex control procedures, and improved training for ATC staff. Fortunately, collisions between commercial aircraft are rare, but not unknown. In Europe, 63 people died when a DC-9 and a Convair 990 collided over Nantes, France in 1973, while a further 176 people were killed in a collision between a Trident and a DC-9 near Zagreb in 1976. In America there have been a few collisions between airliners and light aircraft including one between a Cessna 172 and a Boeing 727 over San Diego in 1978 in which 147 lives were lost. All of these were eclipsed by the collision over India on November 12, 1996, in which all 346 occupants of the two aircraft, a Boeing 747 airliner and an Ilyushin Il-76 freighter, were killed.

Investigators of such events are normally faced with one of two possible causes. Either air traffic control has made an error, or the crews of one or both of the aircraft have not responded correctly to instructions. In either case, a mechanical or technical fault is rare, and the cause will almost certainly lie in a human error of some description. Unfortunately this was very much the case in this major accident. The two aircraft involved were a Saudi Arabia Airlines Boeing 747-168B operating a scheduled passenger flight from Delhi to Dhahran and a Kazakhstan Airlines Ilyushin Il-76TD on a charter flight from Chimkent (Kazakhstan) to Delhi. The Saudi 747 had earlier flown from Jeddah to Delhi and had departed again at 13.03hrs (18.33hrs, Indian Standard Time) for the return sector. Its callsign was SV763 and it carried a total of 312 persons on board, including 23 crew. The flight was under the command of 47 year old Captain Khalid Al-Shubaily, an experienced pilot with almost 10,000 hours flight time although only just over 100 hours as pilot in command on Boeing 747s. The planned route for flight SV763 after departure from

Right: *An example of an Ilyushin Il-76.* Leo Marriott

runway 28 at Delhi involved a PARVI ONE departure and then along airway Golf 452. The requested cruising level was approximately 35,000ft and the initial ATC clearance was to 26,000ft. On departure, the Saudi flight contacted Delhi Approach on frequency 127.9 MHz and was instructed to climb to Flight Level (FL) 100 (flight level is a measure of altitude that roughly equates to one unit for every 100ft: thus FL100 is approximately 10,000ft). However, the 747 was climbing rapidly and was approaching FL100 only four minutes after take-off and the pilot requested further climb at 13.07hrs. The Delhi radar controller cleared SV763 to continue climbing to FL140 but when, two minutes later, the pilot again reported approaching the assigned level the controller told him to, "Maintain flight level one four zero and standby for higher." This instruction was positively acknowledged by the pilot with the transmission, "Saudi seven six three maintain one four zero." At this point the 747 was established on the track of airway Golf 425 which was defined by the 270° radial from the Delhi VOR.

In the meantime, Kazakhstan Il-76TD was inbound to Delhi having departed from Chimkent at 10.25hrs as Flight Kazak 1907. There were ten crew and only 37 passengers aboard the big aircraft which was more often used for cargo flights. In contrast to Western airliners which typically carried a flightdeck crew of two pilots, sometimes supplemented by a flight engineer, the Kazak Ilyushin had a flightcrew of five. In addition to the captain, Alexander Robertovich Cherepanov, there was a co-pilot, flight engineer, navigator, and radio operator. Airlines such as Kazakhstan had come into being following the break up of the former USSR into the Confederation of Independent States (CIS) and many were originally operating divisions of the massive state airline Aeroflot, whose practices and procedures were adopted for the most part. After take-off from Chimkent at 10.25hrs (within five minutes of its flight plan departure time) it had climbed to cruise at FL330 and had contacted Delhi Radio on HF at 11.00hrs to confirm details of its ETA to enter Indian airspace at point TIGER (on airway Golf 452) at 12.43hrs. ETA for Delhi was 13.23hrs. Some ten minutes after passing TIGER, contact was established with Delhi Area Control on the normal VHF frequency (124.55 MHz) and at that time was passing point LUNKA some 177 miles due west of the Delhi VOR. At 12.58hrs Delhi Control cleared Kazak 1907 to descend to 25,000ft and subsequently, at 13.03hrs, to continue descent to FL180 with a request to report passing FL180. However, before this level was reached, the aircraft was asked to contact Delhi Approach on frequency 127.9 MHz.

The pilot of Kazak 1907 checked in with approach at 13.05hrs and reported passing FL230 at 74 miles from the Delhi VOR. The approach controller cleared the aircraft for further descent to FL150 and instructed the pilot to report reaching that level. No report was actually received from the pilot until at 13.10hrs, prompted by a query from the controller, he confirmed that the Il-76 was now level at FL150 and still on the 270° radial. By this time the aircraft had been identified on radar, as was the Saudi 747 which had just leveled off at 14,000ft and was seen to be on a

Right: The Saudi Arabian Airlines Boeing 747-168B involved in the Charkhi-Dadri collision. It is seen in the Philippines being repaired following an earlier incident. ASM Photo

reciprocal track some ten miles ahead. Having received confirmation from both pilots that they were maintaining altitudes safely 1,000ft apart, the controller planned to wait until the two aircraft had passed before initiating further climb for the outbound Saudi and to give clearance for the Ilyushin to begin further descent into Delhi. Most modern air traffic control centers, including all those in Europe and the United States, are equipped with radar displays which show the identity and altitude of each aircraft. This information is derived by a ground based Secondary Surveillance Radar system (SSR) interrogating the aircraft's transponder. Unfortunately the Delhi Center did not have such equipment and the controller could merely see "blips" on his screen indicating the position of the two aircraft but giving no indication of their altitude. He was therefore totally reliant on the accuracy of the pilot's reports, which he had no reason to doubt. Nevertheless, he was able to tell the Kazak pilot that the Saudi 747 was "12 o'clock at ten miles, likely to cross in another five miles." The use of the clock code should have alerted the Kazak pilot to the fact that the other aircraft was closing from straight ahead, but he obviously could not see it as he asked for clarification of the distance. To this, the approach controller replied, "Traffic is at eight miles now flight level one four zero." This information was acknowledged and the pilot said they were looking for the traffic.

This was the last transmission from the Il-76 but a few seconds later a transmission in Arabic was recorded on the tapes although at the time, the listeners on the ground did not understand its significance. The subsequent transcript records the words as "*Astaghfor Allah, Ashhau Unlealaha Ella Allah.*" Saudi representatives confirmed that it had come from their aircraft and that the English translation was "God forgiveness, I witness no other God but Allah."

Initially the controller placed no significance on this transmission but shortly afterward he realized that he had lost radar contact with both aircraft. At 13.12hrs a US Air Force aircraft flying approximately 15 miles north of the point where the blips were last observed reported seeing a fireball or explosion in the sky followed by two distinct fires on the ground. The many attempts to raise the Kazak or Saudi aircraft on the radio were met with silence and realization slowly dawned that the two aircraft must have collided and crashed to the ground. These fears were quickly confirmed as reports began to come in from villages in the Bhiwani district, some 60 miles west of Delhi, that wreckage was spread over two distinct crash sites. It was quickly apparent that there were no survivors in what was now India's worst air disaster and, at the time, the third worst ever in terms of fatalities. There was obvious pressure from many sources to determine the cause of the accident, not least from the Indian Government which would naturally have wished to show that its own ATC services were not to blame.

Investigators were quick to arrive at the scene and an examination of the wreckage indicated that in the actual collision the port wing and engines of the Saudi aircraft had sliced through the port wing of the Il-76. In addition the tail of the 747 had chopped off part of the horizontal stabilizer of the Kazak aircraft. Other indications confirmed the report of the USAF pilot who witnessed the aftermath of the collision that both aircraft had caught fire. They had subsequently disintegrated in the air and spread wreckage over a wide area at two distinct sites. The nose

Above: *The flightdeck of the Ilyushin Il-76. This type of aircraft has been involved in a number of other incidents and fatal accidents including a number of crashes on approach to land.* ASM Photo

section and flightdeck of the 747 were completely destroyed by the impact with the ground and were also badly burned so that nothing of any use to the investigation could be salvaged. In particular no useful components of the two altimeters could be found. The nose section of the Ilyushin was found relatively intact and four altimeters, two calibrated to read in meters and two reading in feet, were recovered. More fortunately, the Cockpit Voice Recorders (CVR) and flight data recorders from both aircraft were recovered intact with only superficial scratching to their outer casings.

Once all available evidence had been gathered a formal judicial court of enquiry was set up by the Indian authorities at which the two airlines and the Indian air traffic control organization were represented. The first point to be established was the exact altitude or flight level at which the collision had occurred. Eventually the evidence from the 747's flight data recorder was accepted as being the most accurate and this put the aircraft almost exactly at 14,000ft to within a tolerance of 100ft.

Although the Ilyushin's altimeters had been recovered, the information derived from them turned out to be confusing as there was discrepancy of 97 meters (319ft) between the captain's and co-pilot's metric instruments, while the other two instruments were too damaged to give any reliable readings although one was set to the standard reference datum 1013 Hpa (Mb) and the other to 1012 Hpa (Mb). This at least indicated that the crew were flying at flight levels and not altitudes (A pilot normally sets the sea level atmospheric pressure on the altimeter sub scale so that the instrument gives an accurate indication of altitude. However as the sea level pressure varies considerably from place to place and over time, the convention is that a standard setting of 1013 Hpa (Mb) is used above specified altitudes by all pilots and the aircraft is then flying at a Flight Level (FL). In this case, if the altimeter read 14,000ft with 1013 set on the sub scale, then the aircraft would be at flight level 140 although this would actually be above or below an actual altitude of 14,000ft above sea level depending on the actual sea level pressure.)

Having established the level at which the collision took place, the inquiry then considered the role of air traffic control. It is apparent from the final report that many members of the inquiry had little knowledge of basic ATC procedures and much time was spent in looking at how ATC actually functioned and what could be considered normal procedures and safety factors. Although the inquiry eventually determined that the Delhi Approach controller had been subject to a very heavy workload and that the radar equipment was old and outdated, it was also accepted that this had no direct bearing on the events leading up to the collision and that the controller had in fact acted safely and efficiently at all times while the radar had provided enough data for the task at hand. The clearances issued to the two aircraft to respectively maintain FL140 and FL150 conformed in every way with normal ATC practice and should have prevented any chance of a collision if they had been followed by the pilots concerned.

As it had been established that the Saudi crew were flying at their assigned level, attention turned inevitably to the actions of the Kazakhstan crew as indicated by the recordings from the CVR. The first point of interest was that all communication between the aircraft and Delhi ATC was carried out by the radio operator and not by either of the pilots. From the CVR transcript it was determined that the radio operator established contact with Delhi Approach at time 13.04:55hrs and he acknowledged the instruction to descend to FL150. This was also heard by the navigator who converted it into a metric reading of 4,570 meters. A couple of minutes later the radio operator was heard to confirm both figures with the navigator and it is certain that this conversation would have been heard by both pilots.

Between 13.06:10hrs and 13.08:50hrs, the controller could be heard clearing the Saudi flight to FL140 and subsequently receiving a report from the 747 that it was level at FL140. In normal circumstances it would be expected that other pilots on the same frequency would hear and understand these transmissions, and be aware of the presence of the other aircraft, and its level. However, it could not be established whether the Kazak pilots did pay any attention to these instructions or, even if they heard them, whether they would have understood what was being said (all the ATC instructions were, of course, spoken in English as is standard aviation practice in

Above: *The Ilyushin Il-76 has a distinctive profile that shows its military ancestry.* ASM Photo

Below: *The Kazakhstan IL-76 involved in the accident seen at Stansted.* ASM Photo

most parts of the world, although not in Russia and the CIS). At 13.08:59hrs, in response to a query from ATC, the Kazak radio operator reported that the aircraft had, "Now reached flight level one four zero." However, analysis of the Ilyushin's flight data recorder showed that the aircraft was actually at an altitude of 16,348ft at that time and was still descending. The reason for the incorrect information passed by the radio operator was unclear although it may have been just a casual approximation or because he failed to differentiate between "approaching" and "reaching" an altitude or level.

Having been told that the Il-76 was level at FL150, the controller then passed information on to the opposite direction Boeing 747 at FL140 but it appeared that the radio operator did not fully understand what was being said and requested clarification. In the background the pilots could be heard discussing the traffic information while the controller updated the traffic information saying, "Traffic is at eight miles, level one four zero." To this the radio operator replied, "Now looking, one nine zero seven." It then appeared that the co-pilot, who was flying the aircraft, mistakenly understood that Kazak Il-76 was cleared to FL140 and continued descending. This action was not challenged by the navigator who should have been monitoring the descent, nor by the captain who appeared unaware of the developing situation until alerted by the radio operator who, at 13.09:57hrs suddenly said "Hold the level!" The captain then asked, "What level were we given?" This conversation took place only 18 seconds before the collision but further confusion resulted from the flight engineer calling out, "Maintain" (this was possibly a reference to FL140 at which the aircraft had just leveled out). However, the radio operator, realizing that the captain was now unsure of the correct level, and being unable to see the altimeters directly, shouted out, "Keep the one fiftieth, don't descend!"

At last the full urgency of the situation dawned on the crew. The autopilot was switched off (at 13.10:05hrs, some 11 seconds before collision) and the captain asked the flight engineer for more power in order to initiate a climb. But it was now too late. Even as the radio operator was calling out to "Get to one five zero. . ." the voice recordings cease as the impact occurred. The final unfortunate circumstance was that both aircraft were almost certainly flying in cloud and the chances of a visual sighting were virtually nil. The official accident report was quite specific in attributing the main cause of the accident to the actions of the Kazak crew. In particular it cites a poor understanding of English and their failure to monitor the general traffic situation by listening to the ATC transmissions. However, even if this could be thought excusable to some extent, it goes on to comment on the poor teamwork on the flightdeck, the lack of positive leadership from the captain, and a failure to monitor each others actions.

Naturally, the Kazakhstan aviation authorities were not happy with this version of events and put forward the theory that the descent below FL150 had been caused by turbulence. This possibility was extensively examined and, while there were some indications of the sort of light turbulence normally experienced when entering cloud, there was no other evidence to support this proposition. In addition the CVR recordings carried no reference at all concerning turbulence.

Finally the actions of air traffic control were closely examined. This was the responsibility of the Airports Authority of India (AAI) who provided the equipment and staff. As has already been stated, ATC was found to have acted efficiently and correctly and could in no way be held directly responsible for the accident. However, the investigation uncovered a number of factors which were undesirable and, significantly, many of the accident report's recommendations were directly aimed at improving the standard and quality of ATC in India. Measures to improve the status and qualification of controllers were suggested, it being found that Indian controllers were not subject to a system of licensing as was standard in almost all other countries. The lack of capacity at Delhi ATCC was also recognized and the AAI undertook to provide an expansion from 2 to 4 sectors to cope with increasing traffic. Another point addressed was airspace management and the structure of the G-452 Airway. From August 14, 1997, this became a unidirectional route with the adjacent Airway Alpha 466 also being made unidirectional. This provided separate routings for arriving and departing traffic and immediately lessened the risk of a head-on collision. One of the reasons that this had not been done before was the poor co-operation between military and civil ATC authorities with the former reluctant to release sections of airspace for civil use—effectively confining civil flights to narrow corridors.

The lack of SSR was also recognized as a factor. If this had been available the controller might well have spotted the impending collision. The installation of an automated ATC system based on the use of SSR was therefore accorded a high priority in the reports findings, although in fact such a system was being installed at the time of accident. Raytheon, a US-based electronics company had been awarded a $120 million contract and this should have been operational by mid-1996 but its commissioning did not actually occur until well into 1997.

On a related issue, the report also recommended that all civil transport aircraft should be equipped with a Traffic Alert and Collision Avoidance System (TCAS). This is a device which receives and interrogates information from transponders aboard other aircraft in its vicinity and, based on the replies, can determine if a risk of collision exists. If such a situation is detected, the pilot is warned and suitable avoiding action triggered if necessary. Such a device is independent of ATC but neither of the two aircraft was so equipped. Following the collision, the authorities subsequently made the carriage of TCAS-II mandatory for commercial aircraft carrying more than 30 passengers operating in Indian airspace after December 31, 1998.

Almost certainly, if any one of the measures had been implemented prior to November 1996 then the collision could have been avoided. As it was, the tragic loss of 346 lives helped to make 1996 the worst ever year for aircraft accidents with no less than 1,840 fatalities from 57 fatal accidents, excluding events caused by non safety related sabotage or hijack incidents. In addition another 364 people were unfortunate victims on the ground at the scene of various crashes. Altogether a depressing picture which required an industry wide global effort to show some positive improvement in more recent years.

18 Long Island, New York, USA, 1996 Trans World Airlines Boeing 747-131
Michael Sharpe

More than three years have lapsed since TWA800 crashed into the waters of the East Moriches, an anonymous area of grey ocean off Long Island, New York. Since that fateful day the incident has attracted an unprecedented level of media and public interest, spawned at least three books and an ever-growing mass of speculative analysis in hyperspace, and continues to provoke fierce debate among experts and concerned onlookers alike.

The NTSB is still engaged in what is already the most expensive and detailed investigation in the history of air accident investigation. Preliminary findings were announced at a public hearing in Baltimore in December 1997 but, lacking firm evidence, so far the NTSB has reserved its final judgment. Pending further scientific analysis the final NTSB report seems some way off. Whatever its conclusions, it seems unlikely that the official explanation will be accepted by the growing band of analysts, many of them with very plausible theories rooted in solid research and analysis, that attribute the destruction of TWA800 and the deaths of its 230 passengers to, variously, a bizarre freak of nature, skullduggery by a foreign power, or another whole host of causes that the US government and its agencies have buried for reasons of national security or self interest. A cynic would say that some of the less coherent theories stem from the American public's great obsession with the intrigues and machinations of government. But it would take a brave person to dismiss the testimony of the growing number of senior politicians, aviation industry professionals and high-ranking military officials, who have refused to swallow the official story.

It must be said that much of the speculation surrounding the accident has been roused by the singular lack of clarity between voices of the FBI, CIA, and NTSB. Public disagreements over the investigations has undermined public confidence in the results of the official investigation and in the Board itself.

Right: *Section of TWA flight 800's wing floats in the Atlantic off Long Island.* CORBIS-Bettmann

When the FBI seized control of the overall Flight 800 investigation it only hampered the NTSB's probe. It ignored and ridiculed expert investigators from other agencies. Furthermore it sustained the theory that the 747 was downed by a bomb or missile long after explosives and aviation-safety specialists were convinced there was no evidence to support that theory. We now have a situation in which a confused, muddled, and often highly speculative mass of theories and counter-theories are batted around the Web, trumpeted or picked apart by often less-than-expert analysts who digest any fragment of evidence or gossip, and try to slot it into a convenient conspiratorial theory. In such a situation clarity is surely a major priority, but in the investigation into TWA800 this has been singularly lacking.

What do we know about TWA800? We know that on July 17, 1996, Boeing 747-131 N93119 was scheduled to operate TWA Flight 800, the mid-afternoon service to Paris Charles De Gaulle. We know that the aircraft was one of the first generation of Boeing 747-100 aircraft and since being manufactured in November 1971 it had accumulated about 93,303 flight hours over 16,869 cycles. On board the airplane were 213 passengers and 17 crew members. The flight was to have been the initial leg of a scheduled three-day sequence for the four-man flight crew. The captain and the captain/check airman, who was acting as first officer, both had worked for TWA for approximately 30 years and were considered senior flight crew members. The flight engineer, who had only about 30 hours as a flight engineer, was on a training flight. The check engineer, who occupied the jump seat, also had considerable experience. The flight was scheduled to depart at 19.00hrs for Charles De Gaulle Airport. but was delayed by more than an hour due to a passenger/baggage mismatch and a disabled piece of ground equipment. Flight 800 took off from runway 22R at 20.19hrs. Visual meteorological conditions prevailed and an instrument flight rules flight plan was filed. The aircraft began climbing to cruising height over Long Island.

Part of the CVR transcript reveals the last moments of the aircraft. (Note Eastwind and Virgin 009 were aircraft in the same area.)

CONTROLLER: "TWA800, climb and maintain one five thousand."
TWA800: "TWA800 heavy, climb and maintain one five thousand, leaving [one] three thousand."

This was the last transmission heard from TWA800. At about 20.45hrs, as the aircraft was ascending through 13,700ft, the primary radar return disappeared from the controller's screen.

EASTWIND: "We just saw an explosion, out here, Stinger Bee 507."
CONTROLLER: "Stinger Bee 507, I'm sorry missed it, yeah you're on 18, did you say something else?"
EASTWIND: "We just saw an explosion up ahead of us here, somewhere about, about 16,000 feet or something like that, it just went down . . ."
EASTWIND: ". . . in the water."
CONTROLLER: (Garbled transmissions)

VIRGIN 009: "Out of my nine o'clock position, sir, it looked like an explosion of some sort, about maybe six to five, six miles out from my nine o'clock position."

CONTROLLER: "Roger that, thank you very much sir, we're investigating that right now."

CONTROLLER: "TWA800, Center . . . TWA eight zero zero, if you can hear Center, ident."

A few minutes later:

CONTROLLER: "TWA800, Center."

CONTROLLER: "TWA800, if you hear Center, ident."

CONTROLLER: "TWA800, Center."

EASTWIND: "I think that was him."

CONTROLLER: "I think so."

EASTWIND: "God bless them."

US Navy, Coastguard and commercial fishing vessels raced to the area but found no survivors in the wreckage-strewn waters. In the days following the incident an armada of ships plied across the six-mile trail of debris marking TWA800's fatal plummet to earth. Much of the heavier wreckage had sunk to the deep ocean floor, but bobbing in the grey ocean swell among the anonymous seat cushions and life jackets they found a depressing flotsam of holiday clothes, briefcases, and children's toys—the debris of a very human tragedy.

The operation to recover the sunken wreckage was a Herculean undertaking. During the summer, deep-water salvage teams scoured the ocean floor to locate the all-important CVR and FDR before winter currents swept them away. At the incident HQ in Calverton, investigators tagged, cataloged, and analyzed even the minutest fragments of wreckage for traces of explosive, scorch marks, or impact damage in their search for a clue. It was quickly ascertained that the bulk of the initial damage had been sustained in the area forward of the leading edge, and a painstakingly reconstruction of the fuselage began. By May of 1997 nearly 95% of the aircraft had been recovered and a 94ft-long portion of the fuselage had been pieced together. An early CVR transcript indicated a routine flight with the captain sitting in the left seat flying the airplane and the check captain sitting in the right seat handling the radio transmissions. Conversation within the cockpit was routine and included all the appropriate checklist requirements. The flight crew discussed a sticky fuel flow gauge, a common occurrence in the 747, and mentioned that they would begin to cross-feed fuel to the engines.

Even as the slow and difficult process of recovery got underway, FBI and CIA agents were alluding to the possibility of criminal activity. The UN policing operation over southern Iraq, to which the US was contributing the bulk of forces, was just one of a long list of possible motives for hostile aggression against US citizens and assets. Lockerbie was still fresh in the minds of everyone. In the ensuing weeks some 91 eyewitnesses were identified, and the process of interviewing them began. But now, with criminal activity long since discounted, an answer to the question

"Why?" is proving somewhat more elusive, and may never be fully satisfied. While the NTSB investigation has focused on a major malfunction in the aircraft systems, leading to a destructive explosion in the center wing tank, at least nine other possible causes have been cited.

The official theory, or at least the one that is being pushed by the NTSB, is that an electrical malfunction, probably due to a short-circuit resulting from contact of worn wiring and most likely specific to older, high-use aircraft, allowed a rogue spark or electrical impulse to enter the environment of a minimally filled, volatile center wing tank and ignite the fuel vapors there. The resulting combustion quickly pushed the front structures of the center wing tank forward, exposing additional areas to the destructive energies originating in the tank. This rapid action then compromised the integrity of the airframe, allowing the fuselage forward of the wings to separate from the aircraft and plummet to the sea. The remainder of the noseless aircraft rapidly climbed about 3,000ft before beginning its fall towards the ocean. As the aircraft fell one or more fuel tanks in the wings ruptured. The large quantity of fuel in the wing tank(s) then ignited, creating the large fireball seen by many eyewitnesses.

Supporting evidence for this theory comes from the known fact that TWA800 sat on the pan at Kennedy on the late afternoon of July 17, allowing a build-up of volatile fuel vapor in the center wing tank. What is less clear is the source of the rogue spark. On earlier models of the 747 thick bundles of electrical wires run aft from the flightdeck. They are thickly armored with aluminum cloth and Kevlar and investigators found no evidence that the wires recovered from the crash site were split or worn. A possible answer is that faulty wiring in the proximity of the wing fuel tanks triggered a flame, which then entered the center fuel tank via a vent hole. A theory that was also cited in the early stages of the investigation by senior NTSB officials is that jet fuel sloshing around in the center tank caused a build-up in static electricity, which then ignited the overheated fuel vapor. If valid, this scenario is virtually unprecedented in the entire operational history of Boeing 747 aircraft and if does prove to be true, it places many thousands of aircraft, not just the 747, at risk.

To support the center wing tank theory, FAA officials attempted to exactly emulate the accident by conducting tests addressing cargo hold hardening on a static ground-parked Boeing 747-100 of similar age and configuration in Bruntingthorpe, England. They also detonated small explosives on the center wing tank of the same plane and recorded the explosions on voice recorders in the hope of aiding analysis of the sound spectrum from the cockpit recorder of TWA flight 800. Crucially, the last 170 milliseconds of the TWA800 CVR recording contained a unique sound signature. Extensive sound spectrum analysis comparing this sound signature both visually and mathematically to other recordings — including bombs, fuel/air explosions and structural failures is still being undertaken.

The CIA has released an animation that purports to show the last moments of the flight, which may be viewed on the Internet.

As it transpired the results of the emulation tests were indecisive, as it has proved impossible to exactly duplicate the purported ignition scenario. This has lent weight to the growing body of opinion that find anomalies in the official story. Their

Above: *NYPD officer watches as flight 800's wreckage is transported from Brooklyn docks to be examined by investigators.* CORBIS-Bettmann

Below: *Map of the crash site.*

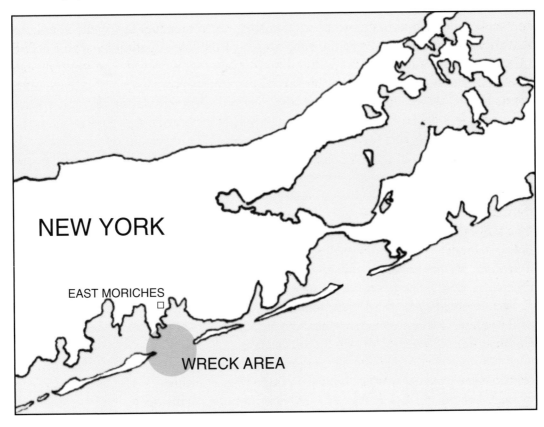

NEW YORK

EAST MORICHES

WRECK AREA

suspicions have no doubt been fueled by the NTSB, which for too long collaborated in cutting off the flow of accurate, detailed information on the status of the accident probe, leading to suspicions that the government was withholding what it really knew about the cause of Flight 800's downing. FBI officials stoked those suspicions with repeated leaks to the media of bomb-damage evidence on Flight 800's debris when in fact no conclusive evidence was in hand.

One of the most coherent voices of dissent comes from a group led by Commander William Donaldson of the Associated Retired Aviation Professionals body. They suggest that pressure from center wing tank ignition would not have been strong enough to detach the nose of the aircraft, that no independent evidence exists of the 3,000ft climb after fuel tank explosion, and that the wreckage reconstruction photographs show that the nose section is not scorched, suggesting it left the aircraft prior to any fire event, not after as this scenario suggests. Eyewitness statements would appear to conflict with the sudden rapid ascent of the aircraft.

Donaldson is a senior ex-US Navy aviator, with considerable experience in air accident investigation, who is proving to be the biggest thorn in the side of the government agencies. His credentials are as impressive as his research. The group also includes Mark Hill—a retired Navy rear admiral, Howard Mann—a former TWA 747 pilot, and Admiral Thomas H. Moorer, former chairman of the Joint Chiefs of Staff. These men believe they have compelling evidence that TWA800 was destroyed not by an explosion triggered by an electrical malfunction, but by a missile which exploded just 60ft from the front of the aircraft.

Since April 1997 ARAP have challenged the official NTSB position in a series of letters to James Hall, Chairman of the NTSB. On July 16, 1998, they released a detailed report that was delivered to the Aviation Subcommittee of the House of Representatives, and more recently have uncovered information they believe provides conclusive proof that TWA800 could have been shot down by one or more shoulder-fired missiles. In May 1999 the Subcommittee on Aviation held a public hearing on the Reauthorization of the National Transportation Safety Board. Testimony was heard from Chairman James Hall of the NTSB, the Rand Corporation and Cdr Donaldson.

Despite the official denials, ARAP was able to present a body of solid evidence that is oddly compelling. Donaldson has interviewed 118 eyewitnesses on 18 boats and 30 locations along 11 miles of shoreline who report seeing a streak of light rise from the surface of the water and merge with the plane before it exploded. He says this streak is the exhaust of a missile. Using global positioning system satellite technology, Donaldson triangulated the locations of the eyewitnesses and the trajectories of the streaks they reported and concluded that the launch site was about three miles offshore.

The voices of some of the many people who back the missile scenario were heard at the public hearing which took place in May 1999. Fred Meyer, a retired Air National Guard major who was flying a helicopter practice mission around Long Island at the time of the incident gave an account of a streak of light arcing through the sky and ending in what looked to him like a military explosion. "I've seen ordnance explosions," said Meyer, a Vietnam veteran. "This was military ordnance."

Another witness, Richard Goss, a carpenter and businessman, said he was having dinner when he saw an ascending streak of light over the Atlantic Ocean, ending in an explosion. He said he twice talked with FBI investigators, but they didn't follow up with him.

The FBI and NTSB have countered that the witnesses saw either burning jet fuel falling from the airplane or they saw the 747, decapitated by a fuel tank explosion, climbing several thousand feet before exploding a final time and falling into the ocean. But says Donaldson, "These people are stretched out along 11 miles of coastline, and they're all pointing to the same place. Now, you get 11 miles of coast and dozens of people who have never met before all pointing to the same place. What's the chance of that being coincidence?" Donaldson has also expressed surprise that federal investigators have not undertaken a similar analysis. "The NTSB literally did not consider the eyewitness testimony," he said. "They were operating under the premise that the FBI was already considering that." And the FBI, he added, has never addressed the eyewitness data as anything more than a series of anomalies. The bureau did not, so far as Donaldson has ever seen, even do his simple triangulation experiment. Instead, as he put it, "The FBI has thrown a cloak over that kind of eyewitness."

The CIA's video proposed that, after losing its nose section, TWA800 shot upwards like a rocket, leading witnesses to believe that they saw a rocket. Donaldson's reaction was equally contemptuous. "It was entertaining but like most cartoons grossly abused universal laws of nature," he wrote to [FBI Director] Freeh. "In my view, the 'Alice in Wonderland' public positions the FBI has taken in this incident have now crossed over from being merely illogical or incompetent to the appearance of obstruction of justice," he added, saying that he had "seen better police work in *Pink Panther* movies."

Another apparent discrepancy that ARAP has highlighted in its alternative hypothesis is the data from the FDR. After studying the documents released at the Baltimore hearing, Howard Mann picked up on a line that had been crossed through in the flight recorder data. Before printing copies of the flight data for distribution in Baltimore, an NTSB official drew a line through the last set of numbers, writing by hand, "End of Flt 800 Data." The official explanation for this action is that the figures represent incorrect readings from earlier flights—flight data recorders use the same reel-to-reel tape several times, erasing it and writing over repeatedly.

This last line of data, ARAP believes, includes readings that prove conclusively that the explosion took place outside the plane. The data indicates that Flight 800's gauges recorded physically impossible conditions, such as dropping 3,645ft and slowing to 100kts from 298kts in just one second. More likely, Donaldson says, the readings record the shock wave of an exploding missile as it ripped past sensors. Such a wave would increase the air pressure enough to skew the altitude and speed measurements, he said. It would also have rocked a device, not unlike a weather vane, which measures from which direction wind hits the aircraft. That reading went from 3° to 106°. The last reading, less than a second later, was again 3°. A shock wave would help explain how the plane's central fuel tank exploded, Donaldson said. Jet fuel, basically kerosene, does not burn easily, not even at the temperatures that the federal government says the central fuel tank reached, he said. Donaldson theorized the shock wave from the outside explosion knocked what little fuel remained in the plane's central fuel tank into the air. That fuel was ignited by a fragment from the missile exploding, he said.

Donaldson doubts that the data that led to his conclusions were left over from an earlier flight and were therefore incorrect. "A lot of the data recovered," he said, "[such as the angle of attack measurement] all fits with what I described." Government officials have responded to this theory by saying there is no evidence of a missile, and that information from the flight recorders was being misinterpreted.

If Donaldson is to be believed, from where did the missile originate? In his version of events a state-sponsored terrorist team acquired shoulder-fired anti-aircraft missiles and having brought them into the United States, took possession of a fast boat and brought down the aircraft. The terrorists then fled the scene. Donaldson believes that the government is trying to cover up evidence of the missile because it failed in its job of protecting airliners from terrorist attacks.

In scenario three, which also supports the missile theory, an air-to-air missile-equipped submarine was sent from its base in Asia to the ocean waters just south of Long Island. The crew of the submarine fired one or more of its missiles at the aircraft. One or more of those missiles struck the aircraft and, from that point, the destructive sequence followed much like any of the other scenarios. The submarine then escaped the immediate scene. This supposition is somewhat leaky and leaves a few questions unanswered. For example, why would a foreign nation not attack American carriers overseas? Very few foreign nations have the ability to carry out submarine operations at the range needed to reach the United States and, in any case, the US uses state-of-art tracking devices to detect submarines far at sea . . . how could this one escape detection?

A better developed argument, which we will call scenario four, has it that TWA800 was accidentally shot down by a stray US Navy missile. It is an open secret that the US Navy and Army were conducting final acceptance tests of the AEGIS-CEC (Cooperative Engagement Capability) system in the Long Island area on the evening of July 17. US Navy guided missile destroyers were on station in the area to test the system, which has been designed to coordinate the defence systems of surface and air forces. The Standard IV missiles they were carrying had been altered to work compatibly with the CEC brain, and would be guided over the horizon — where ship and on-board missile radars couldn't see — via a data link with an airborne P-3 Orion carrying the electronic AEGIS-CEC brain. The three-year old AEGIS-CEC test equipment was designed to discriminate between friend-neutral-foe electronic signatures, isolate the hostile threat and select the weapon best positioned for an assured kill to launch at the target. At around 20.30hrs a drone was launched to replicate an attack on the flotilla of ships. Recognizing the threat AEGIS-CEC system automatically launched a missile from one of the surface vessels. For some reason the co-ordinated link between target tracker, guidance, and missile was broken! Unable to receive guidance commands to keep it on an intercept course with the target drone, the Standard IV reverted to its own programing and began seeking a target. The internal radar acquired the TWA 747 and, seconds later,

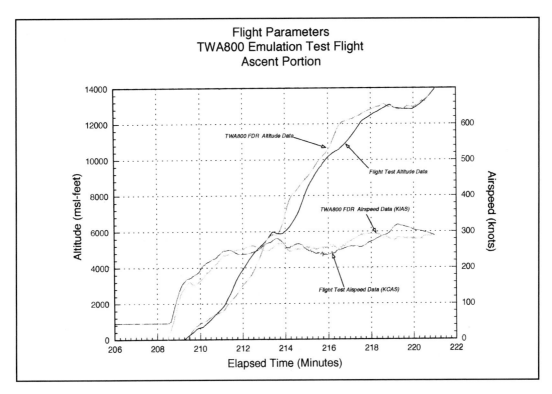

Above: *Emulation flight tests show very little unusual in flight 800's airspeed or altitude.* via Michael Sharpe

Below: *Emulation flight tests showing fuel temperatures in the forward bay.* via Michael Sharpe

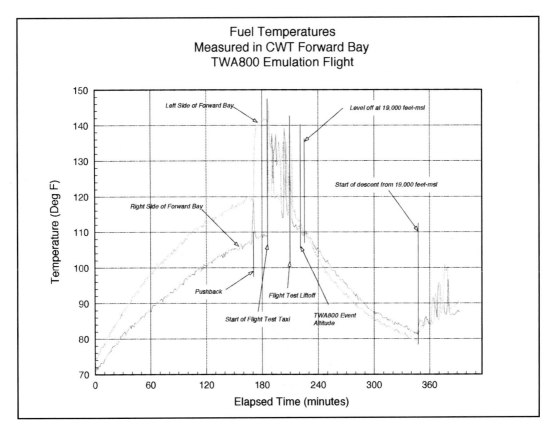

the inert missile struck the fuselage, exiting the left side at the forward wing root. The chief proponent of this theory cites insider knowledge, the eyewitness accounts of 34 people who saw a streak resembling a missile trail, and the unsubstantiated rumors that rocket residue has been discovered on seat backs. Furthermore, he believes that the reconstructed aircraft shows the clean entry and exit holes where the aircraft punched through, that FAA radar tapes verify the track of the anti-missile and that government documents verify the testing in that area and that the military has misrepresented its activities south of Long Island on July 17 repeatedly.

In the fifth scenario, a terrorist or individual with a private agenda managed to place an explosive device aboard TWA Flight 800 either in the cargo, cockpit, or passenger cabin area. The bomb exploded while the aircraft was still climbing to its cruising altitude, just minutes after take-off. Again, this scenario relies to a large extent on rumors of explosives residues of some origin found inside the passenger cabin and other locations and does not explain why the cargo bins were reportedly found in good shape. And yet a relatively small bomb brought down Pan Am Flight 103 over Lockerbie in 1988 and an explosives scenario helps explain the instantaneous nature of the aircraft's systems failures.

There are three other accounts that have been almost entirely discounted either because they lack real physical evidence, or else represent such an unlikely occurrence as to be considered virtually impossible. Some have suggested the cargo door in the forward starboard-side fuselage somehow opened as TWA Flight 800 climbed away from John F. Kennedy International Airport, damaging the surrounding airframe and fuselage skin, which in turn caused the front of the aircraft to become detached and compromised the integrity of the center wing tank. Paint smears on the aircraft's fuselage are presented as evidence that the cargo door slammed against the side of the aircraft while in flight, but among the many gaps are an explanation of how the exterior cargo door could have compromised the structural integrity of the center wing tank, the ignition source for its contents, and why some photographs of the aircraft wreckage reconstruction show cargo door latches clearly still attached to the fuselage.

A least three possible causes have been cited that attribute the crash to a freak of nature. Could it be that military exercises in the area of TWA Flight 800's flight path south of the Long Island coast created powerful electromagnetic fields which enveloped the aircraft, sending powerful electrical currents coursing through the aircraft that disrupted the instruments before igniting the volatile fuel vapors? Or could it have been a large meteorite? No pieces of meteorites were found in wreckage and none of the eyewitness reports are concurrent with a meteorite fall. Or could it, most intriguingly, have been caused by a methane gas bubble that was released by natural processes from the ocean floor under the flight path of TWA Flight 800 as it approached? As the aircraft entered this invisible explosive cloud, an ignition source from the exterior of the plane ignited the gas cloud. Scientists argue that this is unlikely, given the fact that the density of the air at 13,000+ feet is much reduced and a gaseous cloud could not maintain coherence. They have also questioned whether there is there is enough power in a non-contained methane explosion to smash a large aircraft.

Above: *Mourners arrive with flowers to a multi-denominational prayer service for flight 800 victims.* CORBIS-Bettmann

Below: *A TWA 747.* ASM Photo

19 Buah Nabur, Sibolangit, Indonesia, 1997 Garuda Indonesia Airways A300B4-220

Michael Sharpe

At 13.34hrs on Friday September 26, 1997, a Garuda Indonesia Airways Airbus A300B4-220, registration PK-GAI, on scheduled flight GA152 from Jakarta to Medan, impacted into mountainous terrain near the village of Buah Nabar in the Sibolangit district, some 20 miles short of Medan airport, spreading wreckage over an area of 120,000sq ft. All 222 of those on board, including a child and 12 crew members, were killed in what is—to date—the worst air accident in Indonesia's history. The accident occurred as the aircraft was preparing to make an instrument landing in thick haze caused by hundreds of forest fires that had been burning across Indonesia since early summer and which had reduced visibility on that day to about 2,000ft.

As the victims were recovered from the crash site, distraught relatives tried to identify their loved ones at an open air morgue filled with the fire smoke and the stench of bodies decomposing in the warm, humid Indonesian weather. The heat necessitated a mass funeral for the 50 bodies that still remained unidentified the following Monday. Dozens of anxious relatives were prevented from flying to the crash scene because of continued poor visibility over the weekend and President Suharto ordered the unknown victims to be buried in the Mamborano Monument, a cemetery not far from Medan airport that already contained 57 victims from a 1979 crash by a commuter plane from the same airline.

The Indonesian Ministry of Transport launched an immediate inquiry but to date has yet to release its findings. It seems likely that the causes will be attributed to two major factors, namely the disorientating effects of smoke on the pilot and confusing instructions given to him by the ATC at Medan.

Although some press reports were quick to highlight Garuda's less than exemplary safety record, the airline has since been largely exonerated. (In 1997 the airline chalked up three accidents that were traced to pilot error or technical difficulty. In 1996 the US Federal Aviation Administration threatened to ban Garuda from flying to the United States, because it did not meet international safety standards. Garuda later complied with the requirements, and the ban never went into effect.) It has been suggested by Japanese aviation experts that the aircraft may have been

Above: *Investigators sifting through the wreckage.* Associated Press Photograph

brought down by smog particles which blocked minute coolant holes on the surface of engine blades, causing overheating. Past experience has shown that blades which become contaminated in this way can disintegrate after heat expansion and fragments can damage the engine's interior. However, this theory has been rejected by crash investigators probing the GA152 tragedy, on the basis that smoke particles from forest fires are too small to pose any problem to the engines and wings of modern airplanes. Moreover, only the simultaneous and catastrophic failure of both engines causing an in-flight break-up, could bring an aircraft to the ground so quickly that the pilot would not have the time to notice the engine failure and radio for help. There is no indication on the transcript of the ATC transmissions that engine failure had occurred; indeed, sources say the only evidence that the pilots knew they were about to crash was their screams of fear seconds before the plane hit the mountainside.

At the present time the evidence points to a controlled flight into terrain (CFIT) and the Garuda Pilots Association has laid the blame very firmly at the feet of the ATC at Medan. The aircraft was under the command of 40-year-old Rachmo Wiyogo, a pilot with 15,000 hours flight time and 20 years experience with the airline, who was under consideration for promotion to a flight instructor's position. The aircraft, manufacturer's serial No. 214, was delivered new to Garuda in 1982. It had accumulated just short of 27,000 flight hours and approximately 16,500 flights by the end of August. It was powered by two Pratt & Whitney JT9D-59A engines.

Flight GA152 was cleared for an ILS (Instrument Landing System) approach to Medan runway 05 and was flying on a 316° heading on Airway 585/W12. The airport has an elevation of 90ft and minimum sector altitudes range up to 9,500ft within a 25-nautical mile radius of the runway. (Minimum sector altitudes are shown on standard charts and give the safe altitudes within 10 nautical miles of the approach or departure track. So, in this case it means that there are mountains within 25 miles of the runway approach that are 9,500ft high—quite high, and quite close to the airport making for tricky arrivals and departures.) At the time of the incident Medan was equipped with primary radar only, which does not include altitude information.

The recovery of the FDR some weeks after the incident and subsequent independent analysis of both CVR and ATC transcripts provides a useful profile of the last moments of the flight. The following unofficial transcript of radio communications during the approach is believed to be generally accurate. Officials have cautioned that some words may be missing, however, and one line is noted as omitted. The other aircraft mentioned in the transcript are from domestic airlines and include a landing Merpati flight on approach, MNA241, and a departing Bouraq aircraft, call sign BOU683. Transcript wording is verbatim:

Garuda Flight 152 (GIA152): "Medan Approach, GIA152 passing 150."
Medan: "GIA152 radar contact 43 miles. Descent to 3,000ft for runway 05, reduce speed to 220."
GIA152: "Descend 3,000 for runway 05. Reduce speed 220kts, GIA152."
GIA152: "Approach, GIA152, request reason reduce speed above 10,000 to 220kts."

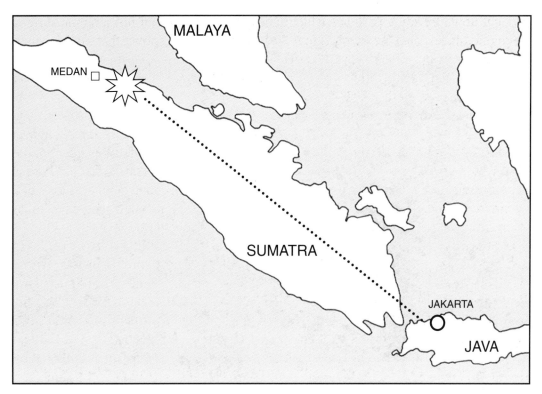

Above: *Diagram showing location of the Garuda Airbus crash.*

Below: *Indonesian rescue workers at the crash scene.* Associated Press Photograph

Medan: "OK sir, your traffic departure sir, now start engine, release traffic departure at or before 27."

GIA152: "152 like to maintain 210kts . . . 250kts, and below 10,000."

Medan: "OK it's approved."

MNA241: "MNA241 passing 10,000."

Medan: "MNA241, your position now 11 miles on W-11. Contact 1212. Happy landing."

MNA241: "*Selamat siang. Terima kasih.*" (Good afternoon. Thank you.)

Medan: "Any time."

GIA152: "GIA152; 3,000."

Medan: "GIA152, maintain 3,000 feet for a while. Maintain heading Medan VOR. Traffic now still taxi runway 23."

GIA152: "Maintain 3,000."

Medan: "Merpati 152, you turn left heading 240 vectoring for intercept ILS runway 05 from right side. Traffic now rolling."

Medan: "GIA152 do you read?"

GIA152: "GIA152. Say again?"

Medan: "Turn left heading a (pause) 240, 235. Now vectoring for intercept ILS runway 05."

GIA152: "Roger heading 235. GIA152."

GIA152: "GIA152 heading 235. Confirm we cleared from a [pause] mountainous area?"

Medan: "Affirm sir! Continue turn left on heading 215."

GIA152: "On heading 215, GIA."

BOU683: "Good afternoon, approach. BOU683 departed left turn."

Medan: "BOU683 continue turn left on heading 120 initial 2,000 feet."

(One line missing from transcript.)

Medan: "GIA152, turn right heading 046, report established localizer."

GIA152: "Turn right heading 040, GIA152, check established.

Medan: Turning right, sir."

GIA152: "Roger, 152."

Medan: "152, confirm you're making turning left now?"

GIA152: "We are turning right now."

Medan: "152 OK, you continue turning left now."

GIA152: "A [pause] confirm turning left? We are starting
turning right now."

Medan: "OK [pause]. OK."

Medan: "GIA152 continue turn right heading 015."

GIA152: [screaming]

So, having descended to 3,000ft the crew was instructed to turn left on heading 240° to intercept runway 05 ILS from the right as the aircraft on the ground was in the process of clearing the airport. At 13.28hrs GA152 was instructed to continue on a

Above: Garuda A300B4-22o PK-GAH was delivered to the airline a week before PK-GAI and is identical to the lost aircraft. Austin J. Brown/Aviation Picture Library

215

215° heading and descend to 2,000ft. At 13.30hrs ATC directed the flight to turn right heading onto 046 and report when establishing the localizer (the VHF component of the instrument landing system used to guide an aircraft onto the runway centerline. It transmits a beam usable up to a height of 6,250ft and a distance of 25 nautical miles). Medan approach radar lost contact at approximately 13.38hrs local time.

Just ten seconds after confirming the right turn, the Airbus crashed in a wooded area, broke up and burst into flames.

The GPA claims the actions of the air traffic controller at Medan pulled Flight 152 off its normal landing approach and brought the plane into a mountainous area where the minimum safe altitude is 7,500ft. One minute before the crash, the controller told the pilot to turn right instead of left bringing the aircraft towards a hill which the pilot noticed too late to avoid due to the low visibility caused by the smog. Their accusations are clearly supported by the data.

If the GPA's explanation is true, the fact that the aircraft was fitted with standard ILS equipment, which allows a pilot to fly with no visibility, is not a factor in the crash because this system may not work properly when an aircraft is not flying on the normal approach course. It is not designed to warn pilots of obstacles but only to steer them toward the runway. Also, the logic on the Mark 2 GPWS, listed as installed on the ill-fated Airbus, disables the warning horn when the flaps and gear are extended for landing. The GPA's claim of an air traffic control error cannot be independently verified, and air traffic control officials at Medan airport continue to deny all requests for interviews and direct all questions to the Indonesian Transport Ministry.

Medan is located on the Indonesian island of Sumatra, which, along with Borneo, was hard hit by fires that raged out of control through Indonesia in 1997. The 2,000ft visibility reported by Polonia Airport was within landing minima, but Polonia had been closed intermittently during the week prior to the incident, and at least three other airports on the island also had closed due to poor visibility. Indonesia's most important natural resource and the major generator of annual income are the timber products of the extensive rainforest. Economic expansion has placed an increasing demand on this resource, driving unscrupulous, profit-driven plantation companies to search for quicker and cheaper means of clearing land that can then be turned over to the production of rubber and palm oil. In October 1997, shortly after the accident, Forestry Minister Jamaluddin Suryohadikusomo announced that 96,000 hectares of vegetation, mainly in protected areas and natural rainforest but including 16,000 hectares of palm oil and rubber plantations, had been destroyed at a cost of $12.5 million in lost production. The government revoked 151 licences from 29 companies, when they failed to disprove allegations supported by satellite images that the fires burning on their land concessions were deliberately set.

In the aftermath of the crash calls have intensified for the addition of minimum safe altitude warning capability to radars at all international airports, as well as enhanced ground proximity warning systems, which incorporate a digital terrain database, on transport aircraft.

Right: *Identification of the passengers by grieving relatives was a harrowing experience.*
Associated Press Photograph

20 Nova Scotia, Canada, 1998 Swissair Boeing (McDonnell Douglas) MD-11

Leo Marriott

McDonnell Douglas first flew the wide-bodied three-engined DC-10 in 1971 and it achieved a moderate commercial success with 386 civil versions being built; the long range DC-10-30 version being the most popular. However, the aircraft's reputation was badly affected by a series of major accidents in the 1970s (see Chapters 1, 4, 5, and 13) although, to be fair, not all were attributable to its design or manufacture. Nevertheless, the damage had been done and DC-10 sales fell off in the early 1980s due to this and other factors including a downturn in the airline market and stiff competition from rivals Boeing and Airbus. McDonnell Douglas responded by redesigning and stretching the basic DC-10 design, equipping it with more powerful and efficient engines, and introducing a modern electronic flightdeck. In this guise it became the McDonnell Douglas MD-11, the new name minimizing any connection with the earlier DC-10. Total orders reached over 175 and the freighter MD-11F proved particularly popular, although by the time McDonnell Douglas was taken over by Boeing in 1997 sales were dropping off and production is scheduled to cease in 2000. From a safety point of view, the MD-11 has fared better than its predecessor and, until September 1998, only one had been lost in an accident. This was a Fedex freighter which was destroyed after a bad landing at Newark, New York, in July 1997, and this was almost certainly caused by human error.

The MD-11's otherwise good safety record was brought to a sudden end in the late evening of September 2, 1998. The aircraft concerned was registered HB-IWF and belonged to Swissair, an early MD-11 customer which at that time operated a fleet of no less than 16 of the big tri-jets. "Whisky Foxtrot" (WF) was one of nine MD-11s delivered in 1991 since when the type had become the backbone of the airline's long range fleet. The entry into service had not been without problems and the Pratt & Whitney PW4462 turbofans had suffered from a series of embarrassing flameouts while McDonnell Douglas had been forced to rectify deficiencies in payload and range performance. However, by the end of the 1990s these problems had been overcome, and the MD-11 was regarded as a reliable workhorse, while its spacious cabin was popular with passengers.

Above: Swissair worked closely with McDonnell Douglas during the development of the MD-11 was one of the first customers for the new aircraft. This shows the airline's first aircraft which was delivered in March 1991. Boeing/McDonnell Douglas

On the evening in question, HB-IWF was operating as flight SR111 on a scheduled service from New York to Geneva and had taken off at 20.18hrs local time (Eastern Standard Time). It was under the command of Captain Urs Zimmermann, aged 50, and his co-pilot was Stefan Low, 36. Both were Swiss. For almost an hour the flight proceeded normally as the aircraft left New York and climbed while flying parallel to the coast of Massachusetts and the Canadian province of Nova Scotia. It had reached its cruising altitude of 33,000ft and on leaving US airspace was transferred to the control of the Canadian Air Traffic Control Center at Moncton.

Almost immediately the captain made a dramatic "Pan" call to Moncton, reporting that there was smoke in the flightdeck and requesting an immediate return to Boston, which he probably assumed to be the nearest suitable airport for an emergency landing. However, Moncton advised that Halifax was much nearer (42nm rather than 190nm to Boston) and the captain decided to accept radar vectors towards runway 06/24. This was nearly 3,000 yards (2,682m) long and perfectly adequate for the MD-11.

The transcript of the radio conversation between Swissair 111 and Moncton Center recorded the time of the Pan call as just after 20.14hrs (Atlantic Daylight Time, ADT). The radio phrase "Pan, Pan, Pan," is internationally recognized as indicating a serious emergency situation, but one in which there is no immediate danger to human life. It is one step below the better known "Mayday" call. The exchange went as follows:

20.14:18hrs, Swissair 111: "Swissair one-eleven heavy is declaring Pan Pan Pan. We have, uh, smoke in the cockpit. Uh, request immediate return, uh, to a convenient place, I guess, uh, Boston."

20.14:33hrs, Moncton controller: "Swissair one-eleven, roger . . . turn right proceed . . . uh . . .you say to Boston you want to go."

20.14:33hrs, Swissair 111: "I guess Boston . . . we need first the weather so, uh, we start a right turn here. Swissair one-one-one heavy."

20.14:45hrs, Moncton controller: "Swissair one-eleven, roger, and a descent to flight level three-one-zero (31,000 feet). Is that OK?"

20.14:50hrs, Swissair 111: "Three-one-zero. [*Unintelligible words obscured by a noise. Possibly the noise associated with donning oxygen masks.*] Three-one-zero . . . one-one heavy."

20.15:08hrs, Moncton controller: "Uh, would you prefer to go into Halifax?"

20.15:11hrs, Swissair 111: "Uh, standby."

20.15:38hrs, Swissair 111: "Affirmative for Swissair one-eleven heavy. We prefer Halifax from our position."

20.15:43hrs, Moncton controller: "Swissair one-eleven, roger. Proceed direct to Halifax. Descend now to flight level two-niner-zero (29,000 feet)."

20.15:58hrs, British Airways 214: "And, uh, Swissair one-eleven heavy, from Speedbird (British Airways flight) two-one-four, I can give you the Halifax weather if you like."

20.16:04.1hrs, Swissair 111: "Swissair one-eleven heavy, we have the, uh, the oxygen mask on. Go ahead with the weather."

The word "Heavy" after the callsign is a standard radio procedure to remind controllers that the aircraft concerned is a large, wide-bodied, aircraft and that smaller aircraft following behind must be spaced at specified minimum distances to avoid the vortex wake of the larger aircraft. It has no particular significance in the context of this accident.

Armed with the Halifax weather information from the British Airways aircraft, the Swissair MD-11 was then instructed to contact Halifax Approach Control for vectors to land on runway zero six. Following initial contact, the conversation went as follows:

20.19:14hrs, Halifax controller: "OK, can I vector you, uh, to set up for runway zero-six at Halifax?"

20.19:19hrs, Swissair 111: "Ah, say again latest wind, please."

20.19:22hrs, Halifax controller: "OK, active runway Halifax zero-six. Should I start you on a vector for six?"

20.19:26hrs, Swissair 111: "Yes, uh, vector for six will be fine. Swissair one-eleven heavy."

20.19:39hrs, Halifax controller: "OK, it's a back course approach for runway zero six. The localizer frequency one-zero-niner-decimal-niner. You've got 30 miles to fly to the threshold."

20.19:53hrs, Swissair 111: "Uh, we need more than 30 miles . . ."

20.21:23hrs, Halifax controller: "Swissair one-eleven, when you have time could I have the number of souls on board and your fuel on board, please, for emergency services."

20.21:30hrs, Swissair 111: "Roger. At the time, uh, fuel on board is, uh, two-three-zero tons. We must, uh, dump some fuel. May we do that in this area during descent?" *(Note: Two three zero tons represented the gross weight of the aircraft, not the amount of fuel on board.)*

20.22:04hrs, Halifax controller: "Swissair one-eleven, uh roger, uh turn to the ah, left, heading of, ah, two-zero-zero degrees and advise time when you are ready to dump. It will be about ten miles before you are off the coast. You are still within about 25 miles of the airport."

20.22:20hrs, Swissair 111: "Roger, we are turning left and, ah, in that case we're descending at the time only to 10,000 feet to dump the fuel."

20.22:29hrs, Halifax controller: "OK, maintain one-zero-thousand. I'll advise you when you are over the water and it will be very shortly.

20.22:34hrs, Swissair 111: "Roger."

20.22:36hrs, Swissair 111: *(conversation between the pilots, inadvertently broadcast on the air)* "You are in the emergency checklist for air conditioning smoke?"

20.24:28hrs, Swissair 111: *(Background phone).* "Ah, Swissair one-eleven. At the time we must fly, ah, manually. Are we cleared to fly between, ah, ten thou . . . eleven thousand and niner thousand feet?" *(Sound of audible signal when the autopilot is switched off)* .

20.24:45hrs, Swissair 111: "Swissair one-eleven heavy is declaring emergency."

20.24:56hrs, Swissair 111: "Eleven heavy, we starting dump now, we have to land immediate."

20.25:00hrs, Halifax controller: "Swissair one-eleven, just a couple of miles, I'll be right with you."

20.25:19hrs, Halifax controller: "Swissair one-eleven, you are cleared to, ah, commence your fuel dump on that track and advise me, ah, when the dump is complete."

20.25:43hrs, Halifax controller: "Swissair one-eleven, check you're cleared to start the fuel dump."

But now it was too late. The controller was talking to himself and no further communications were received from the aircraft, although it remained visible on the radar screens for a further six minutes before it disappeared as it crashed into the sea off the Nova Scotia coast. Subsequent investigations showed that the pilots must have lost control of the aircraft as it descended through 20,000ft and thereafter plunged out of control at around 3,000ft per minute until it hit the sea. Halifax immediately alerted the maritime rescue organization, and coastguard and naval vessels were dispatched to the scene, assisted by many local fishing vessels whose crews had witnessed the disaster.

However, it was already dark and the weather was bad with rain and strong winds whipping up the sea. It soon became clear that there would be no survivors and by daybreak only 36 bodies had been recovered. As luck would have it, a Canadian naval vessel in the vicinity was conducting trials with a multi-beam side scanning sonar capable of providing high definition images of the sea bottom. HMCS *Glace Bay* was immediately diverted to locate the wreckage and made a series of passes over the estimated flight path of the MD-11. This, together with eyewitness accounts and locator signals from the CVR and other recorders meant that the main area of wreckage was quickly found, although recovery of items from the seabed was hampered by the bad weather.

Almost immediately, speculation as to the cause of the accident and the train of events leading up to the plunge into the sea began. It was obvious from the radio transcripts that the aircraft had suffered a serious on-board fire and that the crew had been forced to don oxygen masks, although this was standard airline procedure in the event of any indication of fire or smoke in the cockpit, no matter how trivial. However, in this case, it was apparent that fire had been extensive and serious. As pieces of the wreckage were recovered, the forward section around the flightdeck was seen to have suffered badly from the fire and pieces of molten metal were found embedded in the pilot's seats. Whole sections of electrical wiring were found to have melted and welded together with the insulation completely burnt away. By mid-December, some 25% of the wreckage had been recovered, including the remains of

Above right: The MD-11 has a state of the art electronic flightdeck with computerized displays replacing traditional analog instrumentation. The overhead panel carries controls for the fuel, hydraulic, electrical, and environmental systems. It was in this area, or its associated wiring, that the fatal fire started which caused the demise of flight SR111. Boeing/McDonnell Douglas

Right: The Business class section of a Swissair MD-11 in happier times. Leo Marriott

all three engines. These pieces were taken to a nearby Canadian naval air station where they were assembled on a framework in an attempt to reconstruct the aircraft.

While the painstaking work of examining the wreckage went ahead, the implications of a potential on-board fire were taken to heart by the airline industry which suddenly reported a rash of connected incidents. A faint unusual smell in the cockpit was now reason enough for a crew to seek a precautionary landing at the nearest airfield so that checks could be carried out, and repeat disaster avoided. These included two MD-11 incidents. The first concerned a Delta Air Lines aircraft on a trans-Atlantic flight from Manchester, England, which diverted to Shannon in Ireland for a precautionary landing following on odor in the cockpit; while an American Airlines MD-11 made an emergency landing at Boston after reports of smoke in the cabin while on a flight from Chicago to London. In the seven weeks following the Swissair accident, the Canadian Transportation Safety Board recorded 30 smoke-related incidents compared with a total of only 54 for the preceding eight months of 1998. Fortunately, all of these incidents proved not to have been a major hazard, but it illustrated how concerned pilots had become. Even so, Swissair hit the headlines on November 26 when another MD-11 carrying 223 passengers and crew made a precautionary landing at Singapore after dumping 60 tons of fuel over the sea. The cause was a "penetrating smell" in the cockpit. This incident ended safely with no obvious cause but it forced Swissair to issue a statement confirming the company's commitment to the MD-11 as a safe aircraft.

However, the airline did respond to the possibility that a electrical fault had caused the fire in the Nova Scotia incident by deactivating the electronic in-flight entertainment fitted to the MD-11s (including HB-IWF). While there was no evidence to suggest that this system had been the origin of the fire, some of its wiring did pass through the flightdeck area and, as it was non essential to the operation of the aircraft, it was decided to deactivate it until a positive cause was established.

Continuing investigations located the seat of the fire in the overhead cockpit panel and the avionics circuit bay. The US Federal Aviation Authority therefore issued an airworthiness directive on January 28, 1999, requiring all MD-11 operators to inspect the wiring and insulation in these areas. Some 174 aircraft were affected by this order which, although only mandatory in the United States, would be followed by all operators of the type. The evidence of the ferocity of the fire in the cockpit led to speculation that the pilots had either been rendered unconscious by the flames and smoke, despite the use of oxygen masks, or had actually been forced to abandon the flightdeck after attempting to set the autopilot to keep the aircraft flying. Either picture conjures up an absolute nightmare scenario of the conditions on the flightdeck and the dreadful circumstances forced on the crew.

At the same time, some sources claimed that the CVR recordings showed up a disagreement between the captain and the first officer over the best course of action after the fire broke out. The first officer appears to have been in favor of making a

Right: *Engineers at work installing wiring looms in the tail of an MD-11 on the production line at Long Beach. A large modern jet airliner typically carries 150 miles of electrical wiring. It has now been shown that some types of wire and insulation offer a potential fire risk.* Boeing/McDonnell Douglas

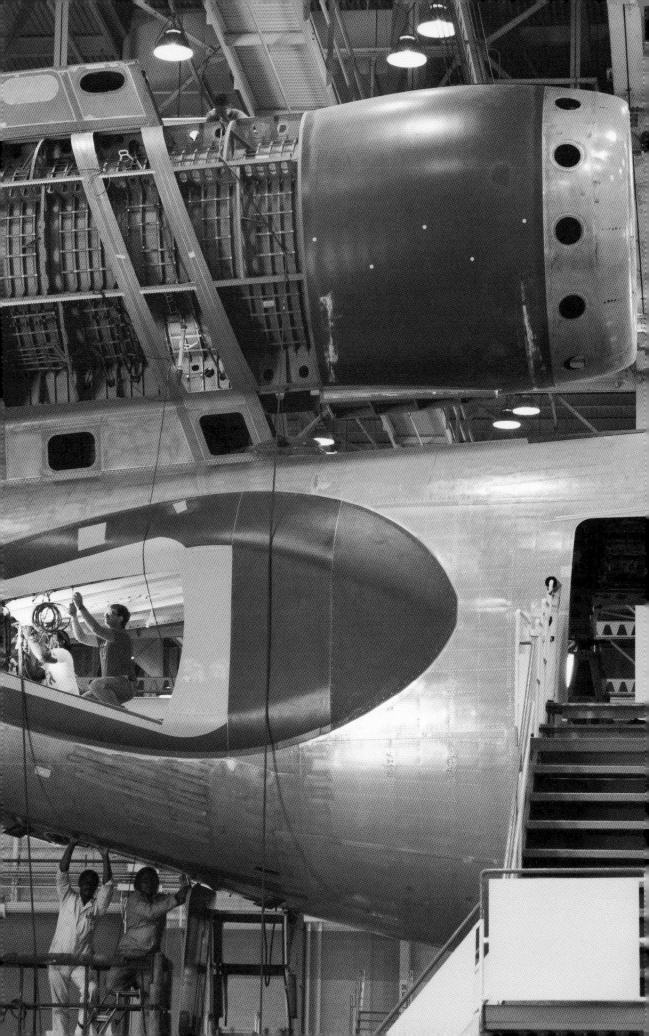

direct approach and landing at Halifax and repeatedly urged the captain to do so. However, the latter seemed more concerned with following the standard emergency procedures and dumping fuel before making an approach. In normal circumstances, an aircraft taking off for a long distance flight will be heavily laden with fuel and well over the maximum permissible landing weight. The engines on an aircraft such as the MD-11 will burn around three tons of fuel each per hour, so that in a typical eight-hour flight the three engines will consume around 72 tons of fuel. This would bring the aircraft's weight well within limits for landing but in the case of SWR111, the aircraft had only been airborne for an hour or so and could well have been 70 tons or more overweight for a normal landing. With hindsight, it would probably have been best to have headed straight for Halifax, although it cannot be established with any certainty that an approach and landing could have been made before the fire overcame the crew.

At the time of writing the exact cause of the electrical fire has not been determined officially and tests and investigations continue. However some sources have pinpointed a type of lightweight wiring which is widely used in modern jet airliners, particularly those with modern electronic flight systems. Known by the propriety name "Kapton," demonstrations have shown that the insulation can become cracked and split if subjected to heat (not necessarily an actual fire) and in this event electrical arcing and ignition can occur. The US Navy was so concerned about these characteristics that it specified the use of alternative wiring materials on its aircraft many years ago. Current Boeing aircraft do not use the material, although it is still installed in Airbus products. The Kapton wiring was used extensively on the MD-11 but no positive proof has emerged that it was specifically responsible for the initial combustion, although it would undoubtedly have fueled any fire which had already started.

Apart from technical considerations, the crash of this Swissair MD-11 has also made aviation legal history. Since the end of World War II, an airline's financial liability in respect of death or injury to any of their passengers has been limited to the sum of $135,000 for each individual under the terms of the Warsaw Convention. In 1996, the International Air Transport Association drew up a new Intercarrier Agreement under which signatory airlines agreed to wave the Warsaw Convention limit, although still retaining the right to contest any claims made. The Swissair accident was the first involving a major carrier since the 1996 agreement and lawyers representing the families of the dead passengers—particularly the 136 Americans on board—were quick to file claims against the airline. Although the legal proceedings will probably drag on for several years as both sides argue over whether Swissair could be held to be negligent in any way, the potential cost of the claims has been conservatively estimated at around $600 million. This would make it the most expensive accident in civil aviation history.

Above Right: *MD-11 general arrangement drawing showing the extra fuselage sections inserted to increase length and capacity over the earlier DC-10.* Boeing/McDonnell Douglas

Right: *Swissair's first MD-11 (HB-IWA) on the ground at Geneva—destination of the ill fated flight SR111.* Swissair

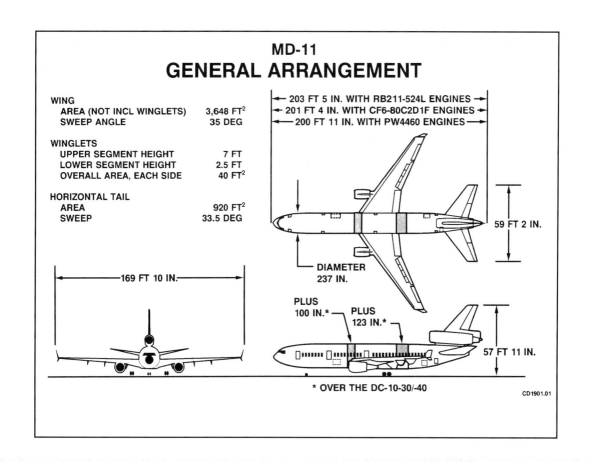

MD-11
GENERAL ARRANGEMENT

WING
AREA (NOT INCL WINGLETS)	3,648 FT^2
SWEEP ANGLE	35 DEG

WINGLETS
UPPER SEGMENT HEIGHT	7 FT
LOWER SEGMENT HEIGHT	2.5 FT
OVERALL AREA, EACH SIDE	40 FT^2

HORIZONTAL TAIL
AREA	920 FT^2
SWEEP	33.5 DEG

← 203 FT 5 IN. WITH RB211-524L ENGINES →
← 201 FT 4 IN. WITH CF6-80C2D1F ENGINES →
← 200 FT 11 IN. WITH PW4460 ENGINES →

59 FT 2 IN.

DIAMETER
237 IN.

169 FT 10 IN.

PLUS
100 IN.*

PLUS
123 IN.*

57 FT 11 IN.

* OVER THE DC-10-30/-40

CD1901.01

Appendices

1 Aircraft Specifications

AIRBUS A300

The Airbus A300 was the first aircraft to be produced by the European consortium and was designed to fill the gap between the conventional narrow-bodied jet airliners and the first generation of American wide-bodied aircraft such as the four-engined Boeing 747 and the Lockheed Tristar and McDonnell Douglas tri-jets. Originally partners in the project were the state-backed Aerospatiale of France and Deutsche Airbus in Germany, with the privately funded British company Hawker Siddeley being responsible for the wing design and production. CASA of Spain subsequently joined and British Aerospace later became a full partner.

The design of the A300 was based on earlier French and British projects and a Memorandum of Understanding between the partners was signed in September 1967. In the course of development the size of the aircraft was scaled down from a 330,694lb 330-seater to a 275,578lb 252-seater in order to avoid direct competition with the DC-10 and Tristar. This became the A300B1 which first flew on October 28, 1972, followed by a second aircraft in February 1973. The production version was the A300B2 which featured a stretched fuselage capable of seating up to 290 passengers and taking gross weight to 302,033lb.

Air France began commercial services with the A300B2 in May 1974, followed shortly afterwards by Lufthansa and then several other European airlines. At the end of 1974 the longer-ranged B4 variant took to the air and offered other improvements including better take-off performance. Sales to Middle East and South American airlines followed but the real breakthrough was a substantial order from Eastern Airlines in the United States. This really established Airbus as a major player and it began to be seen as a genuine rival to the long-established American manufacturers. As if to emphasize this situation, Airbus developed the A300-600 which was based on the B4 but introduced the electronic "glass" flightdeck along with many aerodynamic refinements. When coupled with the inherent economies of the twin-jet

Above: *Kuwait Airways lost two Airbus A300s during the Gulf War. The aircraft were flown to Bagdhad by Iraqi crews and subsequently destroyed on the ground by American bombing. This picture shows one of five A300-600s ordered as replacements for the airline's shattered fleet.* L.Marriott

layout, this gave the A300 a substantial commercial boost in the battle with rivals such as the Boeing 767. The A300-600 supplanted the A300B4 from the early 1980s onwards and was subsequently offered in an extended range version (600R) by additional fuel capacity and higher certified take-off weights. Both the B4 and -600 versions have been offered in cargo and convertible versions and many older A300s are now being rebuilt in a freighter configuration as they are supplanted in passenger service by more up to date aircraft. A total of 520 A300s of all variants had been delivered or ordered up to September 1999.

The A310—over 250 were ordered—has been in airline service since 1983, when Lufthansa and Swissair became the first carriers to operate this shorter-fuselage version of the A300. Typical seating capacity in a two-class configuration is 220 passengers. Two A310 versions currently are available: the medium-range A310-200, and the long-range A310-300. With a full payload, the A310-300 is capable of flying routes of up to 5,200 nautical miles. The A310 and A300 use the same cockpit and have the similar handling qualities. As a result, they share a common type-rating, allowing pilots qualified on one to fly the other without extra training. The commonality also facilitates maintenance for airlines operating both type of aircraft.

Airbus A300-600

Powerplants: 2 x P&W PW4000 or General Electric CF-6-80C2 turbofans
Span: 147ft 1in (44.84m)
Length: 177ft 5in (54.08m)
Height: 54ft 6in (16.62m)
Max take-off weight: 378,535lb (171,700kg)
Country of Origin: International
Capacity: 375 max, 257 in two-class layout

First flight: October 28, 1972 (A300B1), July 8, 1983 (A300-600)
Production: 520 (all A300 variants)
Notes: Versions include B2, B4, C, 600, 600R
Typical cruising speed: 472kts @ 31,000ft
Range (max payload): 4,340nm (8,043 km)
Range (max fuel): 5,100nm (9,450km)

MAJOR ACCIDENTS AND INCIDENTS — 14 Recorded

Date	Type	Identity	Operator	Location	Cause
Dec 18, 83	A300B4	OY-KAA	MAS	Kuala Lumpur	Human factors/ Descent below minima
Sept 21, 87	A300B4	SU-BCA	Egyptair	Luxor	Human factors
Jul 3, 88	A300B2	EP-IBU	Iran Air	Persian Gulf	Military action
Feb 15, 91	A300C4	9K-AHF	Kuwait Airways	Baghdad, Iraq	Military action
Feb 15, 91	A300C4	9K-AHG	Kuwait Airways	Baghdad, Iraq	Military action
Sept 28, 92	A300B4	AP-BCP	PakistanIA	Kathmandu, Nepal	Human factors / CFIT
Nov 15, 93	A300B2	VT-EDV	Indian Airlines	Tirupati, India	Human factors/Fuel exhaustion
Apr 26, 94	A300B4	B-1816	China Airlines	Nagoya Airport, Japan	Human factors
Aug 10, 94	A300B4	HL-7296	Korean Airlines	Cheju Airport, South Korea	Human factors
May 17, 96	A300B4	TC-ALP	Air Alfa	Istanbul, Turkey	On board fire
Sept 9, 97	A300B4	PK-GAI	Garuada	Medan, Indonesia	CFIT/Human factors

BOEING (MCDONNELL DOUGLAS) MD-11

After several years of indecision, in 1985 McDonnell Douglas finally launched a successor to the DC-10 in the shape of the MD-11. This was a derivative of the DC-10 with a lengthened fuselage seating up to 405 passengers combined with a revised wing design, other aerodynamic refinements, an advanced two-crew flight-deck and new generation high thrust turbofans. Production aircraft were offered with either three 60,000lb thrust Pratt & Whitney PW4460 or General Electric CF6-80C2DIF turbofans. It was initially planned to offer a version powered by Rolls-Royce Trents and this was ordered by the British airline Air Europe, but the subsequent demise of this airline terminated the plans to install this powerplant. The MD-11 first flew in January 1990 with the first delivery being made to Finnair at the end of the year after an intensive test program. Although early aircraft suffered from a shortfall in range performance, this was eventually rectified and the standard MD-11 is capable of carrying a full payload over 6,900 miles, while the MD-11ER can carry 298 passengers over a staggering 8,300 miles. The aircraft is also produced in freighter and Combi versions and although sales have been slow with only 174 order to the end of 1996, there have been recent indications that the all cargo MD-11F is beginning to make a name for itself as a better bet than the rival Boeing 747 freighter versions. The MD-11F was launched by Federal Express who ordered their first aircraft as far back as 1986 and currently have 17 of these aircraft in their fleet. More recently, Lufthansa Cargo announced an order in late 1996 for no less than 12 MD-11Fs. With only one major accident so far recorded, the MD-11 seems to be establishing a better safety record than the ill-starred DC-10. Following the take-over of McDonnell Douglas by Boeing, production of the MD-11 is due to end in 2000 after the 200th aircraft has been completed.

At one stage McDonnell Douglas proposed a larger version of the MD-11 under the designation MD-12, but this was abandoned in favor of a four-engined double-deck fuselage capable of carrying up to 700 passengers or, alternatively, around 400 over a maximum range of 8,000 miles. However, the company decided that the risks

Above: *The MD-11 first flew in January 1990 and entered service at the end of that year. The first lost in an accident belonged to Federal Express, the US parcels and freight conglomerate. It crashed as the result of a heavy landing at New York on July 31, 1997.* Boeing/McDonnell Douglas

Boeing (McDonnell Douglas) MD-11

Powerplants: Three P&W PW4460 or GE CF6-80C2D1F turbofans
Span: 169ft 10in (51.77m)
Length: 200ft 11in (61.64m)
Height: 57ft 9in (17.60m)
Maximum take-off weight: 625,500lb (283,725kg)
Country of Origin: United States

Capacity: 405 Max, 293 in three-class seating
First Flight: January 10, 1990
Production: over 200
Notes: Variants MD-11, MD-11F, MD-11 Combi, MD-11ER
Typical cruising speed: 473kts (876km/hr)
Range (max payload): 6,790nm (12,566km)

MAJOR ACCIDENTS AND INCIDENTS — 1 Recorded

Date	Identity	Operator	Location	Cause
July 31, 97	N611FE	Federal Express	Newark Airport, New York, US	Human factors?

involved in such a project were too great and it was shelved, as were later plans for a twin-engined long-range MD-11 derivative known as the MD-XX.

BOEING 727

Although flying over a year later than the rival British Trident (February 9, 1963), the Boeing 727 could seat up to 139 passengers and carry them up to 1,700 miles at a cruising speed of up to 480kts. This combination of range and payload could not be matched by the smaller Trident and the American manufacturer swept the board, turning the 727 into the best-selling jet airliner of its day with 1,831 aircraft delivered up to 1984 when production ceased. Apart from its performance, the 727 was also attractive to passengers and airlines as it retained the same fuselage cross section and standards of comfort as the larger Boeing 707.

The original Boeing 727-100, powered by three 14,000lb thrust Pratt & Whitney JT8D turbofans, was produced in passenger and combi versions but was replaced by the lengthened 727-200 in 1967. With a 20ft increase in fuselage length, the 727-200 could seat up to 189 passengers and more powerful JT8Ds allowed an increase in range to 2,500 miles with full payload. In 1972 Boeing produced the 727-200 Advanced which allowed operation at higher gross weights and had a number of other improvements.

Despite being out of production, the Boeing 727 remains as a workhorse with many airlines, including some US majors.

Above: A Mexicana Boeing 727-200 came down 100 miles northwest of Mexico City on March 31, 1986, killing all 167 people on board. The 727 had been cruising at 31,000ft when an overheated tire exploded, causing substantial damage to the flying controls and other aircraft systems as well as starting a fire. The pilots lost control and the aircraft broke up in the air. AJB Photo

Boeing 727-200

Powerplants: Three P&W JT8D-9A or -15 or -17R turbofans
Span: 108ft (32.92m)
Length: 153ft 2in (46.49m)
Height: 34ft 0in (10.36m)
Max take-off weight: 209,500lb (95,027kg)
Country of Origin: United States

Capacity: 189 maximum
First Flight: February 9, 1963
Production: 1,831
Typical cruising speed: 467kts (865km/hr)
Range (max payload): 2,140nm (3,966km)
Range (max fuel): 2,400nm (9,447km)

MAJOR ACCIDENTS AND INCIDENTS — 52

Date	Identity	Operator	Location	Cause
Aug 16, 65	N7036U	United Air Lines	Lake Michigan, USA	Not determined
Nov 8, 65	N1996	American Airlines Airport	Nr Cincinnati	Human factors
Nov 11, 65	N7030U	United Air Lines	Salt Lake City, USA	Human factors

Feb 4, 66	JA-8302	All Nippon Airways	Tokyo Bay, Japan	Not determined
Nov 15, 66	N317PA	Pan Am	Doberitz, Germany	Human factors/ CFIT
July 19, 67	N68650	Piedmont	Hendersonville, N.Carolina, US	Aerial collision
Feb 16, 68	B-1018	Civil Air Transport	Linkuo, Taiwan	Human factors
Jan 5, 69	YA-FAR	Ariana Afghan Airlines	Horley, Surrey, UK	Human factors
Jan 18, 69	N7434U	United Air Lines	Los Angeles, US	Mechanical defect
June 4, 69	XA-SEL	Mexicana	Nr Monterry, Mexico	Human factors/ CFIT
Sept 21, 69	XA-SEJ	Mexicana	Mexico City	Not determined
Dec 28, 70	N8790R	Trans Caribbean Airways	St.Thomas, Virgin Islands	Human factors
July 30, 71	JA-8329	All Nippon Airways	Morioka, Japan	Aerial collision
Feb 21, 73	5A-DAH	Libyan Arab Airlines	Nr Suez Canal, Egypt	Military action
Sept 15, 74	XV-NJC	Air Vietnam	Phan Rang, South Vietnam	Terrorist action
Dec 1, 74	N54328	TWA	Mt.Weather, Washington, US	Human Factors / CFIT
Dec 1, 74	N274US	Northwest Orient Airlines	Bear Mountain, New York, US	Icing
June 24, 75	N8845E	Eastern Air Lines	New York, US	Weather
Sept 30, 75	HK-1272	Avianca	Barranquilla, Colombia	Not recorded
April 5, 76	N124AS	Alaska Airlines	Ketchikan, Alaska, US	Human factors
April 27, 76	N1963	American Airlines	St.Thomas, Virgin Islands	Human factors
Sept 20, 76	TC-JBH	THY	Isparta, Turkey	Human factors/ CFIT
Nov 19, 77	CS-TBR	TAP Air Portugal	Funchal, Madeira	Human factors
May 8, 78	N4744	National Airlines	Memphis, US	Human factors
Sept 25, 78	N533PS	PSA	San Diego, California	Aerial collision
March 14, 79	JY-ADU	Alia Royal Jordanian Airlines	Doha Airport	Weather
Jan 21, 80	EP-IRD	Iran Air	Near Tehran, Iran	Weather Ground equipment
April 12, 80	PT-TYS	Transbrasil	Florianopolis, Brazil	Human factors
April 25, 80	G-BDAN	Dan-Air Services	Tenerife, Canaries	Human/CFIT

June 8, 82	PP-SRK	VASP	Nr Fortaleza, Brazil	Human factors
July 9, 82	N4737	Pan Am	New Orleans, US	Weather
Jan 16, 83	TC-JBR	THY	Ankara, Turkey	Weather
July 11, 83	HC-BIG	TAME Ecuador	Cuenca, Ecuador.	Human factors/ CFIT
Nov 8, 83	D2-TBNT	Angola Airlines	Lubango, Angola	Military action?
Dec 7, 83	EC-CFJ	Iberia	Barajas Airport, Madrid, Spain	Ground collision
Jan 1, 85	N819EA	Eastern Air Lines	Illimani Mountain, Bolivia	Human factors/ CFIT
Feb 19, 85	EC-DDU	Iberia	Durango, Spain	CFIT
March 31, 86	XA-MEM	Mexicana	Maravatio, Michoacan, Mexico	M e c h a n i c a l defect
Feb 27, 88	TC-AKD	Talia Airways	Arapkoy, North Cyprus	Human factors
March 17, 88	HK-1716	Avianca	Cucuta, Colombia	CFIT
Aug 31, 88	N473DA	Delta Air Lines	Dallas / Fort Worth, US	Human factors
Oct 21, 89	N88705	TAN/SAHSA	Tegucilgapa, Honduras	Human factors/ CFIT
Nov 27, 89	HK-1803	Avianca	Bogata, Colombia	Criminal action
Sept 11, 90	OB-1303	Faucett	180 miles south of Cape Race, US	Fuel problems
Dec 22, 92	5A-DIA	Libyan Arab Airlines	Nr Tripoli, Libya	Aerial Collision
May 19, 93	HK-2422	SAM Colombia	Frontino, Colombia	CFIT
May 1, 96	PP-LBY	Fly Linhas Aereas	Quito, Ecuador	Human factors
June 9, 96	EP-IRU	Iran Air	Rasht, Iran	Human factors
Nov 7, 96	5N-BBF	ADC Airlines	Near Lagos, Nigeria	Human factors (ATC)
June 7, 97	N571PE	Continental Airlines	New York, USA	Not Recorded
Aug 12, 97	SX-CBI	Olympic Airways	Thessaloniki, Greece	Weather
Aug 22, 97	HC-BVU	SAETA	Galapagos Islands, Ecuador	Human factors

BOEING 747

Spurred on by the development of the stretched Series 60 versions of the DC-8 which could carry up to 250 passengers, Boeing investigated a similar version of the 707 but eventually decided on a new design which, while still retaining the basic four engined swept-wing layout of the earlier aircraft, was 80ft longer and would carry three times as many passengers in a single-deck fuselage configured with eight- or ten-abreast seating. The new aircraft was given the model number 747 but soon became known as the "Jumbo Jet" because its massive size dwarfed anything that had come before.

The Boeing 747 used much of the technology which Boeing had developed when competing, unsuccessfully, for the USAF C-5 transport contract eventually won by the Lockheed Galaxy. This included the use of the new generation of big turbofans giving power ratings in excess of 40,000lb thrust: the early 747s were powered by four Pratt & Whitney JT9D-1 turbofans, initially rated at 41,000lb thrust, later increased to 45,000lb thrust in the JT9D-3DW version. This permitted a take off weight of up to 738,000lb, more than twice that of a fully loaded Boeing 707-320C. Passenger capacity varied from around 350 in a typical mixed-class layout to almost 500 in a high-density configuration; in addition, up to 16 tons of cargo could be carried in the capacious underfloor holds.

Pan American ordered 25 Boeing 747s in August 1966 and the epoch-making first flight took place at Boeing's Everett airfield on February 9, 1969, ushering in a new era of air transport. Pan American began commercial operations in January 1970 followed by TWA the next month, while Lufthansa was the first European airline to begin services, in April 1970. The original 747-100 was succeeded by the long-range 747-200 which also offered customer airlines a choice of three powerplants, the 48,750lb thrust Pratt & Whitney JT9D-7AW, General Electric CF6-50E (53,000lb thrust) or Rolls-Royce RB211-524B (50,100lb thrust). Gross weight rose to 833,000lb to allow more fuel to be carried and the first 747-200 flew in October 1970. Subsequently, the original Series 100 was offered in 1973 as the 100SR, optimized for short-range high-density routes, and as the 100B with higher gross weight and a choice of powerplants in 1978.

In a reversal of the normal process of stretching designs, Boeing offered a short fuselage version known as the 747SP (Special Performance) which was intended for ultra-long-range—up to 8,000 miles—services with a reduced passenger load, although only a few of these were built as performance improvements of standard 747s eventually meant that they could also operate economically on such routes. The basic 747-200 could carry a typical payload over distances of 6,000 miles or more and was also offered as a dedicated freighter with an upward hinging nose door (747-200F) or as a Combi passenger/cargo aircraft with a side-loading cargo door aft of the wing.

In October 1983 the first of a new model, the 747-300, took to the air. This was basically a -200 series with the upper deck behind the flightdeck extended to accommodate up to 91 passengers, thus boosting the theoretical maximum seating capacity to 630, although a more typical mixed-class layout carried around 426. As a simple derivative version, the -300 was quickly certificated and entered service with Swissair in March 1983. Maximum weight rose to 833,000lb and range with a full payload was now 6,500 miles. Despite these excellent figures, the 747-300 sold in relatively small numbers with only 81 ordered. However, this was not because of any problems with this version, but simply because Boeing subsequently offered the airlines a substantially redesigned new version, the 747-400, which first flew in April 1988 and entered service, initially with Northwest Airlines, early the following year. This turned out to be the most popular version of the 747 and currently well over 900 are on order or in service, with Boeing raising production to four aircraft a month in order to keep up with demand.

Although retaining the same fuselage dimensions as the -300, the new -400 was almost a new aircraft in virtually every other respect. The flightdeck was completely redesigned for a two-pilot crew using the latest EFIS technology and an advanced flight management system. There were several aerodynamic improvements, the most noticeable being an increased wingspan with upturned winglets, and composite materials were used in several areas to achieve a reduction in empty weight. Finally, uprated engines in the 52–58,000lb thrust rating were offered from all three major manufacturers. The sum of all these changes resulted in an aircraft capable of carrying the same payload as the -300 over ranges up to 7,300 miles at a seat-mile cost reduced by up to 13%. As further evidence of the flexibility of the design, it is offered in Combi and Freighter versions, while the 747-400D is a special variant for the Japanese domestic market. So successful is the 747-400 that it has now supplanted all other versions in production, the last of the so-called "classic" 747s being delivered in 1991. On September 10, 1993, Boeing passed a notable milestone when it rolled out the 1,000th Boeing 747, only the fourth jet airliner to have reached that total, all the others also being Boeing products (707, 727, 737).

After considering even larger versions of the 747 (Series 500 and 600), Boeing are now offering Increased Gross Weight (IGW) versions of the 300 and 400 which will be capable of much greater ranges than the existing models. This development has been spurred on by Airbus's success with the A340-500/600.

Below: *The first major accident involving a Boeing 747 was at Nairobi, Kenya, on November 20, 1974. A Lufthansa 747 crashed on take-off after the crew had omitted to set the leading edge slats. 59 people were killed.* Lufthansa

Boeing 747-400

Powerplants: 4 x GE CF6-80, P&W PW4000 or Rolls-Royce RB211-524 turbofans
Span: 211ft (64.31m)
Length: 231ft 10in (70.66m)
Height: 63ft 5in (19.33m)
Maximum take-off weight: 833,000lb (377,840kg)
Country of Origin: United States

Capacity: Max 550, typically 452 in two-class layout
First Flight: February 9, 1969 (747-100)
Production: 724 (747 Classic), over 550 (747-400)
Typical Cruising Speed: 496kts
Range (max payload): 8,190 miles (13,180km)

MAJOR ACCIDENTS AND INCIDENTS — 23 Recorded

Date	Identity	Operator	Location	Cause
Nov 20, 74	D-ABYB	Lufthansa	Nairobi, Kenya	Human factors
Dec 16, 75		Japan Air Lines	Anchorage, Alaska	Not recorded
Mar 27, 77	N736PA	Pan American	Tenerife	Collision on runway/ Human factors
Mar 27, 77	PH-BUF	KLM	Tenerife	Collision on runway/ Human factors
Nov 3, 77	4X-???	El Al	Belgrade	Decompression
Jan 1, 78	VT-EBD	Air India	Bandra, India	Instrument failure/ Human factors
Nov 19, 80	HL-7445	Korean Air Lines	Seoul, Korea	Human factors
Aug 11, 82	N745PA	Pan American	Pacific Ocean	Criminal action
Sept 1, 83	HL7442	Korean Airlines	Sakhalin Island	Shot down by Military aircraft
Nov 27, 83	HK-2910	Avianca	Barajas Madrid	Ground collision
Feb 19, 85		China Airlines	San Francisco, US	Engine failure
Jun 23, 85	VT-EFO	Air India	Nr Irish Coast	Terrorist action
Aug 12, 85		Japan Air Lines	Mt. Osutaka, Japan	Structural failure
Nov 28, 87	ZS-SAS	SAA	Indian Ocean	On board fire
Dec 21, 88	N739PA	Pan American	Lockerbie, Scotland	Terrorist action
Feb 19, 89	N807FT	Flying Tiger Line	Kuala Lumpur, Malaysia	Human factors/ CFIT
Feb 24, 89	N4713U	United Airlines	Hawaii, US	Mechanical defect
Dec 29, 91	B-198	China Airlines	Taipei, Taiwan	Structural failure
Oct 4, 92	4X-AXG	El Al	Amsterdam, Holland	Structural failure
July 17, 96	N93119	TWA	Off Long Island, US	Fuel vapor explosion
Nov 12, 96	HZ-AIH	Saudi Arabian Airlines	Charkhi Dadri, India	Aerial collision
Aug 5, 97	HL7468	Korean Airlines	Guam	CFIT/Nav error

BOEING (McDONNELL DOUGLAS) DC-9

Although the DC-9 took the air at Long Beach, California, on February 25, 1965, almost two years after the rival BAC 1-11, it was destined to become the most successful of all the Douglas commercial jets with developed versions still in production today. The initial variant, delivered to Delta Airlines, was the DC-9 Series 10 which was powered by two 12,000lb thrust Pratt & Whitney JT8D turbofans and could carry up to 90 passengers. However the main production variant was the DC-9 Series 30 which entered service with Eastern Airlines in February 1967 and this had a 15ft increase in fuselage length to allow up 115 passengers to be carried, a 4ft increase in wingspan, uprated JT8D engines and maximum weight increased from 77,000lb to 98,000lb. Subsequent developments included the Series 40 for SAS in 1967 with an additional 6ft 2in fuselage stretch to raise capacity to 125 passengers, and the Series 50 for Swissair in 1974 with yet a further stretch to accommodate 139 passengers. Each of these versions had more powerful JT8D engines and maximum weight rose to 121,000lb. The flexibility of the basic design which allowed continual growth was a major factor in its success and over 50 airlines eventually bought DC-9s and no less than 976 were produced, with 584 of these being DC-9-30s.

Above: *US Air lost a DC-9-31 at Charlotte, North Carolina, on July 2, 1994. Despite warnings of microburst activity, the crew continued the approach to land and lost control of the aircraft in a sudden downdraft. This accident highlighted the need for more accurate reporting and dissemination of such meteorological information.* US Air

The number of DC-9 accidents recorded is a reflection on the numbers produced and the intensity of short-haul operations. However, it is a statistical quirk that no fewer than eight DC-9s have been lost as a result of collisions in the air and on the ground.

McDonnell Douglas/ Douglas DC-9-30

Powerplants: Two P&W JT8D turbofans
Span: 93ft 5in (28.47m)
Length: 119ft 4in (36.37m)
Height: 27ft 6in (8.38m)
Maximum take-off weight: 121,000lb (54,885kg)
Country of Origin: United States

Capacity: Maximum 115
First Flight: February 25, 1965
Production: 976
Notes: Total built includes variants up to DC-9 Series 50
Typical cruising speed: 431 kts (798 km/hr)
Range (max payload): 1,100 miles (1,770km)

MAJOR ACCIDENTS AND INCIDENTS — 46 Recorded

Date	Type	Identity	Operator	Location	Cause
Oct 1, 66	DC-9	N9101	West Coast Airlines	Wemme, Oregon, US	Human factors/CFIT
Mar 9, 67	DC-9	N1063T	TWA	Dayton, Ohio, US	Aerial collision
Mar 16, 69	DC-9-32	YV-C-AVD	VIASA	Maracaibo, Venezuela	Incorrect data given to crew
Sep 9, 69	DC-9-31	N988VJ	Allegheny Airlines	Near London, Indiana, US	Aerial collision
Feb 15, 70	DC-9-32	HI-177	CompaniaDominicana de Aviacion	Nr Santa Domingo, Dominican Republic	Not determined
May 2, 70	DC-9	N935F	Antillean Airlines	Nr Virgin Islands	Human factors/ fuel shortage
Nov 14, 70	DC-9-31	N97S	Southern Airways	Huntington, US	Human factors
Jun 6, 71	DC-9-31	N9345	Hughes Air West	California, US	Aerial collision
Jan 21, 72	DC-9	TC-JAC	THY	Adana, Turkey	Not recorded
Jan 26, 72	DC-9	YU-AHT	Jugoslovenski Aerotransport	Hermsdorf, Czechoslovakia	Criminal action
Mar 19, 72	DC-9	YU-AHR	Egypt Air	Mt.Shamsam, South Yemen	Not recorded
May 30, 72	DC-9	N3305L	Delta Air Lines	Fort Worth, Texas, US	Vortex wake
Dec 20, 72	DC-9	N954N	North Central Airlines	Chicago, O'Hare, US	Ground collision
Mar 5, 73	DC-9-32	EC-BII	Iberia	Nr Nantes, France	Aerial collision
Jun 20, 73	DC-9	XA-SOC	Aeromexico	Porto Vallarta, Mexico	Human factors/ CFIT
Jul 31, 73	DC-9-31	N975NE	Delta Air Lines	Boston, US	Human factors

Sep 11, 74	DC-9-31	N8984E	Eastern Air Lines	Charlotte, US	Human factors
Dec 22, 74	DC-9-14	YV-C-AVM	AVENSA	Monegas, Venezuela	Not determined
Oct 30, 75	DC-9-32	YU-AJO	Inex Adria Aviopromet	Nr Prague, Czechoslovakia	Human factors
Sep 10, 76	DC-9	YU-AJR	Inex Adria	Nr Gaj, Yugoslavia	Aerial collision
Apr 4, 77	DC-9-31	N1335U	Southern Airways	Nr Atlanta, US	Weather
Jun 26, 78	DC-9	C-FTLV	Air Canada	Toronto, Canada	Mechanical defect
Dec 23, 78	DC-9-32	I-DIKQ	Alitalia	Off Palermo, Sicily	Human factors
Sep 14, 79	DC-9	I-ATJC	Aero Transporti Italiani	Cagliari, Italy	Human factors
Jun 27, 80	DC-9-15	I-TIGI	Itavia	Mediterranean Sea	Military action
Jul 27, 81	DC-9	XA-DEN	Aeromexico	Chihuahua, Mexico	Weather
Nov 8, 81	DC-9	XA-DEO	Aeromexico	Acapulco, Mexico	Human factors
Mar 11, 83	DC-9	YV-67C	AVENSA	Barqusimento	Human factors/ Structural defect
Jun 2, 83	DC-9	C-FTLU	Air Canada	Florence, Kent, US	On board fire
Dec 7, 83	DC-9-32	EC-CGS	Aviaco	Barajas Airport, Madrid, Spain	Ground collision
Aug 31, 86	DC-9-32	XA-JED	Aeromexico	Cerritos, LA, US	Aerial collision
Apr 4, 87	DC-9	PK-GNQ	Garuda Indonesia Airways	Medan, Sumatra	Not recorded

Below: *In a typical human factors scenario, an Alitalia DC-9 crashed while attempting to land in fog at Zurich on November 14, 1990. It was thought that the crew had misread their altimeters and were unaware of known deficiencies in the ILS glidepath indicators at Zurich. Alitalia had previously lost another DC-9, in 1978, when the crew became disorientated at night while on approach to Palermo, Sicily.* ASM Photo

Nov 15, 87	DC-9	N626TX	Continental Airlines	Stapleton Airport, Denver, US	Icing
Mar 18, 89	DC-9F	N931F	Evergreen Int. Airlines	Carswell AFB, US	Human factors
Nov 14, 90	DC-9	I-ATJA	Alitalia	Zurich, Switzerland	Human factors
Dec 3, 90	DC-9-32	N3313L	Northwest Airlines	Detroit, US	Human factors
Mar 5, 91	DC-9	YV-23C	Linea Aeropostal Venezolana	Trujillo, Venezuela	Human factors
Apr 2, 93	DC-9	YV-03C	Linea Aeropostal Venezolana	Margarita Island, Venezuela	Not recorded
July 2, 94	DC-9	N954VJ	USAir	Charlotte, NC, US	Human factors/ Weather
Jan 11, 95	DC-9	HK-3839X	Intercontinental de Aviacion	Cartegana, Colombia	Human factors/ Mechanical defect
Feb 19, 96	DC-9-32	N10556	Continental Airlines	Houston Airport, Texas, US	Human factors?
May 11, 96	DC-9-32	N904VJ	Valujet Airlines	Miami, US	On board fire
May 14, 96	DC-9-15	XA-SNR	Allegro Airlines	Tampico Airport, Mexico	Human factors/ Fuel shortage
Apr 12, 97	DC-9-51	9G-ACM	Ghana Airways	Abidjan-Port Bouet Airport, Ivory Coast	Human factors/ Weather
Oct 10, 97	DC-9-32	LV-WEG	Austral	N. of Montevideo Uruguay	Mechanical Defect?/Weather
Feb 2, 98	DC-9-32	RP-C1507	Cebu Pacific Air	Mount Malagana, Philippines	Not determined

BOEING (MCDONNELL DOUGLAS) DC-10

Design of the McDonnell Douglas DC-10 started in 1966 when Boeing announced its new wide-bodied 747 and American Airlines issued a specification for a smaller, twin-engined, wide-body for use on domestic routes. The McDonnell Douglas team decided that a slightly larger three-engined design would better fit the bill and American Airlines subsequently placed an order for 25 of the new DC-10, followed shortly afterwards by United who ordered a further 30. With these orders in the bag, McDonnell Douglas pressed ahead and by the end of 1970 had no less than three development aircraft flying, while commercial services commenced in August 1971 on the busy American Airlines route from Chicago to Los Angeles. The basic DC-10-10 weighed in at 430,000lb and could carry between 270 and 380 passengers according to cabin configuration and was powered by three 39,300lb thrust General Electric CF6-6D or 6K turbofan, giving a range with maximum payload of 3,300 miles. 122 DC-10-10s were built and delivered to six US airlines and two foreign airlines, among the latter being Laker Airlines who introduced the concept of low fares on the trans-Atlantic routes.

Developments included the DC-10-15 intended for operation from hot and high airports and the Pratt & Whitney JT9D powered long-range DC-10-20, although the

Above: Nigeria Airways was one of the last customers to take delivery of a new DC-10 before production ceased. However one aircraft was written off in a training accident in January 1987. Boeing/McDonnell Douglas

latter only flew in prototype form. The true long-range variant, and the one which sold in greatest numbers, was the DC-10-30 which appeared in 1972 and was powered by various versions of the General Electric CF6-50 giving over 50,000lb thrust which allowed a gross take-off weight of between 530,000 and 590,000lb. This translated in additional fuel, including an extra fuel tank in the after cargo compartment in the extended range DC-10-30ER, so that range with maximum payload rose to over 4,000 miles. The final civil variant was the DC-10-40, developed from the -20 prototype and was sold to Northwest Airlines and Japan Airlines. The more popular DC-10-30 was also produced in Combi and Freighter versions and total civil sales of the DC-10 came to 386 aircraft, although another 60 were completed as military KC-10s. Production ended in 1989.

The DC-10 was a fine aircraft and almost 300 remain in service today, examples of the long-range Series 30 being particularly sought after. However, during its career the DC-10 suffered a number of high profile fatal accidents and earned an undeserved reputation as an unsafe aircraft. These included the loss of a Turkish Airlines aircraft in 1974, shortly after take-off from Paris (see Chapter 1), in which 346 people were killed, another take-off accident in 1979 when an American Airlines aircraft crashed killing 279 passengers and crew (see Chapter 4), and the bizarre loss of an Air New Zealand DC-10-30 which flew into Mt. Erebus in Antarctica (see Chapter 5), again with a large loss of life. While none of these were directly attributable to the basic design, public confidence waned and McDonnell Douglas went through a difficult period.

McDonnell Douglas/ Douglas DC-10-30

Powerplants: Three GE CF6-50C or P&W JT9D turbofans
Span: 165ft 4in (50.40m)
Length: 182ft 1in (55.50m)
Height: 58ft 1in (17.70m)
Maximum take-off weight: 572,000lb (259,450kg)
Country of Origin: United States

Capacity: Maximum 380
First Flight: August 29, 1970
Production: 386 (excluding 60 Military KC-10s)
Typical cruising speed: 475kts (880km/hr)
Range (max payload): 4,000nm (7,413km)
Range (max fuel): 6,504nm (12,055km)

MAJOR ACCIDENTS AND LOSSES — 21 Recorded

Date	Type	Identity	Operator	Location	Cause
Dec 17, 73	DC-10-30	EC-CBN	Iberia	Boston, USA	Human factors
Mar 3, 74	DC-10-10	TC-JAV	Turkish Airlines	Nr Paris, France	Cargo door
Nov 12, 75	DC-10-30CF	N1032F	Overseas National	JFK New York, USA	Bird strike/ Fire
Jan 2, 76	DC-10-30CF	N1031CF	Overseas National	Istanbul, Turkey	Human factors
Mar 1, 78	DC-10-10	N68045	Continental Airlines	Los Angeles, USA	Mechanical defect
May 25, 79	DC-10-10	N110AA	American Airlines	Chicago O'Hare, USA	Human factors/ Maintenance
Oct 31, 79	DC-10-10	N903WA	Western Airlines	Mexico City	Human factors
Nov 28, 79	DC-10-30	ZK-NZP	Air NZ	Mt. Erebus, Antarctica	Human factors/ CFIT
Feb 2, 81	DC-10-30	AP-AXE	PIA	Karachi, Pakistan	Ground fire
Jan 23, 82	DC-10-30CF	N113WA	World Airways	Boston, MA, US	Weather
Sep 13, 82	DC-10-30CF	EC-DEG	Spantax	Malaga, Spain	Mechanical defect
Dec 23, 83	DC-10-30CF	HL7339	Korean Airlines	Anchorage, Alaska	Human factors/ weather
Aug 10, 86	DC-10-40	N184AT	American Trans Air	Chicago O'Hare Airport, US	Ground fire
Jan 10, 87	DC-10-30	5N-ANR	Nigeria Airways	Ilorin, Nigeria	Human factors
May 21, 88	DC-10-10	N136AA	American	Dallas, US	Not recorded
Jul 19, 89	DC-10-10	N1819U	United Airlines	Sioux City, US	Mech defect
Jul 27, 89	DC-10-30	HL-7328	Korean Airlines	Tripoli, Libya	Human factors
Sep 19, 89	DC-10-30	N54629	UTA	Niger, W. Africa	Terrorist action
Dec 21, 92	DC-10-30CF	PH-MBN	Martinair	Faro, Portugal	Weather factors
Jun 13, 96	DC-10-30	PK-GIE	Garuda Indonesia	Fukuoka, Japan	Engine fire
Sep 5, 96	DC-10-10F	N68055	Federal Express	Newburgh/Stewart, NY, US	On board fire

Above: *FH-227 in the colors of the French airline TAT; previously it had been with TABA the Brazilian air-line that lost four FH-227s between 1982 and 1995.* Leo Marriott

FAIRCHILD HILLER FH-227

During the late 1940s aircraft manufacturers were striving to build a replacement for the venerable Douglas DC-3 then in widespread service. In 1950, Fokker initiated the design of the F.27 Friendship, its first new-build airliner since the 1930s and in the two decades following its introduction the F.27 was the biggest selling turbo-prop-powered commercial transport in the world. After studying a variety of config-urations the company opted for a twin Rolls-Royce Dart Mk 507 powered high-wing airplane with pressurized accommodation for 28 passengers and a minimum range of 300 miles with a capacity payload. Production Friendships could carry an addi-tional four passengers and were powered by Dart Mk 511s. In 1956, the Dutch man-ufacturer signed an agreement with Fairchild Aircraft Corporation, which had been building Fokker trainers in the US for several years, to build and market the Friendship on that side of the Atlantic. The first Fairchild-built machine was flown in April 1958. Dutch Friendships are identified by their various Mark numbers, and those produced by Fairchild by F-27 or FH–227 designations.

After the amalgamation of Hiller Aircraft in 1964, the American manufacturer produced its own stretched versions in the FH-227, FH-227B, C, D, and E, which were 52-seaters, 6ft 6in longer than the F-27 and powered by Rolls-Royce Dart Mk 532s. The first FH-227 flew in March 1966 and was delivered to Mohawk Airlines in the following month. The aircraft proved to be extremely popular with smaller air-lines and, notably, with South American operators.

Fairchild Hiller FH-227

Country of origin: United States
Type: 52-seat turboprop passenger
plane
Powerplant: two Rolls-Royce Dart
Mk 532-7L turboprop engines
Performance: normal cruising speed
294mph (473km/h) at 20,000ft
(6,095m); service ceiling 28,000ft
(8,535m); range with maximum

payload and fuel reserves 606 miles
(975km)
Weights: empty 23,200lb (10,523kg);
maximum take-off 45,000lb
(20,638kg)
Span: 95ft 2in (29.01m)
Length: 83ft 8in (25.5m)
Height: 27ft 7in (8.41m)
Wing area: 754 sq ft (70.05 sq m)

MAJOR ACCIDENTS AND LOSSES — 9 Recorded

Date	Location	Type	Operator	Cause
June 02, 80	Nr Yachiba, Brazil	Fairchild F-27J CP-117	Lloyd Aero Boliviano	Crashed
June 16, 82	Tabatinga, Brazil	FH-227B/LCD PT-LBV	TABA	Crashed into tower on approach in poor visibility
Mar 16, 84	San Borja, Brazil	Fairchild F-27M CP-862	Lloyd Aero Boliviano	Crashed
Mar 04, 88	Paris, France	FH-227B F-GCPS	Transport Aerien Transregional	Crashed into power cables on approach in bad weather
Apr 12, 89	nr Valence, France	FH-227B F-GGDM	Uni-Air	Crashed into cliff while off course
May 10, 90	Tuxtla Gutierrez,	F-27J F-GHXA	Aviacsa	Crashed on approach
June 06, 90	Altamira, Brazil	FH-227B PT-ICA	TABA	Crashed on approach
Jan 25, 93	Altamira, Brazil	FH-227B PT-LCS	TABA	Crashed
Nov 28, 95	Santarem, Brazil	FH-227B PP-BUJ	TABA	Crashed on second approach

Above: *Aeroflot Il-76 giving a good idea of the bulk of this substantial transport.* Leo Marriott

ILYUSHIN Il-76

At the end of the 1960s the Ilyushin design bureau, then under the leadership of G.V. Novozhilov, began the design of a heavy transport aircraft to replace the turboprop Antonov An-12. The main requirement of the aircraft was that it be capable of transporting 40 tons of freight over a distance of 3,100 miles (5,000km) in at least six hours, and also that it be able to operate from short unprepared strips, in the most challenging climate conditions experienced in the then Soviet republics of Siberia and in the Far East. The prototype was flying in March 1971, in the form of a four-turbofan aircraft with a wing mounted above the fuselage to ensure the interior remained unobstructed. The same desire influenced the decision to mount the 16-wheel main landing gear in two large ventral fairings. The underside of the rear fuselage is made up of two outward hinged clamshell doors, and loading is facilitated by a loading ramp. The prototype demonstrated exceptional range/payload/altitude performance, and established no fewer than 25 international records during flight trials. Series production of the Il-76T began in 1975, duly entering service with Aeroflot in early 1978 on domestic routes and on the Moscow–Japan service in April 1978.

It was clear from the outset that the aircraft had considerable military potential and the type was evaluated by the Soviet air force. Subsequently, a militarized version designated Il-76M was produced, capable of carrying 140 troops or 125 paratroops or alternative freight and with a rear defensive gun turret with twin 23mm GSh-23L cannon, ECM (Electronic Counter Measures) and IRCM (Infra-Red

Ilyushin Il-76

Country of origin: Russia
Type: heavy freight transport
Powerplant: four 26,455lb
(12,000kg) Soloviev D-30KP-1
turbofans
Performance: maximum speed at
36,090ft (11,000m) 528mph
(850km/h); cruising speed 466-497
mph (750-800km/h); cruising height
29,500-39,370ft (9,000-12,000m),
absolute height 50,850ft (15,500m);
range with 88,185lb (40,000kg) of
freight 3,100 miles (5,000km)
Weights: empty 165,347lb
(75,000kg); maximum take-off
374,786lb (170,000kg)
Span: 165ft 8in (50.50m)
Length: 152ft 10 1/4in (46.59m)
Height: 48ft 5in (14.76m)
Wing area: 3229.28sq ft (300sq m)

MAJOR ACCIDENTS AND LOSSES — 13 Recorded

Date	Location	Type	Operator	Cause
Oct 18, 89	Caspian Sea, USSR	Il-76MD SSSR-76569	Aeroflot	Crashed into sea after engine fire
Oct 20, 89	nr Leninakan, Armenia	Il-76TD SSSR-76466	Aeroflot	Crashed into mountain on approach
Mar 27, 90	Nr Kabul, Afghanistan	Il-76MD SSSR-78781	Aeroflot	Crashed on approach
June 12, 90	Nr Kabul, Afghanistan	Il-76MD SSSR-86905	Aeroflot	Shot down on approach
May 24, 91	Nr Bakhtaran, Iran	Il-76TD LZ-INK	Metro Cargo	Crashed into mountain
Apr 05, 96	Petropavlovsk, Russia	Il-76TD RA-76752	Krasnoyarskie	Crashed into Avialinii mountain on approach
June 06, 96	Kinshasa-N'Djili, Congo	Il-76MD UR-76539	Hoseba	Crashed on take-off, possibly as a result of damage sustained earlier in the day
Aug 19, 96	Beograd, former Yugoslavia	Il-76T RA-76513	SPair	Developed electrical problem shortly after take-off, crashed on final approach
Nov 12, 96	Charkhi Dadri, India	Il-76TD UN-76435	Kazakhstan Airlines	Collided with Saudia aircraft
Nov 27, 96	Abakan, Russia	Il-76MD RA-78804	Russian Air Force	Crashed 8 minutes after take-off; over load suspected
July 13, 98	off Ras al Khaimah;	Il-76MD UR-76424	ATI Aircompany	Crashed after take-off
July 17, 98	Nr Asmara-Yohannes,	Il-76 UR-UCI	Ukraine Aviation Eritea Transport Company	Crashed into hillside on final approach
July 26, 99	Nr Irkutsk, Russia	Il-76 RA-76819	Elf Air/Enimex	Crashed on the edge of a forest shortly after departingIrkutsk

Counter Measures) equipment. Approximately 140 of these were built for the Soviet air forces, Czechoslovakia, Iraq, and Poland.

The Il-76TD is an unarmed military version that became operational in July 1983. This has uprated Soloviev D-30KP-1 engines allowing for increased maximum take-off weight. The facility to carry an extra 22,046lb (10,000kg) of fuel provides an increased range of 745 miles (1,200km). With the breakup of the Soviet Union many of its military aircraft have been sold off to private companies or else passed to the national airlines of the former Soviet republics. Ilyushin currently offers a number of developed versions with powerplant sourced from Western manufacturers.

LOCKHEED L-1011 TRISTAR

The wide-bodied Lockheed L.1011 Tristar flew in late 1970 and was particularly significant in that, from the start, it was offered only with British-built Rolls-Royce RB211-524 turbofans in the 42,000–50,000lb thrust bracket. However, development of both the airframe and engines led Lockheed and Rolls-Royce to the edge of bankruptcy and delayed the development and test program by several months.

Below: The crash of Eastern Airline Flight 401 in the Florida Everglades in December 1972 provoked a flurry of books about the incident including one which claimed that one of the crew members killed subsequently re-appeared as a ghost to haunt other aircraft. The accident occurred because the crew failed to monitor their rate of descent while investigating a problem with the undercarriage.. Although there were only two fatalities, many of the 176 passengers and crew received serious injuries. AJB Photo

Lockheed L-1011-200 Tristar

Powerplants: Three Rolls-Royce RB211 -524 turbofans
Span: 155ft 4in (47.34m)
Length: 177ft 8in (54.17m)
Height: 55ft 4in (16.87m)
Maximum take-off weight: 466,000lb (211,375kg)
Country of Origin: United States
Capacity: 400 max, 256 in typical two-class layout
First flight: November 16, 1970
Production: 250 including 200 long fuselage -1, -100, -200, -250 models and 50 long range -500 series
Typical cruising speed: 463kts (890km/hr)
Range (max payload): 3,680nm (6820km)
Range (max fuel): 4,918nm (9,111km)

MAJOR ACCIDENTS AND LOSSES — 5 Recorded

Date	Identity	Operator	Location	Cause
Dec 29, 72	N310EA	Eastern Airlines	20 miles from Miami Airport	Crew error/ u/c problems
Aug 19, 80	HZ-AHK	Saudia	Riyadh, Saudi Arabia	Fire in cargo Hold
Aug 2, 85	N726DA	Delta Airlines	Dallas/ Fort Worth, US	Weather
May 3, 86	4R-ULD	Air Lanka	Colombo Airport, Sri Lanka	Terrorist action
July 30, 92	N11002	TWA		False Stall Warning after take-off

The original short/medium-range Tristar 1 had a maximum take-off weight of 430,000lb and could carry a maximum payload (between 256 and 400 passengers) over a range of 2,880 miles. It was bought by a number of airlines including Air Canada, Eastern, Delta and TWA, while in the UK it was sold to British Airways and Court Line. As with the DC-10, the Tristar saw considerable development, the first derivative being the Tristar 100 certificated at higher gross weights (450,000lb) to increase range. When fitted with uprated RB211s for operation from hot and high airfields, this became the Tristar 200. To compete with the DC-10-30, the long-range Tristar 500 was developed and this shorter fuselage seating between 246 and 300 passengers, but gross weight was increased to 496,000lb and 50,000lb thrust RB211-524B turbofans were fitted, this combination resulting in a range of 4,310 miles with maximum payload. The Tristar was an attractive aircraft with a good performance but orders were slow to materialize and Lockheed ended production after 250 aircraft had been produced, and in doing so ended their long association in the civil airliner market. However over 180 aircraft remain in service and its accident record is very good considering that many still flying are over 20 years old.

2 Summary of Accidents and Losses by Aircraft Type

How safe is or was a particular aircraft type? This is a complex subject which requires sophisticated examination of all relevant statistics and factors and is certainly not something that can be attempted in a few short paragraphs. However, the table below presents a distillation of the major jet aircraft accidents and losses, so that some simple comparisons can be made.

For each aircraft type the total number of losses recorded is given together with a separate total which excludes all non-flight safety related occurrences such as hijacks, military or terrorist action, and incidents such as hangar fires where aircraft have been destroyed. This figure can then be set against the total number of aircraft produced to give hull losses due to actual accidents and safety related incidents as a percentage. In addition, to provide a further reference point, the aircraft's lifespan is given in years. This is the period from the date of its first flight up to the present if still in service today, or else up to the point at which the last commercial example was retired. From a statistical point of view, if all aircraft were subject to an identical chance of being involved in an accident then the number of accidents recorded for each specific type would be expected to relate to the numbers in service and the period of years in service. The figures are correct to end 1997.

LOSSES (ALL CAUSES)	LOSSES (SAFETY RELATED)	TOTAL PRODUCED	% LOST (ACCIDENTS)	LIFESPAN (YEARS)
Aerospatiale/BAC Concorde				
nil	nil	18	0 %	29
Aerospatiale/Sud Ouest Caravelle				
29	24	282	8.51%	47
Airbus A300/A310				
14	10	718	1.39%	25
Airbus A391/A320/A321				
5	5	702	0.71%	10
Airbus A330/A340				
2	1	175	0.57%	7
Boeing 707/720				
89	75	916	8.19%	44
Boeing 727				
53	49	1,831	2.68%	35
Boeing 737				
50	45	3,000	1.50%	31
Boeing 747				
20	16	1,265	1.26%	29
Boeing 757				
4	4	760	0.53%	16

Losses (all causes)	Losses (safety related)	Total produced	% Lost (accidents)	Lifespan (years)
Boeing 767				
5	2	663	0.30%	19
Boeing 777				
nil	nil	76	0 %	4
Boeing (McDonnell Douglas) DC-8				
46	44	555	7.93%	40
Boeing (McDonnell Douglas) DC-9				
46	44	976	4.51%	33
Boeing (McDonnell Douglas) DC-10				
21	18	386	4.66%	28
Boeing (McDonnell Douglas) MD-80/MD-90 Series				
9	9	1200	0.75%	19
Boeing (McDonnell Douglas) MD-11				
1	1	166	0.60%	8
Bombardier/Canadair Regional Jet				
2	2	159	1.26%	7
British Aerospace 146 / Avro RJ series				
4	3	299	1.00%	17
British Aircraft Corporation BAC-111				
14	13	232	5.60%	35
Convair 880/990				
15	11	102	10.78%	28
de Havilland Comet				
17	13	74	17.57%	30
Dassault-Breguet Mercure				
nil	nil	11	0 %	25
Embraer EMB-145				
nil	nil	24	0%	3
Fokker F28 Fellowship				
16	15	241	6.22%	31
Fokker 70/100				
2	2	326	0.61%	12
Hawker Siddely Trident				
11	9	117	7.69%	25
Ilyushin Il-62				
12	12	285	4.21%	36
Ilyushin Il-86				
1	1	100	1.00%	22
Ilyushin Il-96				
nil	nil	15	0 %	10
Lockheed Tristar				
5	4	250	1.60%	28

LOSSES (ALL CAUSES)	LOSSES (SAFETY RELATED)	TOTAL PRODUCED	% LOST (ACCIDENTS)	LIFESPAN (YEARS)
Tupolev Tu-104 / Tu-124				
28	27	300 +	<9.00%	30
Tupolev Tu-134				
28	27	700+	<3.86%	35
Tupolev Tu-144				
2	2	13	15.38%	10
Tupolev Tu-154				
28	29	1,000 +	<2.90%	30
Vickers VC-10/Super VC-10				
4	2	54	3.70%	25
Yakolev Yak-40				
34	31	1,000+	<3.10%	32
Yakolev Yak-42				
5	5	270 +	1.85%	23
VFW- Fokker VFW-614				
1	1	20	0.50%	30

From the foregoing table it will be observed that, of the airliners still in service, the Concorde, Boeing 777, Embraer ERJ145 and the Ilyushin Il-96 have not yet been involved in a major accident.

Glossary

AA	American Airlines		JAL	Japanese Airlines
AAI	Airports Authority of India		Kapton	lightweight wiring used in modern electronic flight systems
AAIB	Air Accident Investigation Board (UK)			
AD	Airworthiness Directive		LMT	Local Mean Time
ADF	Automatic Direction Finder		NOTAM	Notice to Airman (US Navy designation)
AINS	Inertial Navigation Systems		NTSB	National Transportation Safety Board (US)
Alpha	Angle of Attack (aka AOA)		NZALPA	New Zealand Airline Pilots Association
ANZ	Air New Zealand		PanAm	Pan American Airways
AOA	Angle of Attack (aka Alpha)		PF	Pilot Flying
ARAP	Associated Retired Aviation Professionals		RARDE	Royal Armament Research And Development Establishment (UK)
ATC(C)	Air Traffic Control (Center)			
BARC	Bhabha Atomic Research Centre (India)		RCMP	Royal Canadian Mounted Police
BBC	British Broadcasting Corporation		RLD	Dutch Aviation Authority
BEA	British European Airways		SCD	Side Cargo Door designation
BOAC	British Aircraft Corporation		SP	Special Performance
CEC	Cooperative Engagement Capability		SSR	Secondary Surveillance Radar system
CFIT	Controlled Flight Into Terrain		TACAN	Tactical Air Navigation Aid
CIC	Command Intelligence Center		TCAS	Traffic Alert and Collision Avoidance System
CRM	Cockpit Resource Management			
CVR	Cockpit Voice Recorder		THS	Tail Horizontal Stabilizer
DFDR	Digital Flight Data Recorder		THY	Turk Hava Yollari (Turkish Airlines)
DME	Distance Measuring Equipment		TWA	Trans World Airlines
ECM	Electronic Counter Measures		UAL	United Air Lines
EGPWS	Enhanced Ground Proximity Warning System		UHF	Ultra High Frequency
			USAF	United States Air Force
Emirates RCC	Emirates Rescue Co-ordination Center		V1	go, or no-go decision speed
EPR	Engine Pressure Ratio		V2	safe take-off speed
ESM	Electronic Surveillance Measures		VFR	Visual Flight Rules
F/E	Flight Engineer		VHF	Very High Frequency radio
F/O	Flight Officer		VMC	Visual Meteorological Conditions
FAA	Federal Aviation Administration		VOR	VHF Omnidirectional range
FBI	Federal Bureau of Investigation		VS	Vertical Speed
FCOM	Flight Crew Operating Manual			
FDR	Flight Data Recorder			
FL	Flight Level			
FMS	Flight Management System			
GMT	Greenwich Mean Time			
GPA	Garuda Pilots Association			
GPWS	Ground Proximity Warning System			
"Heavy"	standard radio procedure designating large, wide-bodied aircraft			
HF	High Frequency radio			
IAS	Indicated Air Speed			
IATA	International Air Transport Association			
IFF	Identification Friend or Foe			
IGW	Increased Gross Weight			
ILS	Instrument Landing System			
INS	Inertial Navigation System			
IRCM	Infra-Red Counter Measures			

Conversion tables

Multiply the left column by the center column to convert

inches (in) x 2.5 = centimeters (cm)
feet (ft) x 0.3 = meters (m)
miles x 1.6 = kilometers (km)
pounds (lb) x 0.45 = kilograms (kg)
knots (kts) x 1.15 = miles per hour (mph)
miles/hour (mph) x 1.6 = kilometers/hour (km/hr)
centimeters (cm) x 0.4 = inches (in)
meters (m) x 3.3 = feet (ft)
kilograms (kg) x 2.2 = pounds (lb)
kilometers/hour (km/hr) x 0.6 = miles/hour (mph))
miles x 1.15 = nautical miles (nm)
nautical miles (nm) x 0.87 = miles
°Fahreneit (F) minus 32 x 0.56 = °Centigrade (C)
°Centigrade (C) x 1.8 add 32 = °Fahreneit (F)

Index